Owslebury
Then and Now

by

Evelyn Houghton

with contributions by

Elsie Evans
Gwyn Evans
Elizabeth Harfield
Denis Robinson

George Mann Publications

Published by
George Mann Publications
Easton, Winchester,
Hampshire SO21 1ES
01962 779944

A CIP catalogue record for this book
is available from the British Library

ISBN 0-95-244240-X

George Mann Publications

CONTENTS

This book is dedicated to future village folk in the hope that they will feel a sense of pride in what has gone before and will therefore build on this heritage so that Owslebury will move on into the future as a much loved and cared for place in which to live.

'When man becomes aware of his past, he acquires a sense of responsibility, he feels himself to be a link in an unbroken chain which he is bound to preserve, to increase if he can and, ultimately, to transmit, with respect, everything noble and worthy that he has received.'

Don Antonio Sturmendi
(President of the Third International Congress of
Genealogical and Heraldic Sciences, Madrid, 1955)

FOREWORD

It gives me great pleasure to be writing a foreword to this book, *Owslebury Then and Now*.

The history of the village where I have lived for the last 47 years has fascinated me for a long time. I married someone born and bred here and Alan was a fifth generation Owslebury Harfield. His roots here were deep indeed.

Following the death of Alan's mother, who had been the village nurse and midwife for almost forty years, we discovered a shoebox filled with cuttings and anecdotes of village life. There were enough to fill eight scrapbooks! Having pasted all the pictures and notes into these books, I was well and truly hooked on village history. I became a collector myself of anything and everything relating to Owslebury. The actual name of our village causes such problems and I'm often asked to both pronounce it and spell it! William Cobbett who passed close to the village on his 'rural rides' wrote of the name, *"It is pronounced Uzzlebury – and sounds as it should, purest Hampshire"*. Today true natives follow William Cobbett's example saying 'Uzzlebury', whereas new settlers tend to say 'Osslebury'!

The coming of the new millennium has been a reason for all of us to take stock of the past and wonder about the future. During the last decade, we have celebrated two important happenings in the village, namely the 150th anniversary of the school and then the building of the new Parish Hall. The headteacher, Mrs Adrienne Caplin, approached me with regards to writing a book on the history of the school and I offered unused material to the Parish Hall Committee for a second book as a fund-raiser for the new hall. I hoped these books would not only give pleasure but also preserve for the future, stories which might have remained hidden or become lost.

Recently, some friends who are researching their family history in Owslebury wrote to me with the following suggestion:

"One thing you might like to consider ... is to create a map of the village and show the names of the old houses and buildings, and write a brief history for each: a sort of walking tour guide for those unfamiliar with such details".

I was amazed at these words as this is exactly what Evelyn Houghton has been doing in the main section of our millennium book!

It has been good to have been involved once again in the production of another book about Owslebury, this time as a member of a team; the others being Gwyn and Elsie Evans, Jill Hancock, Evelyn Houghton and Denis Robinson. We felt it would be a good way to mark the millennium, a way to leave our mark for the village of the future. We hope you will agree when you dip into the pages of our book and 'walk through the village' with us.

If you enjoy reading this book as much as we have enjoyed producing it, then our labour of love will have been worthwhile.

Elizabeth Harfield, 2000

The Book Team

This book has been compiled as a joint effort by a small team of village folk.

Gwyn and Elsie Evans: Gwyn and Elsie have lived in the village since 1963 and have been involved in the organisation of many aspects of village life over the years. Gwyn has organised finances and publicity for the book and Elsie has researched and written about areas of the parish outside the village.

Elizabeth Harfield: Elizabeth, who is always known as Betty, came to the village when she married her husband Alan in 1953 and is already the author of two books about aspects of village life in the past. She has steered the rest of us down appropriate paths of research; she has written copious notes at a moment's notice and constantly dipped into her enormous archive of articles, correspondence and pictures concerning the village, in order to help this book come together.

Evelyn Houghton: Evelyn came to live in Owslebury in 1974 and taught the infants at the village school for twelve years. As main editor of the book she has written the chapters concerning homes and families, social encounters, trades and services, the weather, high days and holidays, in loving memory, and beginnings and endings.

Denis Robinson: Denis is the photographer in the team and has lived in Owslebury since July, 1983. His link with the village, however, goes back to the time of the Second World War when he was an RAF pilot flying a Spitfire that had been repaired at Marwell.

OWSLEBURY MILLENNIUM BOOK BENEFACTORS

The publication of this book has only been possible because of the kindness and generosity of the following people:

Gwyn Evans – Roamer Poles	Graham and Margaret Oakley
Kevin Green – Hallmark Builders	Clive and Ali Mansell – Ship Inn
B. L. Emery Ltd	Adrian Hardman
Emery Rees Feeds	Lady Sylvia Rix
Sean Thompson Ltd	Mr and Mrs Pollock-Gore
Margaret Jefferies – Jefferies & Maidment	Peggy Smith (née Merritt)
Fred Houghton	Sharon Lodder
Betty Harfield	Denis Robinson
David Wilkie	Evelyn and David Houghton
Gerald Sanderson	Bob and Carole O'Neill
Mrs Susie Gwyn	Miranda and Edward Sprot
Roger and Brenda Warson	James and Rosie Hoare
Mrs Gray	John and Annette Harris
Jill Hancock	Vivienne and Andrew Sturt
Glen Dawson – DACCOM	
John Stewart	Winchester Area Community Action
Gladys Bradshaw	Owslebury Parish Council
Miss New	OMCA
Betty and Derek Brooks	Quilver Business Services Ltd
Sean Cooper	

ACKNOWLEDGEMENTS

The stories included in this book are mainly those that have been told to us by village folk who have dipped into their memories. Maybe there are other stories that remain untold. We have drawn on memories that have been recorded previously in past Newsletters, in articles and in correspondence, as well as those revealed by today's residents. We value all of these and have tried faithfully to record and interpret all information as correctly as possible. The houses that have been described in the book are those with a history, having witnessed village life during the whole of the last century. Included also are properties that have been built to replace older ones and any with a particular story to tell. Significant village buildings like the school and Parish Hall, have a prominent place in the book.

We would particularly like to thank all those village folk who have given their time to chat and who have offered us old photographs for inclusion in the book. These include:

Doug and Daphne Rogers	*Charmian Jones*	*Stella Jones*
Jane Dawson	*Evelyn Merritt*	*Guy Eddis*
Helen Nelthorp	*Terry Russell*	*Tony and Katherine Sellon*
Alan Ball	*Irene Bliss*	*Betty New*
Frank and Jo Williams	*Jane Ruffell*	*Arthur Berrill*
Kay Westlake	*Ann Boston*	*Philip and Mary Hellard*
Ian and Jackie McLeonards	*Peggy Smith (nee Merritt)*	*Maureen and Bob Niddrie*
Nick and Caroline Perry	*Barbara Crabbe*	*Belinda Martin*
Harold Blackman	*Sally Wickham*	*Duncan and May Pollock-Gore*
Janet Emery	*Melanie Norris*	*Helen Cooke*
Margaret Oakley	*Phyllis Merritt*	*Rachel and Brendan Powell*
Sandy Emery	*Philip Bayley*	*Adrian Hardman*
Dick Lush	*John Seabrook*	*Pat and Daphne Scully*
Michael Lush	*Clive Mansell*	*Sheron Wylie-Modro*
Brian Lush	*Nigel White*	*Lady Sylvia Rix*
David White	*Wendy Wilson*	*Vivienne Sturt*
Walter Trott	*Pearl Hatt*	*Miss Best*
Peggy and Ian Egerton	*Paul and Penny Bowes*	
Sheila and Ray Norgate	*Margaret Jefferies*	

And from Twyford – Stanley Crooks and Sue Sullivan

The Book Team would also like to thank George Mann, our publisher, and Barbara Large, our copy editor, for all their advice and encouragement along the way. For novices such as ourselves, this has been invaluable.

Many thanks to all of the Millennium Book Committee, namely Elsie and Gwyn Evans, Jill Hancock, Betty Harfield, Evelyn Houghton and Denis Robinson. Thanks also to all of the villagers who have contributed to make this book possible.

All proceeds from the sale of the book will be available through OMCA (Owslebury and Morestead Community Association) for deserving causes in our community.

Ann Boston – Chairperson of OMCA

PHOTOGRAPHS AND ILLUSTRATIONS

Photographs and illustrations throughout the book have been contributed by the following people. Initials printed in italic script indicate the actual photographer.

AB • Ann Boston	DR • Denis Robinson	MJ • Margaret Jefferies
AE • Adele Emmans	DW • David Wilkie	MO • Margaret Oakley
AH • Adrian Hardman	EE • Elsie Evans	NP • Nick Perry
AS • Andrew Sturt	EH • Evelyn Houghton	PE • Peggy Egerton
BB • Bob Bennett	GE • Guy Eddis	PM • Phyllis Merritt
BH • Betty Harfield	GW • Gaynor Worman	RM • Dr Morton
BM • Belinda Martin	GT • Gerry Tull	SL • Sharon Lodder
BN • Betty New	HH • Helen Houghton	SS • Susan Sullivan
BMN • Bob & Maureen Niddrie	IB • Irene Bliss	SW • Sally Wickham
BON • Bob O'Neill	IM • Ian McLeonards	TS • Tony Sellon
CJ • Charmian Jones	JB • Jane Briercliffe	VB • Vera Bampton
DE • David Emmans	LC • Lynda Chantler	WW • Wendy Wilson
DH • David Houghton	LK • Lady Kelburn	WT • Walter Trott
DL • Dick Lush	LL • Lucy Lambert	
DPG • Duncan Pollock-Gore	MB • Marilyn Bishop	

WMS • Winchester Museum Service – *all photographs have been reproduced by kind permission of the Winchester Museum Service and come from the William Savage collection. William was a well-known photographer in the second half of the 1800s and used to travel around to take photographs of more wealthy people's houses by invitation. It is something of a surprise to discover that he came to Owslebury! Since William died in 1887 all of the photographs are prior to this date.*

HC • Hampshire Chronicle

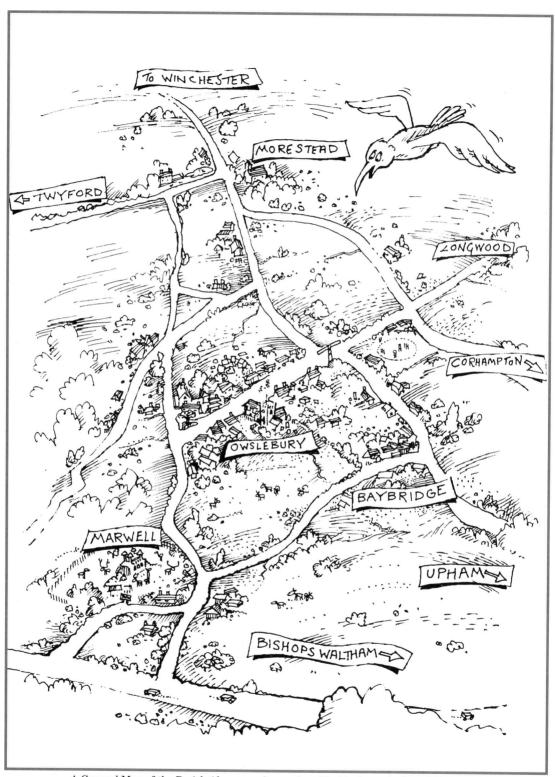

To WINCHESTER

TWYFORD

MORESTEAD

LONGWOOD

CORHAMPTON

OWSLEBURY

BAYBRIDGE

MARWELL

UPHAM

BISHOPS WALTHAM

A General Map of the Parish *(drawn and reproduced by kind permission of Alan Ball)*

1: INTRODUCTION

In 1086, twenty years after the famous Battle of Hastings, William the Conqueror decided that he needed to know details of land occupation and ownership throughout his recently acquired territory. Wheels were set in motion to produce what became known as the *Domesday Book*. This was actually compiled in Winchester, Hampshire, and was kept there until the seat of government moved to Westminster. It was known as *'The Winchester Book'* at this time although, strangely enough, details concerning Winchester itself were not included in it; nor were there any details of Owslebury!

Nine hundred and fourteen years later, the Owslebury and Morestead Community Association (OMCA) had thoughts along the same lines as William's. They decided that it would be a good idea to produce a modern domesday record of the village as a way of marking the beginning of the new millennium in the year 2000. As well as details concerning this present time, they wanted to record the happenings of the previous century, the events and people who had shaped the village and had made it what it is today. They were very happy to make it one of their millennium projects.

Because of its geographical position, the village of Owslebury has always been rather isolated. As well as missing out on a *Domesday* mention, in another publication of 1928 *'Bird Notes and News'* it was written,

*'Owslebury is a small isolated village in Hampshire, south of Winchester, but off the main road and apparently **unknown to history.'***

This 'unknownness' has been partly rectified since, by the publication of two delightful and fascinating books compiled by Betty Harfield, *'Owslebury – a Village School'* (published 1990), and *'Owslebury Remembers' (published* 1994). Although Betty was born in Winchester, she has lived in the village all her married life. What she doesn't know about village life today and yesterday is hardly worth knowing!

The other book that has put Owslebury on the map, was written by Peter Hewett, entitled *'Owslebury Bottom'*. Peter was a schoolboy in the village for a short while during and just after the First World War and has recorded his memories of this time.

By writing this millennium book we hope to reverse the previous notion and to make Owslebury village 'known to history'. The main focus is the village of Owslebury as drawn on the plan, with a smaller section dealing with other areas of the parish which include Downstead, Morestead, Baybridge and Marwell. Along with descriptions of significant aspects of life during the last hundred years, we want to portray a 'snapshot' of the village in the year 2000. It is after all the ordinary happenings of today that become tomorrow's fascinating history. We hope it will be a worthy record.

Whaddon Bottom *(EH)*

Cricket Down *(DR)*

2: OWSLEBURY VILLAGE – A SNAPSHOT FOR THE YEAR 2000

The village of Owslebury enjoys a delightful geographical position. It affords beautiful views over the surrounding countryside, and wherever one lives in the village, there is never far to go to see green fields, wild flowers and hedgerows or to walk a footpath away from traffic. We all hear the birds sing, breathe the fresh air and witness the changing of the seasons first hand, all special bonuses from living in this small corner of our sceptered isle.

Owslebury stands high on a hill, 350 feet above sea level, and is the second highest village in Hampshire, some six miles south east of Winchester, twelve miles north east of Southampton and fifteen miles north west of Portsmouth. It is a small village with just one main street wending its way through, stretching from one end at Whaddon Farm to the Longwood Crossroads at the other. Beyond Whaddon Farm lies Marwell Zoological Park and on the other side of the crossroads is the old Longwood Estate. Branching off the main street there are three side turnings to Pitcot Lane, Beech Grove and Hilly Close. Opposite the old sign post is Crabbes Hill which leads down to a little cluster of houses known as Owslebury Bottom and then on to Morestead. There is also a turning alongside the recreation ground, which leads to Baybridge. Owslebury is closely bordered by other small hamlets; namely, Morestead, Baybridge and Hensting with the villages of Twyford and Upham just a few miles away.

The village has no pavements or street lighting along the length of the main road although the side turnings of Hilly Close and Beech Grove have both of these. Communities in these two streets have main drainage although the rest of the village has septic tanks. Overhead cables bring electricity and telephone to households and running water is supplied directly to each home, although there is no mains gas supply.

As we enter the twenty-first century and the new millennium, our community in the village itself has just over four hundred residents, not counting the children. The civil parish, comprising Owslebury, Morestead, Baybridge, Marwell and Hensting, had a population of 848 at the time of the last census in 1991. In Owslebury there is a church and a primary school, but there is no shop, no resident vicar, doctor or policeman. We have no WI, or Mothers' Union, no drama or horticultural societies. There are no cubs, brownies, scouts or guides and no pre-school playgroup. We do however, have cricket, football, a sports club, keep fit, handbell ringers, senior club, OMCA, the Parish Council and Neighbourhood Watch. We have church and school fetes, harvest suppers and quiz evenings. **And**, almost uniquely, we have our weekly village Newsletter.

Our community today is very different from the one that made up the village at the beginning of the century. Owslebury has a rural setting but is no longer comprised of a predominately rural community. One hundred years ago people were born into families who had been in the village for several generations. Men folk were the breadwinners and most worked in the village. People were drawn together as a community because every aspect of their lives took place within this small village. They depended upon each other, and contact with the outside world was minimal. The church would be full at harvest festival time because so many families were involved in producing the harvest and others relied on it. Everyone knew everyone else and bumped into each other daily as they tackled routine tasks, fetching water, going to the shop, to the blacksmiths, to school and to church on Sundays.

Nowadays, life is very different. Patterns of daily living, routines and expectations have all changed extensively during the passing years of the last century. Our houses, many now being financed by mortgages, all have running water, bathrooms and electricity and are filled with labour-saving devices; we go abroad for our holidays; we travel widely in our cars. Often two salaries are needed to support this life style and today it is taken for granted that women can have careers and jobs even after marriage. Few people living in Owslebury today were born here; most have chosen to live here. Very few people now work actually in the village. It is late when they arrive home from work and they are exhausted at the end of the day. Television is an easy way to unwind and relax. Television, along with much other sophisticated technology not dreamed of one hundred years ago, now keeps us in constant touch with the world beyond the village. Shopping is done in huge supermarkets outside the village or by e-mail from people's own homes. From one week to the next there is rarely the time or the opportunity to bump into one's neighbours or to share an activity with them. Sometimes these changes are hard to accept. But, as the saying goes, 'time moves on' and we must move with it.

Many people who have lived in the village in the past have written and spoken of their time here with great affection and can recount many happy memories. For them Owslebury was a good place to live. As we go forward into the twenty-first century we may be a very different community from the one of a hundred years ago, but a community we are nonetheless. Our village life today is precious to us all and Owslebury is still a very good place to live.

Owslebury Village Plans

The two plans of Owslebury village which follow illustrate the changes that have taken place during the last century. Comparing the two will reveal which houses and buildings have disappeared from our village scene and which are new additions.

The plans are intended as a guide as you turn the pages and so 'walk through the village'.

O.S. Acknowledgement: The road layout is based on the Ordnance Survey Pathfinder 1264 map.

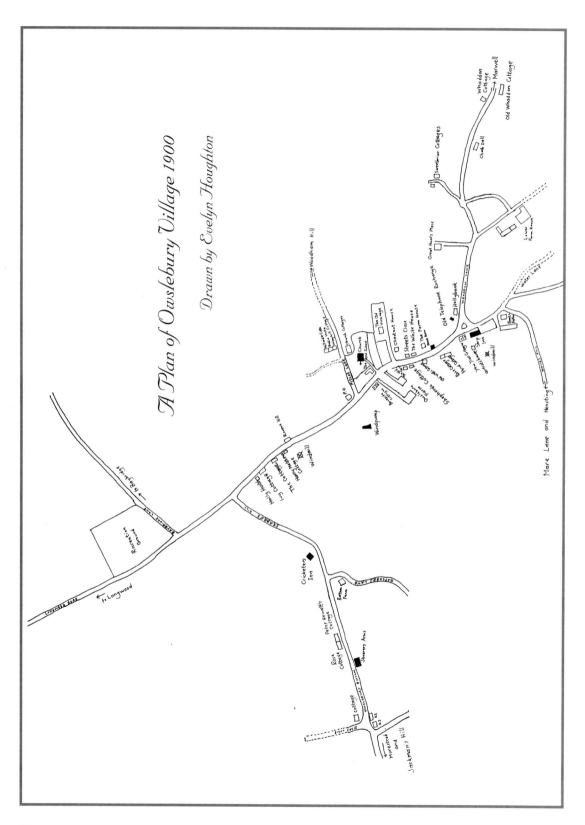

A Plan of Owslebury Village 1900

Drawn by Evelyn Houghton

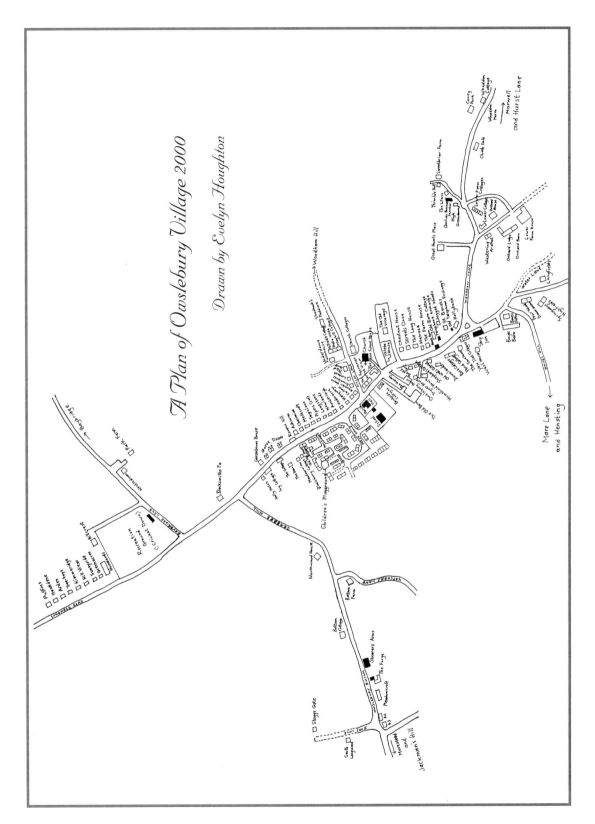

A Plan of Owslebury Village 2000

Drawn by Evelyn Houghton

Marwell Hall (AE)

Longwood House (DL)

3: OWSLEBURY HOMES AND FAMILIES – THROUGH A CENTURY OF TIME

'I think it is often a good thing to look back at the past to encourage us for the future'.
Revd. Charles Buston, friend and pastor, Owslebury Church 1900

One hundred years ago, as the village of Owslebury awaited the dawn of a new century, an aspect of significant difference in village life then was housing. As well as having none of our modern day comforts such as running water, central heating, double-glazing and electricity, homes were rarely owned by the families who lived in them. Often a cottage would be home to more than one family and there might be a lodger, too. Some of today's village properties were actually two or three separate homes early in the century. Often they were tied to a job and belonged to the landowners and gentry of the day, the major two in Owslebury being the Standish and Carnegie families of the Marwell and Longwood Estates respectively. Many little cottages were built from brick and flints dug from the fields and topped with a thatched roof. They were often situated close to the roadside with no front gardens as such. Then of course, roads were for pedestrians and horses only, meaning that pollution, noise and danger were not forces to be reckoned with. Houses were well spaced through the village with areas of green space between them.

Some of the old houses remain today alongside the newer houses that have filled in the spaces although they have all been altered and enlarged, in order to accommodate modern day comforts. Some have sadly disappeared, not having stood the test of time. If the owners had realised what sought after properties their little thatched cottages would become and what high prices they would fetch at the turn of this century, maybe they would have expended more effort to preserve these picturesque dwellings. Now the high value of these old cottages has meant that young people who have grown up in the village are usually forced to move away when setting up home for themselves. Village properties are just too expensive.

Having studied old maps, dipped into past records and chatted to some of our older village folk, a picture of village life has slowly evolved, portraying what it was like for families who made up the Owslebury community in the past. Let us now turn the clock back and take a walk along the length of the village as it would have been at the turn of the last century.

OLD WHADDON COTTAGE

One hundred years ago, approaching the village from Marwell, where today's signpost for Owslebury now stands at the foot of the hill, in a place known as Whaddon Bottom, there stood a large thatched cottage by the road side. It was fronted by a low flint wall and next to it was a

Old Whaddon Cottage (DL)

thatched barn. A gate led into the field behind and a large elm tree grew close by. The cottage and barn were part of the Marwell Hall Estate along with Lower Farm which was tenanted and worked then by Charles Anstey. In the 1930s Doug Rogers, as a young boy, lived in this cottage as his father Mont was employed by Mr Anstey. Doug remembers that when it rained heavily, water would come rushing down the hill, through the front door, along the passage to the kitchen and then down a well actually built in the kitchen! The well was never used to draw water. Later, Doug's father and his brother, Reg, filled it in, covering it with a concrete slab on which they carved their initials. Eventually the cottage was condemned and was demolished just after the Marwell Hall Estate was sold in 1934.

Mont Rogers was a well known and loved figure in the village and a man of many skills. It was he who had thatched the cricket pavilion roof in 1920. He was a dab hand at cutting men's hair for which task he used a pair of sheep shears! He was also skilled in the art of pig slaughter. Many homes kept a pig in those days. He was often helped in this task by Dick Lush who would sit on the upturned belly and hold the throat back while the cut was executed quickly and skilfully with a razor blade. Mont was a member of the bell ringing team and he played football and cricket for the village. He spent 45 years of his life in Owslebury, coming here from Longstock about 1910. He brought up his family here and worked at all kinds of farm-associated tasks over the years before finally being laid to rest in the village churchyard in 1955 alongside his wife, Nellie (née Day).

Today, Doug is one of the few remaining people who was born and bred in the village. His school days were all spent at the village school and following his R.A.F. service during the Second World War, he has always worked close to Owslebury. He has been a keen cricketer, a much valued member of the village side over a number of years. He is one of the few who has scored a century for the team. He has lived in seven different houses in the village and now lives with his wife, Daphne, in Beech Grove. Doug's sister, Margaret Moon also lives in Beech Grove.

WHADDON COTTAGE AND FARM

On the opposite side of the road, just on the bend, is *Whaddon Cottage*, home today to Michael Lush and his family. It is now part of *Whaddon Farm* where the Lush family has lived and worked since 1931. A second house, *Coney Park*, built in 1938 and set back from the road, is the home of Michael's brother, Brian (Bumper) and his wife, Joan. *Whaddon Cottage* is 102 years old having been built in 1898. At this time there was another house behind it but this was burnt down when someone, leaning out of a window holding a lit candle, set fire to the thatch.

Eva Vidler recorded her memories of this cottage in a 1961 village Newsletter. She had lived there as a child, coming to Owslebury in 1885. The house had evidently been large with four bedrooms, four living rooms and two stairways. It also had a bakehouse at the back which housed a large brick oven in which the Sunday dinner was always cooked. The copper was there too.

This was a feature of most homes a hundred years ago and comprised a copper water tank situated above a brick enclosure in which a fire would be lit to heat the water on each wash day. Eva tells how in her home this was used not just for washing clothes, but also for brewing beer. Villagers were certainly resourceful in those days. A few soap bubbles must have blended easily with the froth on the beer!

At the turn of the century the farm at Whaddon Bottom was owned by Corpus Christi College, Oxford. Half a century later it was put up for sale and bought by Dick Lush who had been a tenant farmer there since 1931. Dick came from a farming family in Andover, Hampshire. Seven years after moving into the village he married an Owslebury lass, Edith Bunney. Edith had been born in *Chestnut House*, the daughter of Robert and Mary (née Guy) Bunney. The house where Brian and Joan Lush live today was built then as a first home for the young married couple and it was there that their three children, Michael, Gillian and Brian were born and raised. The house was built by a team of local builders among whom was Harold Harfield, Alan Harfield's father.

When Dick first moved into *Whaddon Cottage* as a tenant farmer, the farm was considerably smaller than it is today. It was mainly arable land to which Dick added poultry houses with incubators. Children used to come to the farm specially to watch the chicks hatch in the granary.

It was two years later in 1933 that Dick bought his first dairy herd of 46 cows. In those days milk could be delivered directly from the farm to people's homes and Dick started a milk round.

At first, he had a motor bike and sidecar into which the churns were placed. He had a helper to assist him. While the helper drove the motor bike he would ride his pushbike so that when they arrived at more outlying places he could use his bike to reach those houses off the beaten track. He would ladle the milk from the churn into a large can and then carry this to people's doors where he would measure it in individual pints into people's own jugs. His round comprised the whole village together with outlying hamlets of Belmore, Baybridge, Hensting, Marwell and Longwood and would take all day. The cows had to be milked at dawn before the start of the round and then again in the evening at the end of it. During the war he would do his round with a horse and cart before eventually owning a van. Peggy Smith (née Merritt) used to help Dick with his round at this time and continued to do so until he gave it up. Peggy remembers Dick scolding her for giving drinks to all the cats along the way while they were doing the daily round! Some homes were served by Raymond Livingstone from *The Farm House* who also had a dairy herd. After the war bottles were introduced for milk deliveries and Dick used to take small third of a pint bottles daily to the school as part of his round. He continued to deliver milk for the next 25 years and was the first in the village to acquire a milking machine in 1944 when the herd was increased to 120. The dairy herd was eventually sold early in the 1980s and today the pastures around the farm are grazed by beef cattle.

Michael and Brian Lush now run the farm together and Dick is enjoying his retirement in his home at Baybridge. Michael's and Brian's children are the fourth generation of the family to have been born in Owslebury.

CHALK DALE

Continuing up the hill on the left-hand side is a chalk pit. A cottage named *Chalk Dale* is located at this point. One hundred years ago this house was named *Chalk Dell Cottage* and alongside was a double forge. The cottage was part of the *Marwell Hall Estate* and the land round the cottage was used as a repair yard for the estate, featuring the wheelwright's and carpenter's shop adjoining the cottage and the separate blacksmith's shop. This had a tyre- fitting platform outside which was for fixing metal tyres to wooden cartwheels.

At the turn of the century *Chalk Dell* was the police cottage for the village. In 1896 James Mills the newly appointed policeman had moved there with his family. His daughter, Sarah, known as Sadie (who later became Sadie Showell) when she wrote her memories of that time recalls how her mother lived in constant fear that one of her children would come to an untimely end by falling over the chalkpit. Shortly after the young Sadie started school, sadly her father died and the family moved to Baybridge. The next tenant of the cottage was Miss Alice May Gurman, always known as Miss **Daisy** Gurman, who was the newly appointed schoolmistress. She continued to live there until her death in 1947 when aged 65 years.

The chalkpit was originally dug to provide chalk to make lime that was used in agricultural and building work. The blacksmith's shop was built onto the front of the lime kilns, some traces of

Chalk Dell Cottage, 1934

Chalk Dale Cottage, 2000, with Nigel White *(EH)*

which still exist behind the forge building. Sites of several other lime quarries are to be found around Owslebury today but *Chalk Dale* is unusual in that it became premises in its own right after chalk quarrying had stopped.

In 1934 *Chalkdell* was sold by auction along with the rest of the *Marwell Hall* estate. It was described as being '*a secluded and attractive small House of brick, plaster and slate, containing Sitting Room, Living Room and Scullery with Three Bed Rooms over. Brick and Tiled Outbuilding. Water from well. Nice Garden*'. The schedule went on to describe, '*Nearby is a Brick and Tiled Smithy and on the other side of the road is the capital Pasture Land*'. *Chalk Dell Cottage* was sold, together with the smithy and the pasture land, for £400.

By 1947 its value had risen to £750. This was what villager, Samuel White, paid for the property and it was he who changed its name to *Chalk Dale Cottage*. Sam ran his agricultural engineering and machinery business from here, alongside Bill Bridle who worked the forge. It was a happy 'partnership' for Bill used to do machinery repairs for Sam.

William Bridle was a much loved village character. Sidney Showell, who used to live in Owslebury, described him warmly in some memories recorded in the village Newsletter in 1961. Bill was evidently a man of many skills, not only with horses, but also in the repair of farm machinery, the curing of crop-bound chickens, the doctoring of cats, the killing of pigs and the emptying of toilet buckets from the school! He

Sam White (NW)

was also part time miller working at the mill between all his other jobs and the mill became known locally as 'Bridle's Mill'. Children used to love to visit the forge and watch him at work there, marvelling at the flying sparks, the red hot metal and the smell of burning hoof. Bill could be seen daily about one o'clock, riding up the hill on his bicycle, leather apron tucked to one side, pipe in mouth, with dog, Jimmy, running behind him. Bill finally retired in the early 1960s but still lived in the village, at *The Sycamores*. He was cared for here during his last days by Mrs Hutchings, the postmistress who lived next door.

When Bill Bridle died in 1963, Sam White wrote the following comments in the village Newsletter: '*Standing at the back of the forge is quite a large sycamore tree which he raised in a small pot, later planting it in its present position, where it has now grown into a well shaped tree*'. Bill's tree is still there today in 2000.

Sam White too was a village 'character', written about and remembered with good reason. He was born at the end of the nineteenth century in 1897 and came as a seven year old boy to *Marwell Farm* in 1905. He learned to fly during the First World War, gaining his license in 1918, as the war ended. He married Isabella Kate Glasspool in 1923 and moved to *Boyes Farm,* initially renting but later buying it. His steam threshing and contracting business was run from *Boyes Farm,* and by the late 1920s he employed 26 men to operate his steam threshing and ploughing engines. It was Sam's engines that were responsible for re-opening the old lane that ran from *Boyes Farm* down to Hensting which had become overgrown and unused. The villagers soon referred to the hill as White's Hill, the hill that Sam made passable again, but it was a great surprise to Sam that the sign markers for Hampshire County Council gave it that name officially! Previous to this, the lane had been known locally as Poorhouse Lane because it led to the poorhouses which were situated at the bottom of the hill in Hensting Lane at the end of the nineteenth century.

Sam was much involved in many aspects of village life. He carried out his duties as a Special Policeman for more than 25 years. He became a sergeant in this job which could perhaps be seen as a forerunner to our Neighbourhood Watch scheme of today. Sam, however, wore a uniform and had particular hours of duty when he would patrol the village looking for anything untoward. Sam was a church warden, chairman of the Parish Council, a rural district councillor and on the planning committee of the Rural District Council. He was very involved in the planning of the council houses in Beech Grove.

Sam's first wife, Isabella, was an accomplished pianist and was often involved in fondly-remembered social gatherings in the village. After her death in the 1950s, Sam married Thora Lush and their two sons, Nigel and Howard, grew up in the village and attended the village school. As children they were often asked to pump the air for the forge fire by winding the handle on the blower. Later Nigel continued to do blacksmithing until the forge was rented out to Nigel Clough, an armourer, in 1982. For the next five years, swords, armour, and even muskets, for museums, collectors and battle re-enactment societies, were made at the forge and sent all over the world.

The forge is currently unoccupied but the building remains as a possible blacksmith's workshop.

Today, Thora still lives at *Chalk Dale* with her sons. Nigel and Howard continue to run their garage repair and breakdown business at *Chalk Dale*, and this has enabled them to live and work in the village in which they were born, an opportunity not available to most of their companions at Owslebury School.

LOWER FARM HOUSE

In order to reach *Lower Farm*, one has to turn left on the bend of the hill and walk down a track marked '*footpath*'. This footpath, number 46, well used by walkers and dog owners, leads across to Marwell. Animals from the zoo can often be seen grazing the fields in the distance. *Lower Farm House* is located at the beginning of the footpath. Today it is a private property, owned by Paul and Penny Bowes. Paul and Penny moved here from nearby Upham in March, 1989, although their link with the village goes back some years before this as they were married in St Andrew's Church, Owslebury. Shortly after moving to *Lower Farm House,* a Winchester City Council official came to survey the property and told them that it was probably built as a medieval hall around 1490 because signs of a timber frame and wattle were evident. Underneath the rendering there were bricks on the façade dating from the Tudor period. At the same time some quarry tiles, that were constantly damp, were lifted. It was found that these had been laid directly onto the soil. Some half-height panelling and a brick fireplace were then removed to reveal an old inglenook fireplace.

A brick and flint extension was evidently added in the 1700s and another in mid-Victorian times. A single storey extension to the original house was probably built on early in the twentieth century.

Before the house became separated from the farmland it was part of the *Marwell Hall Estate* and lived in by the Anstey family. This family had been here since at least 1881. In the census of that year a Robert Anstey was head of the household and farmed 246 acres, employing 4 labourers and 3 boys. A year after this census, the young 11 year old George Harfield started to work here, sheep-minding first and then working in the stables as under carter in the head team. Many years later George told Frank Williams that '*Mr Anstey's flock was about 150 yews and a few tegs*'. He went on to tell him about his work with the horses. '*I used to get up about 5.30 – 6.00 am. I worked along with a man Mr Gilpin who lived in a house on the left as you turn into Lower Farm. We used to go to Botley Mill five days a week with barley – some of the finest barley ever you could set eyes on – what they can't grow today. The harvesting, dung carting – everything was done with the horses*'. In the 1930s it was a farm of '*dairying, stock and mixed holding*' with stabling for nine carthorses and a tiled granary. Water was laid to the house from the Rural Authorities supply, and a large underground rainwater tank was installed. There were flower and kitchen gardens and a tennis court. The farm had good pasture and arable land as well as woodlands well stocked with large numbers of oak and ash '*to provide excellent sporting, being well placed and forming capital cover for game*'.

Lower Farm House, 1934

Lower Farm House, 2000 *(DR)*

During the Second World War, Mr Stern farmed here and initiated many enterprising ideas for the efficient running of the farm. A room was fitted with accumulators and a generator which was used to charge the batteries which supplied the farm with electricity. This was several years before the village itself had a supply. It was Reg Rogers' job then to start the generator up each day. Mr Stern also installed a water pumping station so that there was a tapped supply to the house as well as filled water troughs. During the Second World War the farmhouse was used as a base for the R.A.F.

George and Olive Molden brought up their young sons, Michael and David, at *Lower Farm House* while they continued to farm the land in the fifties and sixties. In the 1970s Michael Molden introduced battery hens and pigs to the farm. They were the last people to farm here. The barns which were situated close by and which were part of the working farm have now been converted to housing. Three terraced brick and flint properties opposite *Lower Farm House* were originally farm workers' cottages, built shortly after the sale of the *Marwell Hall Estate* in 1934. Doug Rogers remembers living here as a child in the 1930s after moving from the cottage at Whaddon Bottom.

GREAT HUNTS

Coming back to the main road from the track leading up to *Lower Farm House* and continuing up the hill, one passes on the right hand side a wide driveway leading to *Great Hunts*. This house, set well back from the road, was built round about the turn of the century but bears no

Great Hunts, 2000 *(DR)*

Sweetbriar Farm, 2000 *(EH)*

resemblance to the house that we see today. It was built originally as a red brick cottage and it was not until the 1970s that it was enlarged and given its present Georgian features. It has been extended again by the present owners Lord and Lady Torrington. They moved to *Great Hunts* in 1981 with their children, Henrietta, Georgina and Malaika. Each springtime there is a wonderful carpet of snowdrops on the bank at the entrance to the drive. Lady Torrington planted these and they were here some time before other snowdrops were planted through the village to mark the new millennium.

In the early years of the last century, *Great Hunts* was home to Charles Anstey's sisters, Louisa and Agnes, who were always referred to by villagers as 'the Miss Ansteys'. In their later years they became very frail and were nursed here by Nurse Mabbitt until they died. Louisa died in 1953, aged 83 and Agnes in 1954, aged 82.

Back in the 1930s on the roadside by *Great Hunts* was one of the village ponds. Dick Lush remembers Charlie Anstey and Arthur Read unharnessing their horses so that they could walk them to the water there to quench their thirst.

SWEETBRIAR FARM

On an old map of the village dated 1909, today's *Sweetbriar Farm* is recorded as *Sweetbriar Cottages*. As recently as the 1970s *Sweetbriar Farm* and what is known today as *Thimble Hall* were considered as one property known by this name. Barbara and Dudley Bryant bought both properties, renovating and living in the renamed *Thimble Hall* part and selling the other cottage to Kay and Christopher Westlake in 1981. Barbara

Bryant used to be chairman of the Parish Council in Owslebury but she no longer lives in the village.

In 1923 *Sweetbriar Cottage* was home to the Hutchings family. Herbert who had been village postman since 1913, was tragically killed in October of this year when he was knocked from his bicycle by a car close to the *Ship Inn*. He had served throughout the First World War in the Hampshire Regiment and the newspaper report of his funeral recorded that he was '*a keen supporter of the local cricket club . . . greatly respected by villagers and won the esteem of all with whom he came in contact*'. After his funeral men of the Oddfellows Perseverance Lodge threw sprigs of thyme into the grave as a token of esteem. A year later Mrs Hutchings moved to *Restholm* with her children, Tony and Peggy, and she then became the village postmistress.

Prior to 1981 the *Sweetbriar Farm* cottage was home to brother and sister Les and Eileen Hutton. Les worked for Dick Lush. Eileen still lives in the village today in a bungalow in Beech Grove.

The two cottages are believed to be over 250 years old. They were built of brick and flint and originally had thatched roofs. Today they look very different because *Thimble Hall* has been extended and the walls have been rendered. *Sweetbriar Farm*, now with a peg-tiled roof, has retained its brick and flint walls. The Westlakes lived in a caravan for five months while they carried out renovations and they finally moved in during July, 1982.

The cottage cannot be seen from the road but it is situated at the end of a drive towards the valley bottom, looking out over a picturesque view of fields, hills and trees. A pedigree flock of Hampshire Down sheep grazed the pastures below until the Westlakes, who were respected sheep breeders and judges, moved from the village in the autumn 2000. Mr and Mrs Brewer now live at *Sweetbriar Farm*, and Louise Westbury lives at *Thimble Hall*.

Hampshire Down sheep were a well known breed in the village in days of old. Frank Williams enjoyed listening to tales from George Harfield back in the 1960s when George explained how he had done the job of sheep shearing. He said, '*The most as ever I did shear was 50 in a day and that wants doing. It takes about nine to twelve minutes to shear a sheep. You had to be on the move all the time when shearing those Hampshire Downs. The wool was tied up in fleeces except the lambs' wool – that was bagged up loose. I've been shearing lambs when they've not been much bigger that a good-sized cat. The wool was taken to the Corn Exchange in Winchester*'.

George's sheep shears were put to good use at other times also because he was in much demand as hair cutter by local men folk!

George Harfield was one of the village characters belonging to a bygone era. He was born back in 1871 and lived to be almost one hundred years old. Evidently Dr Roberts promised him a bottle of whisky to celebrate his century, but sadly he didn't quite make it.

HOLLYBANK

At the top of the hill, on the right-hand bend of the road, where Whaddon Lane joins the main street through the village, stands *Hollybank*. It is obvious that this is not an old property, but it seems there has been a house on this site certainly

Hollybank, 1983 – note the old Telephone Exchange to the left and Southview behind
(IM – photograph © Skyviews Aerial Archives, Leeds)

Hollybank, 2000 *(DR)*

for most of the last century. It is rumoured that back in this period of time, when there was another mill behind the *Ship Inn*, bread was baked and sold from *Hollybank*. Sidney Showell, when he wrote his memories for the Newsletter in 1961, remembered another '*lovely old thatched cottage*' here, where a Mr and Mrs Day lived, along with a Charlie Lee and son, Fred. Mrs Day evidently ran a small general shop from the premises.

Today *Hollybank* is the home of Ian and Jackie McLeonards and their children Mark, Scott and Lisa. When they bought the property from a Mr and Mrs Jennings in 1983 it actually comprised two separate dwellings, *Hollybank* fronting the road with *Southview* immediately behind. It is thought that the building bought by the McLeonards was erected shortly after the First World War. It had to be taken apart piece by piece while the family lived in a caravan on site because planning permission to completely knock down this dwelling in order to rebuild, was refused. *Southview* was demolished and *Hollybank* was discovered to be a very odd dwelling indeed. While building new internal walls to support the roof timbers and add the extension, it was discovered that the original building had been constructed of corrugated iron sheets! Concrete blocks had been added round the outside of the corrugated iron while inside the walls were just hardboard, then fibre board layers with paper on the top. A boarded-up window with a wide sill, which suggested the serving counter of a shop, was also discovered. No wonder it needed to be completely rebuilt! Ian and Jackie have transformed *Hollybank* into the spacious and comfortable

family home that is part of our village today.

Some of our older villagers remember that at the time of the First World War, *Holly Bank* was a corrugated iron building which was used as an army hut.

THE OLD TELEPHONE EXCHANGE

Alongside *Hollybank* stands the old *Telephone Exchange*. This was originally owned by Her Majesty's Postmaster General and was conveyanced to *Hollybank* for private use in 1956 when Colonel Alfred Harvey lived there. Until that date Colonel Harvey had run a post office in this little building as well as the telephone exchange. Today it is used just for storage, although the original battery wells and pulleys are still clearly visible, and it is always referred to by Jackie and Ian as 'the telephone exchange'!

YEW TREE COTTAGES

When walking and puffing up the hill to the main part of the village it is with some relief that the Bank Tree comes into sight at the top, with the three little houses making up *Yew Tree Cottages* behind it. Numbers 3 and 2 are among the oldest houses in the village and are thought to have been built at the same time as the *Ship Inn*, probably by the same builder. The numberings of the cottages today is rather odd for they seem to be in reverse as one goes towards the centre of the village. This ordering is thought to have occurred when the third cottage, Number 1, was added!

Back in 1908 the Victoria County History of Hampshire recorded that at that time there were just **two** '*lichen covered cottages known as Yew*

Yew Tree Cottages, 1904, with trees *'shaped like the trees of a toy Noah's Ark'* (SS)

Yew Tree Cottages, 2000 *(EH)*

Tree Cottages'. In front of them were two large yew trees, *'shaped like the trees of a toy Noah's Ark'*. They evidently gave their name to the properties but it is not very surprising that they are no longer there! The stumps however, can still be seen, one in each garden.

It seems that the third cottage, today's Number 1, was added sometime between 1908 and 1912. When Jessie Tuffs and her family moved to Number 2 in 1912, the family had neighbours on **both** sides; Mr and Mrs Bliss (Irene Bliss' parents-in-law) on the right, Number 3 today, and Mr and Mrs Guy (Vera Bampton's grandparents) on the left, Number 1 today.

Number 3 is now home to Clive and Ali Mansell and daughters Katy and Zoe. This cottage has a large cellar and is thought to have been used as a bakery at some time. When an internal wall was removed, it revealed blackened beams at the site of an old range.

The little cottage in the middle was also a bakery and the curved back wall of the original bread oven still protrudes into a corner of the front sitting room. It is now home to Helen Nellthorp. She came to live here after the death of her great aunt, Dorothy Gradidge. Dorothy was born in nearby Twyford and moved to Owslebury after her marriage to Bert in 1958. For many years Dorothy was organist at the church and at the same time she trained a small choir which sang regularly at services. Behind the cottage is a beautiful garden which Bert created over the years.

Helen Nellthorp's link with the village goes back even before the Gradidge's time. Her great grandfather, Leonard Bealing, attended the village school before the First World War. His family lived at *Greenhill*, in Baybridge, where his father worked as a gardener.

Yew Tree Cottage, Number 1, is lived in today by Sarah and Theo Rye. This cottage used to have a very large garden when it was inhabited by Enid Wynne Jones. Before Mrs Wynne Jones moved from the village she decided to sell part of the garden as a separate plot available for building. As a result, the large modern house, *The Swallows,* came to be built here in the 1980s.

THE SHIP INN

To the left of *Yew Tree Cottages* and the Bank Tree stands the *Ship Inn*. It is believed to have been here since about 1671 and is certainly one of the oldest buildings in the village. It may at one time have been a monastery and tales have been told of King's messengers staying here on route to *Marwell Hall* during the reign of Henry VIII. There is evidence that ship's timbers were used in the building of the inn, hence its name, although rumour has it that at one time it was known as *Britannia*.

If village folk from the turn of the century could come back now, they might well have difficulty in recognising the *Ship Inn*. Gone is the attractive thatched roof of that time, replaced by tiles since 1911, with walls half-hung with tiles too. In 1900, except for the inn sign, it looked almost like another cottage with a low flint wall fronting it and a little gate at the foot of the steps leading to the inn door. In the wall were fastened rings to which horses could be tied. In those days any would-be drinkers would have approached either on horse back or on foot of course.

Ship Inn, c1900 (SS)

Ship Inn, 2000 *(DR)*

At the beginning of the last century there was a mill situated behind the *Ship Inn* and also another house. An artist named Mr North lived in this house. Both the mill and the house were destroyed in a fire during the First World War and neither was rebuilt.

Once inside, yesterday's villagers would have been welcomed by the same warm and cosy atmosphere as today, enhanced by the low beams and the large open fireplace. They might well have found the publican family's dinner cooking over the open fire as they sat on the curved wooden settle close by, each warming both inner and outer man as they enjoyed a drink with friends after work. They would catch up on the gossip of the day and then maybe participate in a game of darts, dominoes or 'tip it' before going home to their own families. In those days it would have been men only enjoying the warmth and companionship of the inn. Ladies did not go into pubs and children were not permitted entry. At the turn of the century George Norgate was landlord at the *Ship Inn*.

Before the Second World War the *Ship Inn* was used for inquests, with the coroner, police, doctor and witnesses all being present.

Half way through the last century it had become acceptable for ladies to be seen in pubs and in the 1960s the *Ship Inn* had its first landlady, Sally Matthews, who ran the pub together with husband, Tony. They were followed in the 1970s by John and Dorothy Law. It was they who introduced the first of the major changes that were to follow in the years to come. The old curved wooden settle which had provided seating for so long was now replaced with small tables and chairs more suited for the eating of meals that were now available. Enhancing the cosy interior and adorning the walls was a veritable gallery of old photographs some of village and other local scenes, along with portraits of Owslebury cricket and football teams over the years. These all remain to this day having been regularly added to and make fascinating viewing, giving today's folk an insight into life in days gone by. It was during the 1970s that the *Ship Inn* began to attract people from further afield. The regular locals would now find the pub visited by strangers who had walked or driven some miles especially to eat or drink there.

The Laws ran the pub for about three years. In 1980 Bob and Carole O'Neill took over as landlords and came with son, James, to live in the accommodation above the pub. They were anxious that the *Ship Inn* should remain a pub that was very much for locals as well as for those who increasingly visited at weekends. They added an extension to the left of the main bar, that had been known as the tap room, and introduced the Mess Deck to provide more restaurant facilities where families could book a table to enjoy a meal out or to celebrate a special occasion. Bob and Carole also introduced several events that have remained annual traditions to this day, namely the Barrel Race, rolled annually each New Year's Day, and the Plank Race. They also organised a bonfire and firework evening each 5th of November for several years. There was much sadness in the village when it became known in 1990 that Bob and Carole were giving up as landlords of the pub. They have remained in the village however, having a new property, *West*

House, built next door to the *Ship Inn*. They have lived here ever since.

When Bob and Carole left the *Ship Inn*, Gervais Head took over the tenancy for the next year. Clive Mansell then came to Owslebury from Winchester in June, 1991. It is Clive and his wife, Alison, who have happily and successfully steered *The Ship* through the last decade of the twentieth century and into the new millennium.

The pub has remained a focus in the village for companionship and sociable get-togethers over the years. More than ever now, people come from many miles away to partake of the delicious food on offer or to participate in a variety of social events devised and organised by Clive and Ali. Although country pubs rely on visitors for their livelihood, much care is taken to retain traditional activities. The annual Barrel Race now takes place between the *Ship* car park and *Boyes Barn*, as today's traffic would make any attempt to roll around the Bank Tree too hazardous. Because of the amount of traffic chaos Firework Night had caused, the display was moved to Longwood in 1997 where it has taken place ever since. Darts is only played occasionally now but the *Ship* has two cribbage teams and dominoes are still played regularly. The *Ship Inn* is headquarters to Owslebury Cricket Club and has its own Sunday team. Photographs of old Owslebury teams are displayed on the bar wall as well as those of members of the Hampshire County Cricket Club who have visited the village three times during the 1990s. The *Ship* has a large petanque terrain which is constantly used by the well supported Petanque Club. Other regular activities include quizzes, cycle rides in France and golf matches.

Harry (Michael) Houghton *(right)* with a friend rolling the barrel, New Year's Day, 1986 *(EH)*

Winners of the Barrel Race with landlord, Bob O'Neill, *kneeling*, 1983
With Bob are, *from left to right*, Graham Bliss, Andy Whittington, Lloyd Williams, Mickey Davis, Trevor Jenkins, John Mahoney.

Winners of the Barrel Race, 1999
from left to right, Kevin Crockford, Mike Wells, Dave King, Pete Charman

SHIP INN CLOSED FOR ONE WEEK

Thanks to Southern Electric who have finally put Owslebury into the 21st Century we can now have third phase electricity which means that "off with the rubbers Clive - you will be replaced by a machine"!!!! (but not for everything) !!! At last Ali can have a dishwasher !
Due to this monumentous occurrence and all the upheaval involved

we will be CLOSED for ONE WEEK from Monday 6th November

We aim to have the Old Bar up and running by Monday 13th November and will hopefully be
serving meals in the Old Bar by Wednesday 15th November
Due to re-tiling and laying a new kitchen floor, the Mess Deck Restaurant will remain closed for a further week and will
re-open on Tuesday 21st November
During this time we will decorate and make some improvements
We are sure you will like them

Book your table now for after the closure and for Christmas

Ship Inn refit notice picturing landlord, Clive, in the kitchen, 2000 *(EH)*

The large garden, patio, ponds, children's play area and pets corner prove very popular with families and have won Clive and Ali many awards.

Towards the end of the year 2000 the *Ship Inn* is to have a refit. Whatever happens in the future it will surely remain an important landmark and play a significant role in the village of Owslebury.

BOYES FARM

To reach *Boyes Farm* one needs to turn left at the Bank Tree and walk past the *Ship Inn* as though leaving the village down Whites Hill. On the right hand side just before the corner stands *Boyes Farm*. This is a house that has witnessed several hundred years of village history, and records of the family who gave their name to the house can be found back at the beginning of the eighteenth century when Robert Boyes was buried in the churchyard in 1715. Perhaps its most famous inhabitant has been John Boyes. He

became well known because, although he was a farmer, he took the side of the farm labourers in their revolt of the 1830s to achieve better working conditions and wages. He paid a price for this, however, because although he was acquitted at his first trial, he was subjected to a second trial and subsequently convicted and sentenced to seven years deportation. He went to Australia where he settled down for a while and raised a family. He is believed to have returned to England some years later. His descendants can still be found in Australia and also New Zealand and have evidently been to this country, to Owslebury, to see the house where their famous ancestor once lived.

There is a legend told concerning another member of the Boyes family who is reputed to have tried to sell his wife under the Bank Tree! Legend does not reveal whether he was successful or not!

Boyes Farm, c1900 (PE)

Boyes Farm with Peggy and Ian Egerton, 2000 *(EH)*

In 1881 at the time of the census the house was inhabited by Joshua and Nellie Heath with their six children, George, Annie, Alice, James, Nellie and Emmy. Emmy believed there was a resident ghost, albeit a friendly one. At night she would hear a rattling noise and on occasions her candle was blown out. Peggy Egerton who lives in the house today revealed that once the roof had been felted and the wind could no longer gust through, Emmy's 'ghost' disappeared!

Sam White lived at the farm in the early years of the last century following the departure of the Heath family. He told of another tradition associated with the house. In the front porch are two oval windows, one on each side. In bygone years when the windows were just open spaces, it was a tradition to pass newly baptised babies through a window of the porch before carrying them into the house.

Boyes Farm today is the home of Ian and Peggy Egerton, and they have lived there for almost half a century. When they came to Owslebury with Ian's parents, Ivy and Robert, in 1947, there were just four cars in the village! There was no water or electricity in the house. Water was fetched from the standpipe at the Bank Tree and Peggy had a wooden yoke specially made so that she could carry two buckets at once. They did better than most villagers for lighting at that time, however, because they had their own petrol-run generator.

The house itself, Ian and Peggy found to be full of features which reminded them of its long history. There is a bread oven to the side of an inglenook fireplace. In the bedroom above, a narrow door in a cupboard can be opened to reveal the soot-blackened bricks lining part of the chimney and a thick oak beam with two stout metal hooks. From these hooks bacon and joints of ham hung to be smoked. Upstairs and downstairs the ceilings have broad oak beams. There is a room in the attic and an apple room which is entered down a deep step and lit by a small low window. There are nooks and crannies, steps up and down, and thick old doors with latches to fasten them. An extension which is now the kitchen was added by Sam White early in the century.

Boyes Farm has been a working farm for much of its long history. When the Egerton family moved in they had a small dairy herd of six cows which later grew in number to 25. The milk would be placed in churns at the farm gate ready for collection each day. Today the dairy herd is gone and the farm yard empty and silent. Barns at the back of the house have been very tastefully converted to make a home for Ian's and Peggy's son, Mark and his family. The old beams of the barn remain evident and the old grain pulley is a feature of their home.

Boyes Farm is believed to date back to the seventeenth century. It seems that many of the oldest properties in the village were built during this century. They include, *Chestnut House*, numbers 2 and 3 *Yew Tree Cottages*, *The Ship Inn*, *Church Cottages* in Pitcot Lane, and Owslebury Bottom cottages, numbers *41 and 42*.

POND COTTAGE AND ROSE COTTAGE

Walking back from *Boyes Farm*, past the *Ship Inn* and then *Yew Tree Cottages*, a pair of white walled cottages come into view. These are *Pond Cottage* and *Rose Cottage*. *Pond Cottage* was built

Pond Cottage, early 1900s (EH)

Pond Cottage, 2000 *(EH)*

Rose Cottage with Clem Hill, c1920, when Sarah (née Fletcher) and Alfred Jeffery were living there (LC)

in 1861 by the Earl of Northesk, who owned a considerable amount of land in Owslebury and lived in *Longwood House*. A plaque on the wall bears the initials E N together with the date 1861. *Rose Cottage*, however, is believed to have been built first, also by the Earl of Northesk, and together they were homes for coachmen from the Earl's estate. The coachmen would shelter the horses and carriages in buildings further along the road, now garages for *Rose Cottage* and *Old Wells Cottage*, while the family attended church.

Rose Cottage was a brick and flint building with a slate roof. At some time the front was rendered although the wall at the rear of the cottage was left with the original brick and flint exterior. *Pond Cottage* was added onto the side of *Rose Cottage* but was built just of brick. To the far side of the

Pond Cottage garden close to *Yew Tree Cottages*, was the pond from which this cottage took its name. It was evidently a large natural pond. It had three stone steps leading down to it and was bordered by trees on one side. In hot weather horses used to enjoy a drink after climbing the hill to the village. In cold weather the pond would freeze, much to the delight of village children who would rush home from school in order to slide on it. This 'village pond' was a feature at least until 1959 but at some time after this the area was infilled and a garage was built on the site.

A sad little story concerning *Pond Cottage* was reported in the press in December, 1935. The report stated '*Early on Tuesday morning, the tragic discovery was made that Mr Arthur Burt Read, 33, a farm carter, and a well known resident in the village, had taken his life with the aid of a single barrel sports gun'.* Arthur was born in the village and had lodged with Arthur George Paige at *Pond Cottage* for three years. He spent his last evening in the *Ship Inn* and had seemed perfectly normal and happy to his friends. The inquest took place in the *Ship Inn* and he was buried in the churchyard.

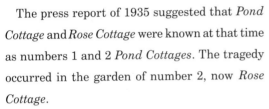

The press report of 1935 suggested that *Pond Cottage* and *Rose Cottage* were known at that time as numbers 1 and 2 *Pond Cottages*. The tragedy occurred in the garden of number 2, now *Rose Cottage*.

Today *Pond Cottage* is home for Evelyn and David Houghton who came to the village with their two young children Michael and Elizabeth in 1974 and over the years they have extended and renovated the cottage. At the beginning of the new millennium *Rose Cottage* stood empty, a somewhat sad little house since Allan Peachey's death in April, 1999. At the end of this year, however, the house has had a total facelift, lights shine from the windows once more, the garden is tended and it is home to Sean Cooper, Fiona and son Jack.

THE FARM HOUSE

Just past *Rose Cottage*, round the bend on the opposite side of the road stands the *Farm House*. It is an attractive, eye-catching dwelling of distinctive architectural style, obviously of great age, with its timber framed walls, small windows, a low front door and a beautiful thatched roof, one of just three remaining thatched houses in the village. The *Farm House* is probably the oldest house in the village and is believed to have been built about 1640 with an extension being added in 1769. On the sidewall of the extension is a wall plaque bearing this date together with the initials IP. The IP was the abbreviation for Joseph Page. The letters I and J were interchangeable at that time. This family took over the tenancy of the *Farm House* from the Soane family in 1752. Joseph Page was a wheelwright and it is possible that *The Barn*, now next door, contains the timber framing of the building in which Joseph made his wheels. The cellar in the house is reputed to have a tunnel leading from it to the *Ship Inn* and was used in years gone by for escapees and smugglers! A house probably existed on this site from the beginning of the sixteenth century. In 1516/17 the manor of Marwell Woodlock and its copyholds were bought by Richard Fox, Bishop of Winchester, as part of the endowment for his newly founded Corpus Christi College, Oxford. Since copyholds were held by tenants and gave very secure tenure together with rents that were fixed for all time, they were much valued. In 1523 the rent was 14s 8d plus a cock and three hens, and this rent remained exactly the same until 1920! By this time the cock and hens were usually commuted to a money payment. In 1920 the last copyholder died and the college then sold the house with some other land for £600. The *Farm House*, one year later in 1921 became the freehold property of Raymond Livingstone.

The copyholder who lived in the *Farm House* for the first two decades of the twentieth century was George Butcher with his wife, Augusta. The

The Farm House, c1956 (W.I. Scrapbook)

The Farm House, 2000 *(DR)*

Butcher family had been tenants since 1813 but the copyhold was finally extinguished when George died on 12 September 1920 aged 88.

When Raymond Livingstone bought the property, true to its name, it was a working dairy farm and supplied milk and dairy produce to the village. Peggy Smith (née Merritt) used to help deliver milk for Raymond Livingstone in the days when households supplied their own jugs to be filled. Peggy would walk down Pitcot Lane, collect eight such jugs, then walk to the *Farm House* to get them filled up. She would then make her way back carrying four jugs in each hand. She delighted in being able to swing these four jugs in a circle, up and over her head without spilling a drop!

In the latter half of the last century this lovely house has been home to the Atchley family and then Barbara and Ron Holden with son and daughter, Nick and Jackie. Barbara and Nick still live in the *Farm House* and daughter, Jackie, now married to Jon Crockford, lives next door in a new house built by Jon on land to the side of the old house, with sons Daniel and Thomas.

THE BLACK BARN

On the bend of the road just before and next to the *Farm House* stands a black corrugated iron clad building, a noteworthy land mark in the village. On the low flint wall fronting *The Barn* is another plaque with the lettering GEY 1808. Frustratingly, what these initials represent remains unknown.

Just behind *The Barn* at the turn of the century was another of the village ponds but this has long since disappeared.

During the Second World War, *The Barn* became a storage area for stirrup pumps and fire drills took place there. Evelyn Merritt remembers participating in these drills.

The Barn has also been a milking parlour for the *Farm House* but today it is no longer part of this property. It belongs now to Gwyn and Elsie Evans who have lived in the village since 1964 in the house on the same site as the *Barn* and which was known then as *The Platt* – the place where calves are reared. The house was built by Raymond Livingstone in 1956 and was intended for his retirement. However he decided to sell. Elsie and Gwyn have added extensions to the house and have renamed it *Old Barn Cottage*. Their children, Sian and David, grew up here.

OLD WELLS COTTAGE

Almost opposite the *Farm House* stands *Old Wells Cottage*, home today to David Wilkie who has lived there since 1974. This is the second of the three thatched cottages in the village and is believed to date back to the early 1600s. It was originally built as two semi-detached cottages which were used as farm dwellings for *Owslebury Farm*. The front doors for these houses were on the sides of the property then rather than at the front. Peggy Smith (née Merritt) remembers living in one of these semi-detached houses for a while as a child. About the time of the First World War, one of these cottages was well known in the village for its home-made sweets. Jessie Norman (née Tuffs) has told how she used to buy them on her way to school then.

Old Wells Cottage, c1900, note *two* cottages with front doors on the side (DW)

Old Wells Cottage, 2000 *(DR)*

Looking back down the village street towards Old Wells Cottage from the Old Shop and Shepherds Cottage, c1900 (SS)

The same view, 2000, with Frank and Jo Williams and neighbour Margaret Oakley. David Houghton is walking his dog *(EH)*

Looking up the street in the other direction towards the church (BON)

During the years of the Second World War, the vicar of that time Revd Francis Barker, moved out of the vicarage so that it could be used to house evacuees from Acton County High School. *Old Wells Cottage* then became his home until the evacuees left in 1943. The house was converted to a single dwelling in 1968. David Wilkie extended the back of the cottage in 1985.

In the early 1950s the garden of *Old Wells Cottage* extended right along the side, in front of the place where *Downlands* stands now, to the two garages on the corner. A hedge bordered the garden. The garages were evidently used at this time as shops. Brian Lush remembers seeing as a child, an assortment of garden tools for sale inside the open doors of what is now David Wilkie's garage. A Mr Lees was involved with the garden tools. It is possible to see where the old door from

that time, fronting the road, has been bricked up. Next to it, the garage for *Rose Cottage* had a sign over the wooden doors reading, *'licensed to sell wines, spirits and tobacco'*. Setting up shop like this is something that belongs to a bygone era, a time that was much more relaxed for individuals to do what they fancied, without the red tape and form filling that accompanies everything in this twenty first century.

SHEPHERDS COTTAGE

Shepherds Cottage is another of the older properties in the village although it could very easily have disappeared from our village scene in the 1950s because of its appalling condition. It was rescued from this fate by Frank and Jo Williams who were house hunting in Owslebury in 1956. The letter they received from the agents,

Shepherds Cottage, c1920 (SS)

George Smith & Son from Parchment Street, Winchester, advised, *'You would however, need to come to an early decision as the property will shortly have to be demolished unless a satisfactory repair scheme is submitted to the Rural District Council'*. Frank and Jo came to an early decision and decided to make an offer, beating the price down to a cash payment of £125.0.0, and early in 1957 the house became theirs.

At this time the house was completely uninhabitable. It comprised just two main rooms downstairs, along with an outhouse, storeroom and scullery and two bedrooms upstairs. The previous tenant, Peter Merritt, had lain in bed at night upstairs looking at the stars through a hole in the thatch where a thistle had also taken root. When it rained he put up an umbrella and collected the rainwater in an old tin bath! Peter

and Dolly (née Lawrence) Merritt had lived in *Shepherds Cottage* for several years and daughter, Peggy, married husband, Jack Smith from this house.

Frank and Jo Williams moved into the village, living in a caravan built by Frank, while they began work on the cottage and awaited the birth of their first child. The caravan was named 'Happy Prospect' after a winning horse that they had heard about on a chance listening to a racing programme before they moved in. Later, as the family expanded, the caravan became known as 'Nappy Prospect'! In those days the thought of nappy washing must have been grim because the water had to be fetched from the standpipe, fortunately close to the front of the old cottage, carried and then heated. The toilet then was a privy at the bottom of the garden.

Frank Williams standing through the thatch, 1957 (FW)

inglenook fireplace. On the main wooden beams could be seen Roman numerals, incised by the carpenter's chisel, to help match up the joints when the frames were later being re-erected on the site.

It took Frank and Jo three years of hard work before they finally moved into *Shepherds Cottage*. Their four children, Lloyd, Elaine, Claire and Erica were all born and grew up in the village. Jo and Frank later set up their successful hand-crafted wooden toy-making business, known as *Chisellers,* from a workshop at the bottom of the garden. As we enter the new millennium, they have decided it is time to retire from toy making.

As Frank began work on the cottage he found it to be of 'post and pan' construction. The roof had no ridge board and the joists were adzed larch poles, slatted to support a thatch. This construction indicated that the cottage could date back to Tudor times. The walls were constructed of brick and had at some time been painted white. It had been built originally as a simple tithe cottage and was named after the successive generations of shepherds who lived in it.

Frank and Jo lovingly restored the little cottage over the years doing all the work themselves, adding a tiled roof and extending closer to the road edge at the front as well as to the rear. As they excavated the floor at the front of the cottage, they discovered an old floor made of brick, laid in a beautiful herringbone pattern. They would have dearly liked to restore this floor but the bricks proved too thin and brittle. All the old beams were cleaned and left exposed, along with the large

Jo and Frank may well have been newcomers when they moved to the village in 1957, but today, having witnessed almost half a century of happenings and changes in Owslebury, they are firmly established as 'village folk'.

THE SHOP

Next door to *Shepherds Cottage* with only a few feet between them is another cottage named *The Old Shop*. It is so named as a reminder of the time when it actually **was** a shop serving the village folk of Owslebury. Changes in twentieth century life styles and the advent of huge out-of-town supermarkets helped to bring about its demise. This little shop closed its doors for the last time on 31 October 1989. It has left a gap

Shepherds Cottage and The Old Shop, 2000 *(DR)*

which no supermarket can fill. The friendly personal service, the chance for a chat to other shoppers, a reason to go out and somewhere to walk to, are all much missed. It is understandable however, that a small shop such as this, serving a small community, is no longer a viable business proposition in today's world.

Villagers have fond memories of the shop. It was one of two general stores in the village at the beginning of the last century. The other was at *Hollybank*. It was built in brick and flint in 1857, the date being inscribed on the wall above the door. The initials BB are engraved underneath but what these initials represent no one can say for certain. They might stand for a member of the Boyes family who was involved for some time with the shop in the previous century and until 1905. The building was bequeathed to Alice Sophia Boyes by Mary Lavington, her aunt, from *Bottom Farm*. On the same wall but above where the present double doors are, there is a tiny china face embedded in the cement between the flints. Frustratingly no one knows why this came to be placed here either. It has been suggested that it might have been a tobacconist's sign as the little figure is smoking a pipe.

Jessie Norman (née Tuffs) who grew up in the village before emigrating to New Zealand, remembers the excitement of going to the shop to buy a sherbet dab with her weekly farthing allowance, round about the time of the First World War. At this time *The Shop* was known as 'Granny

The Old Shop, 2000 *(DR)*

Baker's', and Peter Hewett also records his memories of the shop in his book 'Owslebury Bottom'. 'Granny' was Mrs Caroline Baker, known affectionately as Mossy Baker to villagers, and she took over *The Shop* from Henry Boyes in 1905. Peter Hewett evidently used to go there from school during the lunch hour. He too enjoyed the sherbet dabs – *'tissue paper triangles of sherbet with hollow liquorice tubes in two corners through which you sucked up the powder and got a fizzy mouthful'*. They had doubled in price since Jessie Tuffs had bought hers and Peter had to pay a halfpenny for his! Among his other treats were locust beans at 1d for 8oz, or broken pieces of Packer's chocolate which he described as being *'greasy, sweet and powdery on the surface'*. Granny Baker, he remembered, was a tiny person,

a little on the deaf side, with thin hair and gold-rimmed spectacles, arthritic and veiny hands. She wore a long black skirt with an apron and she had a parrot which lived in *The Shop*. If children came into the store while Granny was in the garden, the parrot would shout out 'shop Mossy'! Almost 80 years later when Margaret and Graham Oakley took over the store, this custom was resumed as they too had a parrot which would shout out 'Shop'!

Granny's daughter, also Caroline Baker, took over the shop from her mother. Then in 1931, after her death, it was sold for the sum of £260 to Constance Thatcher from *Bottom Pond Cottage* in Morestead. She was quaintly described in the documentation of the sale as *'a stranger in blood'* and the property was stated as being *'a freehold cottage with shop and stable adjoining'.* Connie Thatcher, known as Auntie Connie to village children, was to run the store for the next thirty years. Her son, George, took over in 1960 for the next three years before Harold and Marjorie Blackman came to live at *The Shop* in February, 1963 with children, Jill, John and Janet. The shop premises then were on the right of the door, with a bakehouse alongside. Harold's father, Bernard, who lived at *Deeps Cottage* at Marwell used to cart wood up to the shop for the bakehouse. It was a grim first winter for the family in 1963 when the weather was bitterly cold. All of the unlagged pipes froze and mice came in by the score to run along by the fireplace and shelter under the floorboards which were simply balanced on bricks at that time. At least the family had an inside toilet! Harold and Marjorie had a new floor laid and a solid fuel Aga stove installed and they also built an extension at the rear of the property.

In *The Shop* itself was a cream and green Lyons Maid freezer containing amongst other things, frozen faggots, fish fingers, ice cream and lollies. This was at a time when few families would have had a freezer. In the kitchen at the back they had a big old fridge where they kept butter, fats and bacon.

When Marjorie and Harold Blackman took over *The Shop* there was no post office; that was to come a few years later, and it took over the front room of *The*

Shop on the left hand side of the door. They sold groceries and all sorts of household necessities and made regular weekly visits to Nurden and Peacock in Eastleigh to stock up on their supplies. Greengroceries came from Morley's at Horton Heath. Bacon was sliced from the joint as required and cheese was cut with a wire. These would both be weighed, then wrapped in greaseproof paper and placed in a white paper bag pulled off a string. Broken biscuits could be bought from a tin with a see-through lid. Many village folk at this time would shop daily, and some would record their purchases in a notebook and pay at the end of the week. Some liked to pay into a Christmas Club week by week so that they would be able to afford extra treats when the festive season arrived.

The Shop used to open from 8.30 to 5.30 each day from Monday to Saturday with half day closing on Wednesday. They closed for lunch from 12.30 to 1.30. On Saturdays they stayed open for an extra hour in order to await delivery of the Football Echo. The Evening Echo newspaper was sold daily.

In 1981 Marjorie and Harold Blackman decided to retire and *The Shop* was taken over then by Margaret and Graham Oakley who saw it through to the day when it closed its doors for the last

Declaration for the sale of the Shop in 1930. Note the phrase *'stranger in blood'*. *(reproduced with kind permission of Margaret and Graham Oakley)*

time eight years later. When they first moved in they discovered stalls still in position at the back of the room used as a storeroom behind the double doors. These were remnants of the time when it was as a stable and a pony and trap were kept there.

Owslebury Stores as the shop was known for its last few years, continued to serve the village community, carrying on the traditions of high quality and friendly personal service both in the post office and the general store. Among Margaret Oakley's best-known and favoured products were the hams which were cooked on the premises and sliced straight from the bone for customers. There were always three on the go – one being sold, one chilling in the fridge and one being cooked. Margaret maintained the Christmas Club and also had a special Christmas evening when the store would open again after normal hours and people would come to make their Christmas purchases and enjoy a pleasant social occasion at the same time. The ground floor of the house would be opened and Margaret would serve everyone with ham sandwiches, mince pies, a glass of wine and coffee.

Margaret employed several village folk to help in the shop. These included Sheila Allen, Betty Wood, Mary Taylor, Sheila Gough, Pat Payne and Pat's daughters, Rebecca and Josephine. During these last years as in years gone by, customers would come daily to the shop to make their purchases. Margaret would sometimes notice items on lists not bought, but on pointing this out she would be told –'I'll get that tomorrow; I'll come back'.

As we enter the new millennium sadly we can no longer 'come back'. There is no tomorrow for our village store. Margaret and her husband,

Inside the Shop – Josephine Smith serves behind the counter (MO)

The White House, 1904 (SS)

Graham, have remained in the village however, and have been able to keep the old shop premises as their home.

THE WHITE HOUSE AND STREETS CLOSE

One hundred years ago, opposite *Shepherds Cottage* and *The Shop* were two more picturesque thatched cottages named *The White House* and *Streets Close*. There were only the narrowest of gardens and a low flint wall between them and the road. These are two more cottages that have disappeared from the village scene today.

The White House was inhabited by Mr and Mrs Joe Froud and their family. Joe's son, Will, grew up to marry Jessie Tuffs' sister Marjorie. The next generation on, grand-daughter Daphne Fousler, now living in Beech Grove, was born in *The White House*. This cottage was the first of the pair to be demolished. The dwelling on this site today, now set well back from the road and renamed *The Long House*, is a distinctive single storey, timber framed, cedar wood building, designed and built by Martin Kibblewhite in the late 1950s. Martin, his wife, Mary, and daughters, Helen, Celia and Anna lived here until 1985 when they moved away, and today's owners Derek and Bet Brook, came to live in the village.

Early in the century *Streets Close* was home to Charlie Glasspool. The Glasspools had been in the village for many generations and, in fact, theirs is the first ever name recorded in the ancient burial registers of the church. In 1508 it was recorded, '*The will of Nicholas Glasspool who desires to be buried in the churchyard of Santa Andree of Ozilbury'*.

The last residents in the cottage were Mrs Alice McDermott and her lodger, William Odger. The cottage was in a very frail state before it was demolished. This was done in April, 1969 by Gwyn Evans and John Mahoney, who virtually just pushed it over with a stout pole! John and Di Mahoney had the present *Streets Close* built, again this time set well back from the road. Their children, Lois and Joseph, grew up in the village.

Streets Close (FW)

The present owners are Edward and Miranda Sprot who moved in to *Streets Close*, together with daughters, Rachael and Arabella, in August, 1998.

The Owslebury Women's Institute produced a scrapbook about village life back in 1965. In the book they recorded details about significant houses in Owslebury and one of these was *The Long House* which had been built in the late 1950s. Their concluding words were as follows; *'This is the last house to be built in the village and it will be one of the last for a few years because of the green belt restrictions'*. It seems that they

were looking through rose coloured spectacles at the time. Since then there have been many new properties built where there were none before. These include *The Lilacs, High Greendowns, West House, The Swallows, St. Benets, Jagged Woods, Melrose, Downlands* which was originally known as *Cedrine, Homefield House, Tryner House, Glebe House, Gamefair, Underdown Farmhouse, Shadracks Paddock, Newlands, Ashiana, Blackberry Cottage, Meadowview, The Dean, Gorsedown House, Blacksmiths Farm, Greenacres, Kimmeridge, The Forge, Meadowcroft*, and *South Longwood*. As we enter this third millennium there is concern amongst villagers that more of their green spaces will be taken in the future for more housing development. People who have chosen to live in Owslebury love it for its rural setting and accompanying limited facilities. They fear that more houses will mean the loss of all they hold most dear about village life. Only time will tell.

CHESTNUT HOUSE

Next door to *Streets Close* is *Chestnut House*, which has been a home to various villagers for almost 350 years. Like many other properties in the village it used to be owned by Corpus Christi College, Oxford. It was the last such property in Owslebury to be sold in 1959. The first private owners then were Arthur and Lily Pritchard who purchased the house for £300. In 1962 the Pritchards sold the house to Raymond and Pauline Aitchison who began major renovations. They, in turn, sold it to Commander and Wilhelmina Lutyens and it was they who did the most extensive work on the house, restoring many of the old features while adding others to make it a comfortable and beautiful home. It was in 1982 that *Chestnut House* became home to the present owners, Eddie and Sandy Emery and it was here that their daughter, Joanne, was born and grew up.

Chestnut House is a brick construction with a peg tiled roof. It has a cellar below and rooms extend up into the roof cavity with beamed sloping ceilings. The original bread oven is still there as well as a large inglenook fireplace and each room is ceilinged with thick oak beams.

To the right of the property but joined to the front wall is the room housing the treadmill. This is a unique feature of the house and was restored by the Lutyens in the early 1960s

shortly after they had bought the house. Today the treadmill room has become the main entrance to the house. As one enters it is an awe-inspiring sight. The wheel itself is 12 feet in diameter, and 4 feet wide. The shaft is 15 inches in diameter and has two sets of spokes. The well is 400 feet deep and can still be viewed through the doors which the Emerys fitted above a short circular brick wall constructed over the

top. One wonders at the original engineering feat of digging out such a well. Evidently at one time it used to supply water to a small brew house.

In 1832 Revd Charles Maberley and his family became tenants at *Chestnut House* briefly, while waiting for the vicarage to be finished. His daughter, when writing as an old lady of eighty, could still remember her '*delight in running in the big tread wheel in the cottage . . . and playing at ghosts in the empty house*'.

In 1892 the copyhold for *Chestnut House* was extinguished. Robert Bunney then became the leasehold tenant at a rent of £10.0.0 per year.

Chestnut House, 2000 *(EH)*

About 1910 the Bunney family had lodgers when Sadie Mills came to live here with her mother and brothers and sisters. Her father had been the village policemen but had died. She also remembered the existence of the tread mill which

Chestnut House, c1880 (BH)

'to fetch water from the well gave us children some good fun and healthy exercise'. The wheel was last used to draw water in 1913.

Robert and Mary Ann (née Guy) Bunney had nine children, one of whom was Edith, who grew up to marry Dick Lush and become mother to Michael, Gillian and Brian. Edith's father, Robert, as well as being a carpenter by trade, was undertaker for the village, and in the front garden of *Chestnut House* was a sawpit which was used to saw the planks that would be made into coffins. These coffins were described by George Harfield when talking to Frank Williams as being *'black all round and polished'*. Robert Bunney died in 1923 but Mary, or Polly, as she was always known, continued to live here with her children until she died in November 1939.

Another village family was to live in *Chestnut House* as the Second World War began. Pearl Hatt (nee Pritchard) remembers coming here as a young girl. She married Christopher Hatt in the village church in 1941 and the young couple began their married life living with Pearl's parents in *Chestnut House*. Their first child, a daughter Christine, was born here just after Chris was called up for the war. Like many other children born at this time she wasn't to see her father again for several years. She was almost 4 years old when Chris came home again, on VJ day in September 1945. Pearl's parents, Arthur and Lily Pritchard continued to live in *Chestnut House*. In 1959 the opportunity arose for them to buy rather than rent the property. Three years later they sold *Chestnut House* to the Aitchesons.

Edith Bunney with her mother, Polly, c1930 (DL)

THE OLD VICARAGE

Next door to *Chestnut House* and approached down a long drive is the house known as *The Old Vicarage,* even though today it is no longer a vicarage. It is a large, elegant house with extensive land around it and beautiful views over open countryside towards Baybridge. The drive is flanked with an avenue of trees which includes horse chestnut, beech, lime and sycamore and these are underplanted with bulbs which make a colourful display each spring.

The Old Vicarage with its stable and coach house was built in the 1840s, on land known as Spencers Paddock, at the same time as the school and school house. Money for this was generously given by Alice Long from *Marwell Hall.* She was much loved by village folk because of her

kindness, compassion and practical help for those in need. A stained glass window above the altar in the church was later placed in her memory. John Froud, who was Daphne Fousler's grandfather who lived at *The White House,* was one of those who helped build the vicarage. The barge boards under the eaves are of a similar unusual and attractive design as those on the *School House* and also *Owslebury Farm* (now *Owslebury House*) which is opposite the church. The first resident incumbent was Revd Charles Maberley with his wife and twelve children. His eldest daughter, many years later when recalling her memories of those days, described the Parish as being '*in an awful state of wickedness and my father had to work hard when he went to live there*'.

In 1973 the diocese made the decision to sell the *Old Vicarage* house and build a new smaller vicarage on land adjoining the site, at the front of the Glebe. The Revd John Pringle was the last incumbent to live in the old house built 140 years previously. The new vicarage became home to Revd Colin Howell but only for a very short time. Due to the reorganisation of benefices in the Winchester diocese, Owslebury and Morestead joined once again with Twyford. The vicarage was no longer needed and so was sold as a private residence in 1980 and renamed *Glebe House.*

Today the *Old Vicarage* is home to Susie Gwyn, and Lea and Caroline Shipley live at *Glebe House.*

A previous owner of the *Old Vicarage* was Mrs

The Old Vicarage, pre 1887 (WMS)

A back view of the Old Vicarage, pre 1887 (WMS)

A back view of the Old Vicarage, 2000 *(DR)*

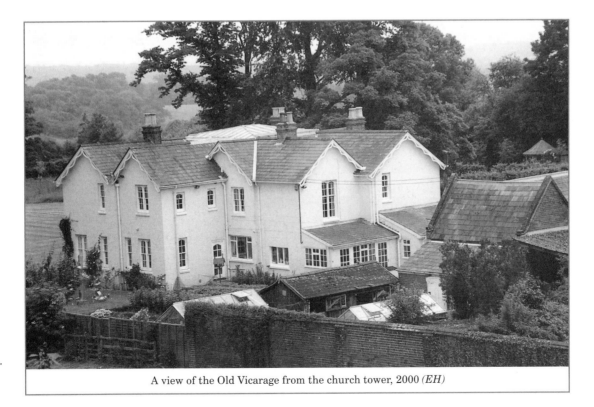

A view of the Old Vicarage from the church tower, 2000 *(EH)*

Sarah Wadham. She evidently decided to move from the house because she was convinced that she was sharing it with the ghost of a young Victorian girl. She saw this young girl, aged between 12 and 14 years and dressed in a nightgown, both up the stairs and in the kitchen. She had been told that one of the past vicars had had a daughter who died in the house and she thought this was the ghost of that child. Sarah actually had an exorcism carried out but felt she could no longer live there. Today's owner, Susie Gwyn, is happy to share her house with the ghost but to date has not actually met her!

The Church

Alongside the green space known as the Glebe, stands the church which has stood sentinel over the village for almost seven hundred years. Its long history is enough to fill a book by itself. It is set back from the road and approached through a pair of gates, which were placed in 1953 to mark the coronation of Queen Elizabeth II, and along a short winding path before a couple of steps lead down into the porch through to the church itself. As the 1800s became the 1900s, the feet of nearly every villager would tread along that path and down those steps each Sunday week by week in order to worship in church. Nearly all those folk who have written their memories of Owslebury, record this particular event as a significant feature in their lives. Miss Maberley, the daughter of the first resident incumbent, Revd Charles Maberley, writing in 1906 as an old lady of eighty, describes the high backed pews 'lined with torn green baize, haunted by beetles and earwigs'. The Longwood pew even had its own fireplace. The chimney for this can be seen on photographs taken early in the century. Ada Betteridge (née Taylor) recorded how children from the school often went into the church to sit on the hot pipes there to keep warm and were then in trouble from Mrs Pierce, the schoolmistress. The pipes were warmed from a boiler in the cellar which was kept going by 'Stumper' Lee. Jessie Norman (née Tuffs) tells how she fainted when she tried to pump the bellows for the organ.

Any building of this great age needs ongoing restoration work, some of which causes changes to be made to the actual design and fabric of the building. St Andrew's Church is no exception. All such work is costly. In the past a regular source of income for the Church came from tithes which were a tenth part of the main produce of the land and of both labour and stock such as wool, pigs and milk. The payment of tithes was abolished in 1936. Other monies came from more-well-to-do local folk. During the nineteenth century a most generous benefactress for Owslebury was Mrs Alice Long from *Marwell Hall*. It was she, who in 1832, enabled Owslebury to become a parish in its own right, separate from Twyford, with a grant of £3000 which was to provide a stipend for the incumbent. Almost a hundred years later, in 1921, Owslebury joined with the parish of Morestead making them a single benefice, Revd Albert Briggs being vicar of both. Alice Long's generosity continued when, in 1836, she gave a further £1,200 to pay for the building of a vicarage on a piece of land near the church, known as Spencers Paddock, which was also a gift. This was given by the Countess of Northesk from Longwood. The Earl of Northesk gave yet more

The Church, 2000 *(DR)*

money during the last decade of the nineteenth century when much restoration work was needed. This included the removal of a gallery, the unbricking of the west arch and the adding of a new stone parapet. An early photo and the first we have of the church, shows that this had a flat top with no crenellations at the time. Today's crenellations were probably added to the tower sometime between 1887, when the photographer of this photo died, and 1898 when the clock was added. A previous weather vane is recorded as having blown down during a gale in 1883.

In 1905 a porch was added to the church. This replaced a moth-eaten curtain and at the same time the doors were widened in order that coffins could pass through more easily. Previously to this, one of the doors had had to be removed whenever there was a funeral service. In 1928 a vestry safe was given to the church by Major Phipps Foster of *Longwood House*. In 1930 the Pen Gate between the churchyard and the Glebe, known as Litton Paddock then, was replaced by an iron structure. In the same year the weather vane was regilded, this being financed by the vicar of that time, Revd Albert Briggs. A new pole was given by the Earl of Eldon from Longwood.

It was during the Second World War that the Children's Corner came into being. This was dedicated on St Stephen's Day, 1943. Pictures were given by Mrs Florence Lush who was an infant teacher in the Sunday School and by Mrs Sharp who was a relative of the then vicar, Revd Francis Barker. Candlesticks were given by Mrs Florence Palmer. A statue of the risen Christ was

Inside the church, early 1900s – note the pews on the right for the gentry, organ on the left, iron pillar on the left (SS)

Inside the church, 2000 – note the Millennium Tapestry on the right *(EH)*

Probably the earliest photograph of St Andrew's Church, pre 1887 – note no crenellations on the tower and no clock (WMS)

placed in the corner along with a bookshelf of books which could be read and borrowed by the children.

At the end of the Second World War in 1945 the candle lighting in the Church was replaced by five Tilley lamps. Then just five years later, on 19 December, 1950, these were replaced by electric lighting, which we take for granted nowadays but which must have seemed magical at that time. In the same year the nave roof was retiled at a cost of £333. One year later, cracked lead on the tower roof was replaced by asphalt, and a year from then all the timbers were sprayed against death watch beetle. In 1956 more death watch beetle damage was repaired and major work was done on the supporting structures of the building. This involved replacing the cracked

iron girders and plates with steel girders and encasing them in oak. In 1980 the plaster between the beams of the aisles was replaced by insulating board and the lead on the roof was renewed, along with the bell tower floor. In the same year a new ladder to lead from the clock to the roof of the tower was given by villager, Tony Wilson.

At the top of the tower hang the bells, six of them, which ring out regularly to announce church services and other significant events. The first bell, a tenor, was hung almost four hundred years ago in 1619. In 1622 it was joined by a second bell, a fifth, both probably cast by John Higden. In 1674 the third bell, a fourth, was hung, this being cast by Ellis and Henry Knight. And so these three remained through the next two centuries until Revd Charles Buston initiated a

Crenellations now added to the tower – note the chimney for the fireplace in the Longwood pew, no houses yet next to the school, no vestry (SS)

This postcard picture of the church was posted in 1906 – note the houses next to the school are now built (SS)

move to raise money at the beginning of the twentieth century to acquire three more bells. In 1905, a third, a second and a treble, all cast by Mears and Stainbank, were hung alongside the others in the bell tower, making possible now a peal of six, to be rung out across the village for all to hear. Our bells joined those across the nation at 12 noon on 1st January, 2000 to celebrate the birth of the new millennium.

One of the few times when our bells have had to remain silent was during the Second World War. Revd Francis Barker tells us in the Parish Notes on 13 June, 1940 – '*At the time when the invasion of England was expected, the ringing of church bells was forbidden. Bells were to be rung as a warning of threatened invasion only. Owslebury bells were so rung – tho', as it turned out, the warning was issued in mistake – on Saturday September 7th 1940*' He tells us that the bells were first rung again on Sunday, 15th November, 1942 after victory at El Alamein. The village ringers then were Sam White, Ernest Merritt, Mont Rogers, Jim Heath, Mr Stansbridge and Edith Lush. It was surprise to find one lady in the team. The bells were again rung on VE Day, Tuesday, 8th May 1945 at the conclusion of the war in Europe.

The church is now warmed by electricity, which generates heat from beneath the pews and from overhead. This was installed in 1959.

Hanging in front of each pew in the church are some beautiful kneelers. Each one is of a different and unique design, often of some significance to village life, such as the Brownie badge motif, and the birds and flowers of the area. Each was chosen by the person who stitched it. It was the Mothers' Union who initiated the idea in 1979 after a visit to Chichester Cathedral. They were inspired by the kneelers there and so wool and canvas were bought in bulk from the Wilton Carpet Factory and everyone was asked to work the kneelers in certain background colours and in cross-stitch to provide uniformity. A photographic record was made by David Houghton and each photographed design was signed by the embroiderer. It was however a real village project with many other people being involved beside those who did the sewing.

The dedication service for the kneelers took place at Evensong on 1st June, 1980. Revd Geoffrey Holland was the vicar then but Revd John Pringle was invited back to the village for this special occasion and he gave the address.

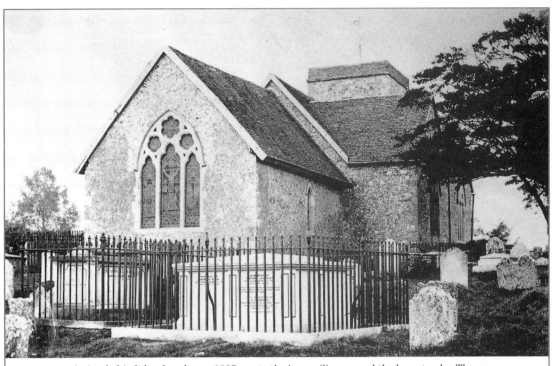

A view behind the church, pre 1887 – note the iron railings round the large tombs. These
were removed and melted down for munitions early in the Second World War (WMS)

Brownies, Cubs and Guides paraded at the service
and the new Brownie flag was dedicated at the
same time. After the service, tea and sandwiches
were served to parishioners and people were able
to look at the kneelers in detail.

As we enter the new millennium it is a
satisfying thought that these kneelers are a
heritage that we shall pass to the next generation
of worshippers.

Inside the church there are several unique
artefacts of great historical interest. There is a
beautiful silver communion chalice dating back
to the time of Edward VI. In a glass case in the
south west corner of the nave there is a serpent,
a musical instrument, not a snake! This was used
to accompany the singing of the choir. It was
introduced in 1840 and was played from the

gallery along with the barrel organ. The present
organ was dedicated on 20th July, 1987 to the
memory of Richard Tryner Boston, organ builder.
Dick and his wife, Ann, lived at *Owslebury Farm
(now House)*, opposite the church.

Charles II Royal Coat of Arms can be seen
hanging over the west arch of the nave. It was
restored in 1970 and was thought to have come
in 1682 from Sir Charles Brett, a friend of the
King's, who lived at Marwell at the time.

A photocopy of the Tithe May and Schedule can
be seen in the ringing chamber. The original was
made in 1840 so that tithes could be assessed in
cash instead of produce in kind.

Also in the bell-ringing chamber is a large oak
chest. This was carved from a single log and was
provided at the beginning of the seventeenth

century following the order issued to church wardens in 1602 to provide a 'coffer with three locks' in which to keep the registers. The burial register was begun in 1678 and the marriage and baptism registers in 1696. The registers are no longer kept in the church but like those from all churches nationwide have been removed for safe keeping to the local Record Office.

These artefacts along with other details are depicted in a beautiful tapestry which has been designed and stitched as a village millennium project.

On the west wall of the church tower, facing the Glebe Field, hangs the church clock. This was installed on October 12th, 1898 and was purchased to mark the Diamond Jubilee of Queen Victoria at a cost of £78.5s.2d. It was made and erected by John Smith and Sons of Derby. The face has been repainted twice during the last century, in 1922, and again in 1952, and the hands and figures have been regilded. Today the chimes of the clock can be heard regularly striking the hour across the village, and this is due to the dedication of the clock- winding team. This is led by Terry Russell, who climbs the vertical ladder to the clock chamber in the tower to rewind the clock each Tuesday. It is wound for a second time each week by Andrew Bailey on Saturday. Bob Brown helps out when either of these is unable to do the winding. Alan Ball from *The Old School House* had been a chief clock winder for 16 years

Charles II Royal Coat of Arms *(EH)*

before he moved from the village. There are two weights from the clock which hang down into the corner of the bell ringing chamber below, where they are encased behind wooden boxing. One of these regulates the clock and the other provides the power to chime the hours, like a big Swiss cuckoo clock! A large metal handle, rather like the old-fashioned starter handle on an early day car, needs to be turned fifty times to raise these heavy weights to the height of the clock, in order to wind it up, and thus keep it telling and tolling the time for Owslebury.

Just under the clock over the west window can be seen a plaque on the wall bearing the initials JF and TC with the date 1675. These were the initials of John Friend and Thomas Cawte who were churchwardens at this time.

At the beginning of the last century, villagers approaching the church would have been confronted by the village stocks and maybe their occupant at the churchyard gates! These were removed early in the century and now we see only the peaceful graveyard surrounding the church where stand the gravestones of those villagers who have gone before. A path through the churchyard leads down to Pitcot Lane. In front of the church is a low flint wall bordering the Glebe Field. Seats are positioned here enabling both village folk and walkers to enjoy its peaceful setting and the lovely views across towards

Baybridge and the Isle of Wight.

When people walk through the village at night after dark, they see the church attractively illuminated by floodlighting, which surrounds it with a soft orange glow. Such floodlighting became possible after a most generous donation from parishioner, Joyce Wayment. She was adamant at the time that her gift should remain anonymous. She had been a regular church worshipper all her life, until her death early in 2000, when she was aged 90. But now her story can be told. The lighting was dedicated in 1994 by Revd Scott Joynt, the then Bishop of Winchester.

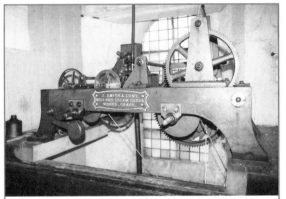

The church clock inside the tower *(EH)*

Throughout the twentieth century vicars and villagers have continued to raise money for the upkeep and repair of their village church. It is an ongoing commitment that is as necessary at the beginning of this new millennium as ever it was. Revd Charles Buston who was vicar at the turn of the century, recorded that much work was paid for by *'subscriptions, concerts and rummage sales'*. A century on from then it remains the same! In 1922 the Free Will Offering scheme came into being and today churchgoers and parishioners give weekly both at services and by deeds of covenant to ensure the much needed income for the church. In 1978 the 'Friends of St Andrew's' group was formed and this group have raised funds over the years to pay for the cleaner, the organist and the gardener. In 2000 this system

of provision is about to change but the support of the 'Friends' will continue to be much needed.

In 1975 a major reorganisation of benefices in the Winchester diocese was decided upon and this had a huge impact on Owslebury. The gift of Alice Long, 150 years previously was no longer enough to ensure that the village could have its own vicar. Once more Owslebury and Morestead joined with Twyford to share a vicar who would live in Twyford. The village vicarage was sold and this it how it remains today as we move into the new millennium. The vicar at this time is Revd Mark Bailey who began his ministry with us in February, 2000. In the gap between Mark's arrival and Revd Dr Peter Lippiett's departure in September, 1999, we continued to receive support and pastoral care due wholly to the *voluntary* dedication of Revd Vivien Moffitt and lay reader, Jonathan Kemp.

The Church remains a dominant and significant influence in village life today due to a small army of dedicated village folk, some of whom hold formal offices within the church and others who fulfil those duties essential to its ongoing upkeep and care.

The organist on most Sundays is Betty Harfield. The church is regularly cleaned by Gwen Barney. The flowers are masterminded by Marilyn Hamilton who took over from Lady Sue Torrington who had done this job for many years

The Glebe. In the Victoria County History of 1908 the land between the church and the Old Vicarage was described as *'the recreation ground'* (SS)

Picket fencing fronting the Glebe – note the two large trees close to the road (SS)

previously. The churchyard is cared for by Andrew Bailey. For many years Fred Gray devotedly looked after the churchyard, pushing his lawn mower through the village street when it was time to cut the grass. Fred was a familiar figure walking his dog round the village and during such walks he would make sure that the steps leading down to Pitcot Lane were kept clear of leaves. Fred died in July, 2000, a much loved and much missed villager. John Dewdney had taken over the churchyard job from Fred and Andrew followed John.

The official body that is responsible for the church is the Parochial Church Council. They hold regular meetings to discuss church affairs. At one such meeting in 1967 a heated argument took place as to whether **women** should be allowed to read the lesson in church. It was a difficult decision but eventually it was conceded that they should!

THE OLD SCHOOL HOUSE

The Old School House was built in 1840 as an integral part of the village school with the intention that the headmaster would only have to open a door each morning to be 'at work'. In those days too, there was no transport available; consequently, to be close at hand was essential. It was due to the generosity of the Countess of Northesk from Longwood that the building became a reality.

The house was built in brick and flint as were so many of that time. The very first resident was actually a schoolmistress – a Miss Sarah Lindour, who shortly became Mrs Sarah Blundell. In the year 1900 the schoolmaster was Thomas King who had been in post since 1881. In 1905, Mr George Pierce, who was to become one of the school's best known and loved headmasters, took over the post. In the early sixties, Frank Williams chatted to an elderly Mr Pierce and his son, also George. Mr Pierce senior remembered seeing the house for the first time. He told Frank, *'It was in a shocking state; no one had been living in it. The windows were naturally full of holes, having stones inside on the floors. The grate in the kitchen was covered in rust. There were stone floors, no back garden; the door opened into a yard. I didn't think much of it. It was covered in ivy'.*

Mr Pierce remained headmaster at the village school until 1931. He is remembered, among other qualities for instilling in the children a great respect and love of the countryside. It was during his time that the school repeatedly won the Bird and Tree Competition which was offered to all schools in Hampshire. He left Owslebury to take up a post at Wellow School and it was written at the time, 'When it was first learnt that Mr Pierce had been appointed Headmaster at Wellow School a gloom was cast over the whole village, where he had been a friend to both rich and poor for the last 26 years'. As a leaving gift he was given a solid silver tea set and a set of W. H. Hudson's Nature Volumes. He was awarded the MBE in the Queen's Birthday Honours in June, 1931.

Another much loved person from the school was May (Daisy) Gurman, the infant teacher for many years when George Pierce was headmaster of the

where she always stood watching her charges while she was on playground duty. The wording was as follows:

> In loving memory of Miss May Gurman,
> Pupil, Monitress, Prefect, Teacher.
> A lifelong friend to all the village children.

Sadly, this memorial has now disappeared.

The last person to live in the School House was Lyn Casson, who was the infant teacher in the early 1970s. With the building of the new school, the house and school building was sold to become a private property. The Lumkin family became its first new residents. They did most of the original conversion to the house and used the outside toilet block and the infants' room as a very successful carp breeding farm. Shirley and Alan Ball became the next residents in the Old School House and lived here for the next sixteen years. Shirley was able to use the large old schoolroom as a studio for her pottery. Alan used the old staff room across the playground as an

The School House, c1900 – note the house on the corner of Pitcot Lane (BH)

school. She must have been a very special teacher as the parents of her pupils collected enough money to erect a memorial to her. This was placed on the boundary wall of the church, behind the schoolhouse, in the corner

The School House, 2000 (EH)

animation studio, producing many films and television commercials there. The animation for the famous Christmas favourite 'Snowman', based on the well-known children's book, began here from Alan's creative pen. During their time in the village, Shirley was renowned for the painting of wonderful backcloths for village pantomimes and drama productions and Alan for delightful cartoon type drawings which regularly appeared in the Newsletter. He also drew many of the pictures for Betty Harfield's book 'Owslebury Remembers'.

The present residents in the *Old School House* are Justin and Sheena Passfield and their two small daughters, Flora and Cecily. They have done extensive work on the property to make it a comfortable family home. Outside they have given the property its first garden. Gone is the old concrete playground, now replaced by grass and flowerbeds. They have had an attractive brick and flint wall built on the boundary in keeping with the brick and flint of the old school building and have been able to use one of the original old doors as a gate between the front and back gardens. In the utility room the old school coat pegs can still be seen.

OWSLEBURY FARM

Almost opposite the church stands an imposing large house approached by a wide driveway. Today the sign on the brick and flint wall fronting the property reads *Owslebury House*, as it has been known since the house was sold, separately from the farm buildings alongside it. These were tastefully converted to two new homes known as *The Granary* and *The Old Barn*. The three properties together made up *Owslebury Farm* in the early years of the last century and were

Owslebury House, 2000 – until the 1960s this was 'Owslebury Farm' *(DR)*

another part of the *Marwell Hall Estate*. In the sale schedule it was described as '*a well placed dairy farm, practically all pasture with a commodious farmhouse*'. The commodious farmhouse was entered by a '*short carriage sweep*' and as part of its appeal had two staircases, six bedrooms, a bathroom **and** W.C.! The farm buildings comprised '*Nag, stable and coach house; Six-bay open shed; Two-bay cart shed; Cooling room; Granary; Carthorse Stable for 5 and Harness room; Good Cow Shed for 20; large Barn;*

Two Pig Styes and Small Open Shed'. The property also had a flower garden, a good kitchen garden and an orchard as well as a large underground tank for rainwater storage. It was sold in 1934 for £1450.

Just after the Second World War, the Worthington family lived at *Owslebury Farm*. In 1952 Dick Corbett farmed here, and at this time it was still a working dairy farm. Mrs Harrison from Marwell then moved here briefly, but by the time Richard, who was always known as Dick, and

Owslebury Farm, 1934

Owslebury Farm, 2000 *(EH)*

Ann Boston came to Owslebury, the farm was no longer operating. They moved to the village in 1966 and it was here that their two daughters, Hilary and Philippa grew up. The original farm buildings came in extremely useful when Dick and Ann very kindly offered hospitality to the annual Horticultural Show each year. Following Dick's death, Ann sold the house and had the farm buildings converted in 1989 to two houses. She now lives in *The Granary* and her daughter, Philippa Conyngham, lives in *The Old Barn* located behind *The Granary,* with husband John, and daughters, Katie and Jo-Anna. Philippa has a livery yard and stables for a number of horses and it is a picturesque sight to see her on occasions driving a carriage and pair through the village.

Timothy Jobling, with Lorna and her daughter, Katie Cramond, now live in the original farmhouse. Katie recently achieved the distinction of becoming one of the first girl choristers in Winchester Cathedral.

BANKSIDE COTTAGES

Continuing through the village from *The Granary*, the next few houses on both sides of the road, have seen almost a whole century of village life pass across their thresholds. The style of windows and the slate roofs indicate their longevity.

On the left hand side is a pair of semi-detached houses known as numbers 1 and 2 *Bankside Cottages*, very aptly named as a steep bank has to be climbed to enter both of them. At number one lives Roy Denbury, who is amongst our newest villagers. Next door at number 2 live John and Sue Tickle with their young family, Hannah and James. John and Sue moved into the village in 1994. Both children were born in Owslebury, Hannah in 1996, and James in July, 1999.

At the beginning of the last century, both of the *Bankside Cottages* housed farmworkers from *Owslebury Farm* next door and were part of the *Marwell Hall Estate*. They each had a front sitting room, a kitchen and three bedrooms upstairs. In addition, Number 1 had a larder in its kitchen and Number 2 had a range and copper. Their water came from a standpipe situated at the top of Pitcot Lane.

Just along from the cottages the steep bank continues along the road edge. Above it today is the boundary fence of the school playing field. This area was in fact earmarked as a playing area

Bankside Cottages, 2000 *(EH)*

for school children in the early years of the century long before it became the present school playing field. In the *Marwell Hall* Sale Schedule it was described as *'A Small Grass Enclosure'*. It went on to state that

> *'The children of the village have for upwards of 40 years been permitted by the Vendor's predecessors in title to use this lot as a playground'*.

Peggy Smith, a villager of today, was actually born Peggy Merritt, at Number *2 Bankside Cottages*. Her parents were Peter and Dorothy (née Lawrence) but her mother was always known as Dolly. Peter's parents also lived in the village in *Church Cottages* down Pitcot Lane. Peggy spent all her school days at the village school just across the road, remaining there until aged 14. She thinks back fondly to happy days with teacher Miss Gurman, and headteachers, Mr Pierce and Mr Matthews. Some village children graduated to schools in Winchester if they passed the appropriate exam, but for many this was not an option. There was no school bus in those days and the cost of books and uniforms were beyond the reach of many families. Peggy lives today in Beech Grove in the same house now that headteacher Mr Matthews helped the family to obtain many years ago, when priority for houses here was being given to agricultural workers.

THE SYCAMORES, POST COTTAGE AND WEST VIEW

Opposite *Bankside Cottages* is a set of three terraced properties, which were originally owned by Charles Anstey from *Lower Farm*. They were not actually built until the last century was a few years old. In 1900 the land, where the houses now are, was used as the school garden. For many years, the first of the houses, *The Sycamores* on the corner of Pitcot Lane, was the home of villagers, Frank and Doris Harfield. Prior to this time, way back in the 1920s it was the village police house and home to police officer, William Banks. It took its name from the sycamore tree that stood in the corner of the garden.

Next door is *Post Cottage* and the two properties together are now the home of Kieron and Melanie Norris and their small daughter, Tara. *Post Cottage* was at one time called *Restholm,* but today's name is far more appropriate as it was this house early in the last century that served as the village post office. Mrs Lane was the first postmistress at *Restholm,* moving there in 1911. She was well practised in all the necessary skills as she had previously assisted her mother, Mrs Ellen Taylor, when she operated the postal service from the cottage on the other corner of Pitcot Lane at the end of the previous century. This is long since gone and is now the garden for *Gamefair*. The first public telephone was installed in the front room here and if it was required after hours a 'disturbance fee' of one shilling (5p) could be charged although this was never actually made. The telephone finally became automatic in 1946.

At some time in the 1960s Frank Williams from *Shepherds Cottage* had a conversation with Bill Bridle and Mrs Hutchings during which he asked them about their memories of the early postal services in the village. Mrs Hutchings had taken over from Mrs Lane, the widowed Mrs Taylor's daughter, who later became Mrs Hayter. Mrs Hutchings was postmistress for over 32 years,

A view looking down the street from the corner of Pitcot Lane towards Bankside Cottages on the right. The house on the left located on the corner of Pitcot Lane, is the Post Office of this time (BH)

The same view, 2000 *(DR)*

The Sycamores, Restholm and West View on the left and Bankside Cottages on the right (AE)

remaining so until August 1956. Her husband, Herbert, had been village postman until he was tragically killed when knocked off his bicycle close to the *Ship Inn* in October 1923. Their daughter, who became Peggy Churchill, grew up in the village and later lived with her husband, Jack, in the cottage at the end of the terrace, *West View*. The reminiscences from Bill Bridle and Mrs Hutchings included the following fascinating details.

In 1912 the village mail was placed in a letter box fitted into the front wall of the house. This was cleared by the post office staff who cancelled all the stamps manually. The letters were then placed into mailbags which had the string ends sealed with red wax and an impression made with a special stamper. This showed the name of our village and the Royal Cypher. Letters could still bear an Owslebury postmark as late as 1957.

In 1923 the post office was open during the week from 8am until 7pm daily. There was a half day service on Saturdays and surprisingly it was open again from 9am until 10.30am on Sundays. During the war the opening hours were shortened to 9am - 6pm daily but the Sunday morning opening continued until 1950. Until just before World War 1 there was a delivery of mail on Sunday.

Under PO regulations all telegrams, regardless of contents, had to be delivered as soon

as possible. This sometimes made huge demands on post office staff. On one occasion when the weather was terrible, the snow lying deep and drifting, a telegram was phoned through, 'Happy Birthday John'. This had to be taken to *Honeyman's Farm* on the Longwood estate, an isolated homestead

Fanny Hooker, the Owslebury postmistress from 1878 until at least 1889. She is buried in the churchyard – note the windmill in the background (BH)

nearly three quarters of a mile off the road. On return from an exhausting trip the poor postmistress was greeted with the news that another telegram had arrived for the same farm! Perhaps even more ironic would be the telegrams received explaining that the sender could not visit the recipient as the weather was so bad. Bad as the weather was it was still a priority for the postmistress to deliver such telegrams, which might be for addresses as much as four miles away.

The third cottage in the terrace, nearest *The Old School House* is home to Andy Gwynn and Elsa Morris with daughter, Rosie, and baby son, Charlie. Charlie was born in July, 1999 making him our newest village baby and youngest Owslebury resident as we actually entered the

new millennium. This house is known as *West View* and it was here that Bill Bridle, the village blacksmith, used to live.

CARTMEL

Crossing over the corner of Pitcot Lane, past the post box in the wall, stands a new bungalow named *Gamefair*. This was built in the 1980s in what was the garden of another dwelling built at the turn of the century, namely *Cartmel*. *Cartmel* is another attractive brick and flint property which is now the home of Hazel and David

Reproduced by kind permission of Melanie and Kieron Norris

Cartmel, 2000 *(DR)*

Crowsley. As with so many of today's houses it was built on the site of a previous dwelling which in the 1860s was Mr Bunday's Bakery. Many of the flints from this bakery were used to build the new *Cartmel* and when the house was recently extended, more flints were used for the building so that the new part is very much in keeping with the old. Mr Bunday, the baker, had as his next door neighbour, cornering on Pitcot Lane, Mrs Taylor who ran the village Post Office. It is appropriate perhaps that today's postbox is sited at this place.

CHURCH COTTAGES

To find *Church Cottages* one has to turn off the main street into the little side turning immediately past *The Sycamores*, now known as Pitcot Lane. The naming of this lane has been a matter for discussion and argument over many years. Many villagers recording their memories from the early years of the last century refer to it as Church Lane. Betty Harfield chatted to an elderly gentleman recently who on seeing the sign marked Pitcot Lane, remarked to her, *'They've got that sign wrong at the top of the lane – that's always been **Church Lane**. Tis the bottom end*

Church Cottages, Pitcot Lane *(DR)*

that's Pitcot Lane'. Betty explained to him that it was the Post Office that would often use this labelling but his response to this was as follows: *'When the new houses were built opposite Hilly Close in the early 50s, I had mates working there and they said the contractors didn't like the address of Main Road – thought the houses wouldn't sell – and so they were advertised – by the builders – as being in Church Lane – and no one queried it so that's how it was – the Church anyway was further up the road'*.

Pitcot Lane or Church Lane is an unmade road which is often quite difficult to negotiate because of the huge and heavy lorries that turn here regularly to reach the egg farm further down the lane. As one walks there is a high bank on the right hand side which marks the boundary of the churchyard. Steps lead down from this higher level to the lane further along, just before reaching the boundary of the garden of *Church Cottages*. Opposite are several more houses built during the twentieth century. *Church Cottages* is another building that has seen many changes with the passing of time. Miss Maberley, the first resident vicar's daughter, remembered another house alongside *Church Cottages* back in the 1830s, as being thatched and serving as the village school. She wrote, *'There was a play yard in front of it, opening onto the street or road, and a very nice garden behind it, running down the field from the street'*. At the beginning of the 1900s the thatched school had disappeared but Charles Anstey told villager, Evelyn Merritt, many years later, that as a small boy, he had attended a Dame School in *Church Cottages*. Dame Schools were private schools charging a small weekly fee and were usually run by women teachers. Arthur Thatcher and Brian Lush relate that their mother and grandmother respectively went to school there and paid 2d a week to do so.

Evelyn Merritt came to live in *Church Cottages* after her marriage to Len in 1948. Len's mother had lived here previously with her four children. Evelyn was no stranger to the village as she grew up in Mare Lane, the other side of Whites Hill and attended the village school when Mr Pierce was headmaster. She was told that the house was 400 years old. It was actually divided into three connecting cottages at the time, and was owned by Mr Limebeer who was out in South Africa. His sister, Mrs Sharpe, lived in the middle part of the cottage and Mr Rogers in the end nearest the church. One of the windows at the front had been bricked up many years previously, probably at the time of the window tax which came into being in 1696. There was no sanitation or electricity in the cottage. Cooking was done on an oil stove and all hot water boiled in a kettle. The clothes were boiled in a copper and then wrung out by being passed through the rollers of a mangle. The door of Evelyn's kitchen opened onto a little porch on the side of the house, which is no longer there, which led to the garden. Beyond the garden were open fields and beautiful views towards Woodham Hill and Baybridge. *Church Cottages* remained home to Evelyn until 1983 when the property was sold as one private residence. She has stayed in the village, however, and now lives in Hilly Close. Revd. Geoffrey

Holland and family were the first people to move into the cottages as one house and they carried out much renovation work to restore this lovely old house with its mellow brickwork and peg tiled roof. The lost window has also been restored! Today it sits tucked cosily away in this corner of the village, just where the little wooded lane narrows and leads off down the footpath towards Woodham Hill at the bottom. It is an area enjoyed by ramblers and dog walkers.

BELLA VISTA

Continuing down Pitcot Lane one reaches a driveway on the left leading to a terrace of three old brick and flint cottages. They enjoy wonderful views down into the valley below looking towards Baybridge. The middle one of the terrace is thus very aptly named *Bella Vista*.

Irene Bliss has lived here ever since her wedding day on 13th October, 1951. She married village lad, Bob, in St Andrew's Church just across the lane and came straight back to the cottage as Mrs Bliss, without any honeymoon. Those were the days of rationing following the war and it was a struggle to get enough tokens together to buy a new outfit for this special day. Their son, Graham, grew up here and went to the village school. He was actually born in Southampton because Irene

(HH)

Weyhill, Bella Vista and Hillside Cottage down Pitcot Lane, 2000 *(EH)*

went back home to her mum there for this important event. Irene thought that her mother, having brought ten children safely into the world herself *'knew a bit about it'*!

Irene grew up in Southampton but came to live for a while in Lower Upham after the family's house was bombed during the war. It was then that she met Bob who had been born in Owslebury, in *Yew Tree Cottages*. He had worked at Marwell before the war and then at the sawmills at Longwood like his father before him.

Bob completely transformed *Bella Vista* over the years, doing all the work himself. When he and Irene moved in, it was owned then by Charles Anstey who lived at *Great Hunts* with his two elderly sisters. Irene used to walk down there each week to pay the rent. Making the cottage into a comfortable home was a challenging task. The walls were all painted a dark brown and there

was no sink, cooker, toilet or electricity. Lighting was by oil lamps or candles; cooking was done on a Valor oil stove with an oven on top. If this stove was not adjusted perfectly, it would cause black smoke and smuts to fill the room. Heating came from the black range in the living room which was a fire with an oven alongside. Lighting this was always the first job of the day in the winter months. The primitive toilet facilities were outside the back door in a nearby corner. They did have the luxury of a cold tap inside the house but there was no means of heating it other than by a kettle on the stove. They had a wash stand and a bowl and bathing was done once a week in a long tin bath in the kitchen. When bath time was over the bath and its contents had to be laboriously carried through the living room and tipped away in the garden at the front. After wash day, the ironing was done with

(HH)

81

a flat iron heated on top of the range. This had to be checked for black smuts so that all the effort of wash day would not be ruined.

The cottages were originally built of brick and flint, either at the end of the 1800s or very early in the next century. After Bob and Irene moved in, the flints were proving very porous. As a result Bob tiled the top of the front wall. He added small extensions at both front and back and transformed the cottage to a modern and comfortable home such as we all take for granted today. The path to the cottages from Pitcot Lane used to come straight to the front doors but once cars needed to have access a new driveway was made further back. The lane itself then was much narrower and very overgrown. Irene made a beautiful garden in front of their cottage and was to win many prizes for 'Best Garden' at village horticultural shows.

HILLSIDE COTTAGE

In the house nearest the valley, *Hillside Cottage*, Bob and Irene had as neighbours for many years, Bert and Peggy Derrick. Bert was another lad born and bred in the village. He was a much-valued member of the cricket team, and Peggy worked at the school for a considerable time looking after the children during the lunch hour. Now *Hillside Cottage* is home to Keith and Jackie Wake. They have tastefully extended their home using flints and old roof tiles so that the new blends in perfectly with the old.

WEYHILL COTTAGE

Weyhill Cottage is the first of the terrace reached down the driveway from Pitcot Lane. The little cottage is set well back and most of the old brick and flint walls have been rendered. John Seabrook lives here today. He moved from nearby Whiteflood in Baybridge to *Weyhill Cottage* with his wife, Hazel, in 1960. Their daughter, Maxine, was four at the time and John and Hazel wanted to be near the school. Many years later Maxine was to have another link with the village when her husband built *The Lilacs* in Whaddon Lane.

Prior to actually living in the village John already had a link here. His brother-in-law, Cliff Lush, had set up a garage and small engineering workshop, on the site where Quilver is now located. John joined him in a business partnership here in 1946. The garage disappeared some time during the 1970s but the workshop remained until 1990. John spent much of his working life contracted to Hampshire County Council and was also involved at the planning stage with Marwell Zoological Park.

John has witnessed many changes that have taken place in the village during the last 40 years, and has been very involved in village life as he has been a parish councillor for 20 of those years.

THE WINDPUMP

Two famous landmarks in Owslebury village at the turn of the last century were the windpump and the windmill. They are both long since gone. Owslebury was a good place for such wind-driven power sources, for being situated at such altitude, wind is something the village has always had plenty of!

The windpump was built about 1870 and was well set back from the main street through the village. Later the Parish Hall came to be built in front of it and today the school car park is located where the windpump once was.

The windpump was built in order that villagers could have access to running water, albeit not from taps in the comfort of their own homes, but from one of three standpipe taps at various points through the village. There was one by the Bank Tree, one at *Shepherds Cottage* and one at the top of Pitcot Lane which was then known as Church Lane. By the 1930s two more had been added, one down Pitcot Lane by *Church Cottages* and one near the newly built Hilly Close. Everyone used these taps but there was often a problem in the winter when they froze. People would then have to boil some of their precious water to carry there and pour over the tap, or they might set fire to the straw packed round the pipes, in order to defrost them that way. Bill Bridle, the village blacksmith of bygone years told Frank Williams, '*many a time people would hide behind the curtains and wait for others to thaw out the pipes and taps*'!

Outside the building was a steam boiler installed by Dean and Smith, Winchester. This had a pulley wheel on it; the spindle went through the wall and cogs inside drove the windmill which in turn pumped the water. This was installed so that water could still be pumped even when the wind wasn't obliging. Bill Bridle maintained the machinery.

Pumped water was stored in a reservoir tank close by. This held about 45,000 gallons and was kept filled to a depth of 6ft. It measured 22ft long and was almost as wide and was covered over. During the Second World War it was used as an observation post by the army. The reservoir was demolished early in the 1950s and much of the concrete and rubble was used as foundation for Beech Grove houses.

The shaft below the windpump was an amazing construction. It was dug to a depth of 284ft. Bill Bridle had a string with a lead weight attached which he let down into the well to test its depth. He pulled it straight across the playing field to

The Windpump with steam boiler, known as Bridle's Mill (WMS)

The Windpump without its sail behind the Parish Hall, after 1907 (SS)

measure. *'Is that the depth of it – Never!'* he would exclaim.

Deep down on the chalky sides of the shaft there is evidently a beautiful carving of Owslebury Church. It is reputed to have been done by whoever it was who originally dug out the well shaft. It was discovered by a Southern Counties man who used to be let down the well on a big winch at intervals to clear a recurring air lock. Bill Bridle remembered *'when he was down there with a candle he only looked like a fly'.* He used to carry a candle down to check there was no foul air.

Sometime during the First World War an engine pump was installed by Duke and Ockenden, Littlehampton, and the old handle and windmill became redundant. The windpump building however, remained and was used as the engine house.

There used to be iron ladders going down into the shaft but when the pump was installed they were deemed unsafe and removed. They were bought by a Jack Gill from Winchester and were used on board ships in Southampton.

It was Bill Bridle who looked after the mill and it was always referred to by villagers as 'Bridle's Mill'. He was cajoled into doing the job rather against his will. He told Frank Williams, *'I didn't want the job and told him I didn't want the job but he'd come and beg me that I do it and at last I said I'd do it and took it on and done it for 30 years'.*

Owslebury finally had main drainage laid through the village in 1948. The windpump building remained a feature in the landscape until about 1960 when it was demolished by villager, Jim Pritchard.

The Parish Hall, 1907 (BH)

THE PARISH HALL

The village of Owslebury gained its first Parish Hall in 1907. It was built close to the water works and opposite the post office of that time. The present Parish Hall occupies the same site. It cost about £300 in 1907 and the money was given by Revd Charles Buston and fifty other subscribers. Many villagers at the time helped to actually build the hall. The land was owned by the Rural District Council but was let to the Trustees of the hall on a lease which would terminate in June 2006. The purpose of the building was stated to be as follows:

'First, as a reading room with papers and games for recreation, second as a room for technical education, such as cookery classes etc., third as a drilling hall with a miniature rifle range, fourth as a room for meetings of all sorts, irrespective of religion or politics.'

The Trustees at the time were Revd L Haslope and Mr Charles Anstey. They had been appointed for life, without the power of resignation, the last survivor to be succeeded by his legal executors.

In 1947, just after the end of the Second World War, a meeting was called to discuss the possible building of an extension to the hall as well as a lych gate for the church. The complicated legal structure was discussed. Villagers were told that unless a new constitution, not based on the lives of individuals, was adopted, no funds raised by public subscriptions could be applied to an additional building on the present site. It was agreed that if one or both of the lessees were agreeable, application would be made to the Charity Commissioners to issue a new scheme.

The rest is history, as the saying goes. The building of our new Parish Hall, proudly opened in November, 1996, was only possible because of the new scheme organised in 1947 and which was updated in 1994. It enabled us to apply for a variety of grants and many villagers fifty years on gave generous donations or committed themselves to covenant-giving to help towards the required total. The book 'Owslebury Remembers' was compiled by Betty Harfield and published by the Parish Hall committee in order to raise funds for the new hall. The Parish Council dealt with an outstanding deficit at the end via the Parish annual precept which was part of the community charge. The final cost of the new hall, designed by architect John Alexander, was £240,000. At the time this was a breathtaking target and the fact that we achieved it was really quite remarkable. The idea of a new Parish Hall was a dream of today, realised for villagers of tomorrow.

The Parish Hall is run as a charity; it has a committee and a constitution and the books are audited annually. Any Parish organisation has the right to be represented on the committee. In 2000 Terry Russell is chairman of the committee having taken over from Lady Kelburn in the 1980s. Representatives from Parish organisations include two from the Parish Council, and one each from the PCC, the Cricket Club, the School Governors, the Sports Club, the Football Club and until recently, the WI. The objectives for the Parish Hall are as follows:

'The provision and maintenance of the Village Hall for use by the inhabitants of the Parish of Owslebury, without distinction of political, religious or other opinions, including use for meetings, lectures and classes, and for other forms of recreation and leisure time occupation with the object of improving the condition of life for the said inhabitants'.

As we enter the new millennium, Terry Russell is the acting caretaker for the hall as he has been for the last four years. He performs many duties tirelessly that the rest of us in the village take for granted. He will unlock the doors for most activities and then lock up again at the end of the day, even if it is after midnight on some occasions. He supervises the heating, checks the toilet rolls, puts out tables and chairs and periodically cleans out the gutters. Terry's deputy is Pete Juggins, and the hall is kept impeccably by Helen Pritchard and her mother, Eileen.

People who have lived in the village for some time have many fond memories of the old hall. Wally Trott remembers enjoying numerous concerts, dances and whist drives there. Village

---

CHARITY COMMISSION

HAMPSHIRE.
PARISH OF OWSLEBURY.

In the matter of the Charity called the

PARISH HALL

and

In the matter of the Charitable Trusts Acts, 1853 to 1939.

I HEREBY GIVE NOTICE that, under the authority of the Charity Commissioners for England and Wales, I shall be at the

PARISH HALL, OWSLEBURY,

at **7.30** p.m.

on FRIDAY, the 21st MARCH, 1947, for the purpose of inquiring into the endowments and administration of the above-named Charity, and that I shall be ready at the time and place above-mentioned to receive evidence concerning the same.

THE INQUIRY WILL BE PUBLIC

Dated this 1st day of March, 1947.

Charity Commission,
St. James's,
London, S.W.1.

R. L. DANIELL,
Assistant Commissioner.

Inside the Parish Hall, sisters Vera and Joyce (née Trott) say a fond farewell before its demolition in 1996 (WT)

keep fit, painting and upholstery. Christian Fellowship worshippers used to hold their Sunday services there. In the 1960s a welfare clinic took place in the hall. There was a billiard table permanently in position and many village clubs and societies used the hall as their meeting place. The kitchen facilities meant that there would always be a good cup of tea on hand.

Since we have no doctor in the village the Parish Hall was an ideal place to hold a surgery for those unable to get to Twyford. This situation still holds true today. Prescribed medicines are very kindly collected regularly from Twyford and delivered personally to people's doors by Terry Russell. Ray Norgate performed this same kind service for 30 years before Terry took over. Johnny Jones was also much involved in the past. Today other willing helpers who fill the gap when Terry is away, include members of Terry's family, Doug

'hops' were organised every Saturday night during the Second World War when soldiers in the area would help fill the hall to capacity. Harold Harfield used to run these and being an exceptionally fine dancer, he taught many a young village lass to dance during these evenings. In days before we all had televisions for entertainment, the Parish Hall was the place to go to relax, to catch up on the news of the day and to find fun and laughter, companionship and friendship together.

Before the new school was built the children used to go to the hall daily for their school dinners and also for PE lessons. The village Drama Society performed their plays and pantomimes there. It was used as a polling station on election days, as it still is, as well as for coffee mornings, fetes in wet weather and various evening classes, including

The Parish Hall, 2000 *(DR)*

Rogers and occasionally, Clive Mansell.

Since the closing of the last village shop in 1989 the Parish Hall has also been home to post office facilities each Monday and Thursday. Celia Thompson has become our postmistress on these days, relieving villagers of the worry of how to get to town to a post office when the bus service is a limited one.

For much of the last century villagers rarely thought of the Parish Hall without thinking at the same time of Doris Harfield. She lived with husband, Frank, in a house almost opposite, *The Sycamores*. She served on the hall committee, held a key to the hall, took bookings and money for the hall, cleaned the hall, made countless pots of tea in the hall, kept an eye open for anything untoward happening in the hall; in fact, we sometimes wondered if she didn't actually **live** in the hall! Everybody knew Doris and Doris knew everybody. It was a sad day and the end of an era when she had to move from the village because of increasing frailty.

It seems almost that as we begin the new millennium Terry Russell has taken over from Doris! Terry has pointed out that this is only by happenstance and that he doesn't make the tea! He has been a villager since 1961 and his two daughters, Anna and Heather, were born here as was Anna's first child, Zack. Zack also now attends the village school as did his mother and aunt before him.

The Parish Hall is still a focus for village meetings, events and activities. During 2000 we have enjoyed a Quiz evening there, a delightful Handbell concert and a delicious parish lunch after the dedication of the millennium tapestry in the church. It will surely continue to be used and enjoyed in future years.

THE SCHOOL

A sign by the roadside announcing 'school' is to be found in the main street of the village, but to reach the school one has to turn left into Beech Grove and then left again into the little cul-de-sac that leads to Owslebury Primary School. The building is a modern one surrounded by mature hedges and backed by a spacious playing field. It has been the place where village children have been educated since 22nd October, 1976. This was a long awaited day of great excitement and pride and which opened the second chapter of the story of our village school. Fourteen years later in 1990 a book was published to celebrate the school's 150th anniversary. It was compiled by Betty Harfield who put together a fascinating collection of old documents and letters from past pupils, to make a detailed and absorbing record of the school's long history. It deserved a book to itself.

As we enter the new millennium the school remains a hugely significant feature of village life even though our teachers no longer live in the village as they did one hundred years ago. It is here that our next generation is being nurtured and taught, with the best traditions being continued along with new ones to prepare our children to become tomorrow's citizens.

New legislation for British schools and good transport facilities has brought about a major change to Owslebury school numbers. Fifty per cent of the 89 children now on roll come from outside the village. Children now start school when they are 4 years old and to accommodate

The back of the school and playing field *(DR)*

the extra numbers a new classroom was added in 1995 and an extra class was formed in 1998. Most of the money for this tremendous achievement was raised by parents. Friends of the School, led by Tracey Dicks with a committee of 15 other parents, continually work at raising money. Their latest ambitious project concerns a new school hall. If their dream is realised it will mean that children from the temporary classroom alongside the main building will be able to move into the present hall as a classroom, thereby uniting them with the rest of the school. The new hall would be built between the present hall and the temporary classroom.

Hampshire County Council is very supportive of small schools and we are fortunate that there is no threat of closure here in Owslebury. The overall responsibility for the management of the school rests with the governors who were known as 'managers' in the past. Today they manage their own budget, as well as monitoring standards. The village school, like all others nationally, is subjected to regular OFSTED inspections. New curriculum areas have been introduced such as the Literacy and Numeracy Strategies in order to promote and maintain high standards in these areas, and the learning of spellings and tables still features prominently in the daily programme. The school now has twelve computers which are permanent aspects of today's learning.

There are many opportunities for children to participate in a wide range of sporting and musical activities. A new venture of the last decade has been the production of a termly school magazine OSMAG, written by the children for the children. Pupils are helped to recognise their place in the wider community by being encouraged to be aware of the needs of others less fortunate than themselves. They have supported such ventures as the Magpie Scanner Appeal, an animal at Marwell Zoo, Blue Peter Appeals, and the Kosovo refugees.

Although not a church school, Owslebury school has always had strong liaison with the church and today, Revd Mark Bailey and Val Corcoran from Twyford come to take the school assembly about twice a term.

The school continues the tradition of three houses known as Robins, Yellow Hammers and Woodpeckers. They can score house points for good work, good behaviour and sporting achievements. The children look distinctive in their royal blue sweatshirts with the ouzel bird logo on the front. There is a mini-school group for three year olds who gather together once a week and thereby gain a taste of their future school life.

As we enter the new millennium the headteacher continues to be David White who has been in post since 1989. He leads a team of dedicated staff who include the following:

Dorothy Storry – deputy head and reception teacher

Liz Wilson – Y1 & Y2 (infants)

Barbara Clancy – Y3 & Y4 (lower juniors)

Pauline Gilbert – Y5 & Y6 (upper juniors)

David himself teaches one and a half days a week. Janet Emery is a learning support assistant and Eleanor Tomkins is an information technology assistant.

The children are able to enjoy a tasty and hot meal at lunch time if they choose. These are cooked by Jane Rennison and the assistant cook,

Diane Butt. The children are cared for at lunch time by Jackie Pretty and Pat Rudgley. It is Jackie Pretty who also keeps the school premises clean and tidy.

In the school brochure, David has written:

'It is our intention to create a secure and happy environment in which all children have the opportunity to succeed and reach their full potential... it is our aim to give as wide a range of experiences and opportunities as possible and to allow all talents and achievements to be valued and recognised'.

It would seem that these aims continue to be a focus in the school although it is a concern of David's today that the pace of life and the challenges of the modern curriculum sometimes make it difficult for children to reflect and revisit. In spite of this, judging by the increasing numbers on roll, Owslebury School remains a place where the children's first learning experiences are good ones and a place where they are happy to be.

THE WINDMILL

The village of Owslebury had a small moment of fame back in 1890, when the Hampshire Independent Newspaper described it as having *'the last windmill at work in Hampshire'*. This windmill was sited on an appropriate high spot behind where *Bressay* and *Old Mill House* are found today. It was built there in 1870 and provided a milling service to the village for the next thirty years. At first it was owned and worked by Alfred Young's grandfather, described by Alfred when he recorded his memories of the village in the late 1800s. Bill Bridle, when talking to Frank Williams, remembered that mill well.

He told Frank that there were four sails or shiftings as they were known. Evidently a shifting would sometimes blow off and then Bill would climb up to the platform outside, and with the help of a mate because they were very heavy, he would fit the shifting back into its socket and replace the bolt. The windmill had two floors, one at ground level and another reached by means of an iron ladder.

Bill Bridle was involved in the demolition when the time came to take the windmill down. He must have had a quiet chuckle to himself when thinking back to this occasion. He told Frank, '*I helped pull them all down and bought it – in fact I bought it all before the government inspector came down to value it. I went and saw an old gypo chap who lived at Owslebury Bottom and got him to take it away before the inspector came*'!

Today in 2000, we are left with only an old photograph to remind us of an aspect of village life which has gone for ever.

OLD MILL HOUSE AND BRESSAY

At the turn of the last century there was a space where now stand these two semi-detached properties. They were built at the end of the first decade of the century and many of the bricks for the two houses came from the old windmill which had recently been demolished. The properties had large sash windows, little porches over the front

Owslebury Windmill. Seen behind is The Cottage and Harry Matthew's Cottage (WMS)

Old Mill Stores with Lillian Cobb (BH)

Bressay and Old Mill House, 2000 (EH)

doors and the walls were half-rendered. It was the house on the left, now known as *Bressay,* which became the second general store for the village. Peter Hewett in his book 'Owslebury Bottom', remembers walking up Crabbes Hill to the main village, delightfully referred to by him as 'Owslebury Top', and then along to Mr Cobb's shop. He says, *'it was frankly modern, with purplish-red brick and mustard- yellow stone facings'*. Mr Cobb's shop later became Mr Sawyer's shop and remained so until 1947 when the shop closed and the two properties were sold together and became private homes. Today *Old Mill Stores* has been renamed *Bressay* and is home to Gerald and Joyce Sanderson. Next door,

Old Mill House, is lived in by Gerry and Sue Tull.

When Lillian and Percy Cobb ran the stores, many postcards of local views were published, and these were sold from the shop. Today they have become collectors' items giving a pictorial record of how things were long ago.

Percy Cobb also worked as a carpenter in the village. Cricket Club minutes in 1920 record that *'It was decided to accept Mr Cobb's tender of £7.50 to repair the Cricket Pavilion'*. Percy died in January, 1945, aged 67.

RAVENS HILL

Almost opposite *Old Mill House* and *Bressay* stands *Ravens Hill,* right on the road edge. Evidently this house began its life as a barn which was later converted to three brick and flint cottages. These were known as *Windmill Cottages* due to the fact that they were situated opposite the village windmill. Later still, the three houses became one, changing the name to *Ravens Hill* as it is now known. Cynthia and Stuart Mariner live here today having moved into Owslebury with their baby daughter, Elizabeth, back in 1976. Their son, William, was born in the village a few years later.

HARRY MATTHEW'S COTTAGE

A hundred years ago, a villager walking towards Longwood would next have passed a tiny cottage built right on the roadside. Its name is unknown today but in the 1950s it was inhabited by Harry Matthews and his wife. This is another of the lovely thatched cottages which has long since disappeared from the village scene. Harry was a 'lengthman', a term we no longer use today, but which meant that he had his own length of road to care for and keep tidy, to trim hedges, clear ditches and sweep up. Villagers evidently used to chat to Harry on summer evenings when he sat outside his cottage weaving straw beehives known as skeps.

THE COTTAGE

The Cottage, on the left-hand side of the road, is the first of a little cluster of very old properties situated just before the turning to Crabbes Hill. Although now named *The Cottage*, this building was originally three cottages when first built nearly three hundred years ago. The section of the cottage on the right at the end, would originally have been a barn in which animals were housed.

The present owners of this attractive and eye-catching cottage are Hume and Charmian Jones. They moved there in April, 1979 with their two small children, Teddy, aged 4 and Dolly, aged 3.

Bill Bunney with Dick and Nadine Corbett from Owslebury Farm outside The Cottage (CJ)

Their family was soon to grow to include Augusta, now 16, and twins, Geoffrey and Theo, now 13, all of whom were born in the village. When Hume and Charmian bought *The Cottage* there was much restoration and renovation to be done. The house had actually been empty for two years after the deaths of the previous owners, Bill and Eileen Bunney.

During Bill Bunney's time, the three dwellings had become two. It was he who had built the ornamental well to the left of the house and also fitted the eye-catching stained glass windows in the walls to either side of the property. The beams used for the well had come from the old granary at *Boyes Farm*. It cannot have been a particularly comfortable house for him to inhabit because he was a very tall man and *The Cottage* had very low ceilings! Before coming to live in Owslebury, Bill had been publican at *The George* in Warnford. His daughter, Sally, was later to become landlord with husband, Tony, at the *Ship Inn* in Owslebury.

As they grew older, Bill's wife became very frail and needed much care and support which Bill gave unfailingly to her. It was a shock when Bill himself suddenly collapsed and died, and only three weeks were to pass before Eileen died too. They are buried together right at the end of the churchyard a little apart from the rest of the graves. This was evidently at Bill's request, as was the lead-lined coffin in which he was buried. Special permission was granted by the Bishop for such a burial as this was before the land at the far end was part of the graveyard. Bill had looked after the horses for Dick Corbett from *Owslebury Farm* and wanted to be buried near them. Sally remembered that it seemed quite uncanny that

The Cottage – note the roof thatched at the back and tiled at the front (SW)

The Cottage, 2000 *(DR)*

when the cortege arrived, the horses followed behind and just stood there, almost as if they knew it was Bill.

Hume and Charmian Jones were the first people to live in *The Cottage* as just one dwelling. When they moved in they found low wooden-beamed ceilings, diamond-shaped leaded windows, and a large inglenook fireplace with an old bread oven to the side. Sadly the bread oven collapsed and disintegrated during restoration work. The plumbing was of the most primitive sort and the electricity supply very limited. The roof needed urgent attention and looked rather odd at the time as the back of the house was thatched while the front was roofed with slates. The old wooden beams were believed to have started life as ships' timbers. Outside, the path leading round the property was made of bricks laid in an attractive herringbone pattern. Steps led up to the path from the road and there was an old brick and flint wall fronting the house.

When Charmian and Hume moved into *The Cottage,* a fire-mark from the Sun Insurance Company was fixed to the front wall. During the eighteenth century and the first half of the nineteenth century, fire fighting was on the whole organised by various fire insurance companies. Anyone who had paid his premium had a metal fire-mark fitted to his wall.

Usually the insurance policy number was engraved under the company emblem so that it also advertised the company. It has been said that if the first fire fighters to reach the scene were rivals of the company who had insured the property, they were most likely to leave the fire burning!

Before Bill Bunney's time, when the property would have been tied with a job of work, Mont and Nellie Rogers lived in one of the cottages here. Doug Rogers was born here and spent his first few years in *The Cottage* before moving to Whaddon Bottom.

IVY COTTAGE

Ivy Cottage is one of the few houses actually named on old maps, and is therefore easily identifiable as well as being a very picturesque and elegant old building. This is a house that has witnessed the dawn of three new centuries. It stands close to the road edge as the turning to Crabbes Hill is approached, a brick property with

Ivy Cottage with Holly Hatch behind, 2000 *(DR)*

Agreement for sale by auction of Ivy Cottage to William Trodd in 1882
(reproduced by kind permission of Nick and Caroline Perry)

a peg tile roof. True to its name, it has ivy climbing to roof height on part of the front wall. The house is fronted by a pair of staddlestones and there is a narrow strip of garden alongside the road edge. The cottage, built in 1731, has a long and interesting history which has been well researched by the present owners, Nick and Caroline Perry, who came to live in Owslebury in 1982. Exactly one hundred years previous to this, William Trodd had purchased the cottage by auction, together with the three tenements next door, now known as *Holly Hatch*, for the sum of £480. His family had actually lived and worked in the cottage as copyhold tenants since 1846. As recorded in the 1851 census William Trodd Snr was a blacksmith and licensed victualler employing two men. With William at this time lived his wife, Marian, his nephew, another William who was also a blacksmith, and Marian's father, Richard Lush, aged 87. They carried out their blacksmith's trade at the three forges on the same site. In 1859 William Snr bought the freehold of *Ivy Cottage* for £80. By the time of the 1871 census William Snr had moved to Hursley, although he still owned the cottage, and nephew, William, now lived there with his wife, Jane, and daughters, Mary and Frances. Birth and marriage certificates for Frances are framed and hanging in the *Ship Inn* where her father was publican at the time of her birth. *Ivy Cottage* remained as home to members of the Trodd family until 1909 when William died. His daughters then rented it out during the next ten years until it was purchased in 1919 by a William Perry which is a strange coincidence but has no connection to Nick Perry of today. During the next few decades the cottage had several changes of ownership and also of name, being known for a while as *Ivy Clad Cottage*, and then as *Cobblers* before reverting to its present name.

One of the difficulties that has occurred in researching for this book has been the scarcity of street names on old maps and the failure to record house names in census records and on electoral rolls. Often properties were just recorded as 'the dwelling', or 'cottage', or 'village'. Even in records which do exist, as for *Ivy Cottage*, often the information is conflicting. *Ivy Cottage* has been listed as being situated in Owslebury Street (1827), The Street (1851 census), Main Road (1919) and more recently, in Church Lane, – confusing to say the least!

HOLLY HATCH

Next door to *Ivy Cottage* is *Holly Hatch*, a detached house, the last one on this side of the street and standing on the corner at the top of Crabbes Hill. Beyond *Holly Hatch* are fields that stretch as far as the Longwood crossroads.

Holly Hatch is another old dwelling, with a slate

Ivy Cottage and Holly Hatch at the end of the 1800s – note the house on the right hand side of the road. It is possibly the Trodd Family pictured outside (PE)

Ivy Cottage and Holly Hatch with Lucy Day crossing the road. Lucy, born in 1868, was daughter of Robert and Sarah (née Smith) Bunney (DL)

just one dwelling and for the last decade has been home to Major Richard and Mrs Susan De Salis. They moved from the village in September, 2000, and Roger and Liz Porteous and their family then came to *Holly Hatch,* becoming some of our newest village residents.

roof, built of brick and flint and painted white today. On the 1841 tithe map, *Holly Hatch* is shown as a small building, and together with *Ivy Cottage* was described as a *"House, Garden and Smith's Shop",* owned and occupied by George Smith. In 1882 it was purchased by William Trodd along with *Ivy Cottage* next door and was described then as being three tenements. It is now

Bordering the land alongside the house is a very old hedge containing eleven different species, - beech, ash, dog rose, lonicera nitida, bramble, yew, elder, privet, old man's beard, ivy and of course, holly, from which the house took its name. There are two acres of land to the side and back where there are paddocks and stables for two horses.

Back in the 1950s this house was evidently

Holly Hatch, 2000 *(EH)*

Harfield's book about the school. This family was preceded by the Glasspools, Annie and Frank, and during their time, the inn was a popular gathering place for farmers and farm workers of the area. At the time of the Second World War soldiers from the Hazeley Camp would make their way to the *Cricketers* for one last night of cheerful and carefree fun and camaraderie before leaving to go into battle. Mrs Sam White, and her brother, Fred, would play the piano and violin to accompany the songs. As Sidney Showell poignantly commented in his Newsletter memories, *'to many a soldier, Owslebury was the last of the country he saw that he died for'*.

painted black and occupied by Mr Dark! At a time when very few people were car owners, he used to drive a huge black car that looked like a hearse.

THE CRICKETERS INN

When walking down Crabbes Hill, having turned left off the main village street, after passing through a tunnel of trees and rounding the bend, a white walled house comes into sight on the right hand side. A hundred years ago this house was the *Cricketers Inn*. Today the building is an inn no longer, having become a private residence in 1933 when the last landlord, Mr Wort, moved away from the village. His daughter, Hilda, has recorded some of her school memories in Betty

The old cast iron signpost with its block lettering, at the top of Crabbes Hill (BH)

After the *Cricketers* demise as an inn, alterations took place to make it a comfortable family home. Jack and Mary Shaw were to live there for many years with their family. To the front of the house was a barn or coach house which had provided stabling in days gone by. On the wall of this building is a benchmark indicating the height above sea level. This is regularly inspected to make sure that it has not been defaced or destroyed. There used to be a grove of ancient yew trees surrounding the house while it was home to the Shaw family. Sadly, recent storms have taken their toll and many of the trees are now gone.

Northwood House, 2000 – this house used to be known as the Cricketers Inn *(EH)*

A view of the back of Beech Grove houses from Crabbes Hill *(EH)*

The *Cricketers Inn* was believed to have been named after the cricket field which stood opposite at the end of the 1890s. Once the present recreation ground had been given to the village, the field was adopted by the village football club before they too came up to Owslebury Top, to the recreation ground there. The deeds of the old house date back to 1832 although Jack Shaw believed there had been another house on the same site before this date. Another document dated 1867 names the house as *Rumbolds*, suggesting that it was not yet the inn that saw in the beginning of the twentieth century.

During the last years of the twentieth century the house changed its name again to *Northwood House* and became home to Jane and Laurence Ruffell who continue to live there with their daughter, Laura, and son, Thomas. The name change was made after the family bought an extra piece of land on the northeast side of the house, following the sale of the Longwood Mereacre estate. They felt it was fitting to make a change of name, to mark its new identity as a home rather than an inn, and thus move it on into new times.

When the Ruffells moved into *Northwood House* they were somewhat surprised to discover that they were not the only residents. It seemed they had a ghost in the house, a female figure in brogue shoes, thick, dark stockings and a long tweed skirt, someone remarkably like Mary Shaw! They felt that she was unhappy with the alterations that they were making to the house. Jane visited Mary's grave to try and make her peace with the ghost and following this, it has all

A view of Bottom Farm with the Shearers Arms behind as seen from the footpath behind Beech Grove *(EH)*

HAMPSHIRE

BOTTOM FARM HOUSE,
OWSLEBURY, NEAR WINCHESTER

FOR SALE BY AUCTION AT

THE ROYAL HOTEL, WINCHESTER

On TUESDAY, 10th, OCTOBER, 1967

AT 2.30 P.M.

(unless previously sold privately)

Solicitors:
MESSRS. SIMPSON NORTH, HARLEY & Co.,
1 Water Street, Liverpool, 2.

Auctioneers:
MESSRS. JAMES HARRIS & SON
Jewry Chambers, Winchester.   (Tel: Winchester 2355—3 lines)

Sale notice for Bottom Farm in 1967 *(reproduced by kind permission of Don and Marilyn Bishop)*

felt better at home whenever they work on the house.

BOTTOM FARM

Shortly after passing *Northwood House,* or the *Cricketers Inn* that was, there is a narrow turning to the left called Hatchers Lane. On the corner here stands *Bottom Farm,* the entrance to which is reached from the lane.

In the early years of the last century *Bottom Farm* was a busy dairy farm, managed by James Lavington. In the 1881 census, it was described as being *'200 acres and employing 4 men and 2 boys'.* James' father, also a James, had died four years before the end of the century in 1896. He had been married to Mary Boyes, the daughter of Benjamin and Mary Boyes, another village farming family of long-standing.

Peter Hewett, when writing 'Owslebury Bottom', records how it was a daily task of his to walk to the farm to collect the family's milk in *'a dark-blue-and-white enamel can with a wire handle and a cup top.'* He describes how it became *"a ritual opening to the day as well as contributing to my growing sense of the seasons: each day in spring a little softer and brighter, with the early leaves of the elder and the first daisies starring the verges; each day in autumn a trifle darker until frosts glazed the roadside puddles with white ice and there were angry red skies'.*

Today *Bottom Farm* is a farm no longer although animals are still very much in evidence. Goats and horses can be seen grazing the fields close by and geese and chickens strut the yard. Donald and Marilyn Bishop live at *Bottom Farm*

Bottom Farm House, 2000 (MB)

House today with sons, Mark, Paul and Matthew. They purchased the farm by auction in 1967 and established a kennels for dogs 'on holiday' in the outbuildings, although they closed this down in 1993.

Don and Marilyn purchased the farmhouse from Michael Packenham who farmed at Upham. He had bought it from a Mr Dunster who had farmed the land in Owslebury for many years previously. In his time, water for the house and for the cattle was drawn from a well, which can be seen in the garden behind the house today, although it is no longer functional. When Don and Marilyn moved in, an old flint wall ran along the boundary, staddlestones from a former granary marked its position in the yard and there was a pond just inside the farm gate. To the front of the house were several old fruit trees. The pond was filled in and became a garden. A new ornamental pond has now been made at the front of the house.

PETER HEWETT'S COTTAGE

Continuing down the hill after passing *Bottom Farm*, back at the beginning of the last century, a pair of semi-detached cottages with thatched roofs would have stood on the right hand side of the road just before reaching the *Shearers Arms*. It was to one of these that Peter Hewett had come with his mother, sister and brother at the time of the First World War when his father was away fighting in the trenches of France. Many years later he recorded his memories of this time at the cottage and in the village in his book 'Owslebury Bottom'. The two little cottages are now gone, along with two others close by, described by Peter Hewett as being built of brick and tile and *'at right angles to the road, backed by the huge beeches of Jackman's Hill'*.

The cottages were tiny. The front door opened straight into the main living room, one wall of which was taken up with the basket fire, oven alongside, then shelves and cupboards. The room was lit with an oil lamp. The small amount of furniture owned by the family had arrived from Twyford where they had briefly lived previously, roped onto a cart. The rent was 2/6 a week. There were two small bedrooms upstairs, the windows of which were so low that when the postman Bert Hutchings arrived early in the morning, he would ring his bicycle bell, open the little wicket gate, walk up the brick path and hand the letters straight into the outstretched hand reaching from the bedroom window! There was a well with rope and windlass in the front garden, and this was the family's only source of water. Nearby was a large tumbledown barn and next to that was an earth closet toilet.

Peter has vivid memories of the road at Owslebury Bottom. He wrote thus: *'After a heavy summer rainstorm the narrow little road was almost impassable: no wonder we mostly wore heavy, clumsy boots. Sometime the road became a mire of cow droppings and straw-yellow puddles, edged with the little pineapple weed and merging vaguely into nettles and grasses'*.

The road here, throughout the last century, has always been flooded after heavy rain. At the end of the first year of the new millennium the rainfall was so continual and heavy that flooding occurred here again, the severity of which was within no living memory. Properties in this area had water flowing inside them, pushing up the foundations, and owners were forced to move out until the floods abated several weeks later. The road was impassable to traffic.

Back in the nineteenth century one of these cottages was known as *Rose Cottage* and it was home to Eva and George Witt, who were grandparents to Margaret Jefferies who lives in the village today. Eva was a Glasspool before her marriage and her parents were William and Henrietta (née Young) Glasspool who had married at Twyford Church in 1860. William died in 1908 while living in *Rose Cottage,* Owslebury Bottom.

Rose Cottage / Peter Hewett's Cottage at Owslebury Bottom, c1895.
In front of the cottage, *from left to right*, are Eva Witt (née Glasspool),
Emily Glasspool (Eva's sister), William Glasspool and his wife Henrietta (née Young) (MJ)

William Glasspool seated in the carrier's cart with wife, Henrietta, c1895. Miriam Witt (daughter of George
Witt from his first marriage) is seated between them. George is standing by the horse. Eva, George's wife, in
hat, is standing by Louisa Witt, another of George's daughters from his first marriage (MJ)

GREEN BUNGALOW, OWSLEBURY BOTTOM

In 1972 when the Longwood Estate was being split up and sold, there was another old property at the end of the bridleway now known as Stags Lane, to the right of the crossroads at Owslebury Bottom. This property was *Green Bungalow* and was described as being '*an ideal subject for redevelopment*'. It obviously was redeveloped and a new bungalow called *Staggs Gate* stands on this site today. Nichola and Alan Snudden live here. Their house was one of those badly affected by the flooding that occurred at the end of 2000. Also along this little unmade-up lane is another new house, *South Longwood*. This is built on land at a slightly higher level where there used to be an assortment of old farm buildings. This is home to Bernard and Sandra Dunford.

THE SHEARERS ARMS

Almost at the end of the hill, approaching Owslebury Bottom, on the left-hand side of the road, stands the *Shearers Arms*. Like the *Ship Inn* at the other end of the village it has a long history. Henry VIII is reputed to have hunted deer from the *Shearers,* but how long before then the inn had stood at this spot, no one really knows, although a building on this site seems to have had a mention in the Domesday Book. In the last decade of the nineteenth century the *Shearers Arms,* which at this time was thatched, suffered a bad fire which virtually destroyed it. It was rebuilt, without the thatch in 1895. Judging from the name, it would seem that at one time it must have served a shepherding community. Alfred Young when writing about village life as it was at the end of the nineteenth century commented that '*in those far off days, nobody tried to farm those chalk lands without a flock of sheep*'.

Peter Hewett in his book 'Owslebury Bottom' describes the *Shearers* at the time of the First World War as being of '*crude brick with gravy brown woodwork*'. He lived almost opposite and his mother sometimes worked there. At the beginning of the last century there was a well situated very close to the house which was covered by the roof of the licensed premises. This well house featured in a story told about a group of Owslebury friends who had been invited by the landlord, Frederick Jewel, to share a glass of

The Shearers Arms with Christine Sutherden in the doorway *(DR)*

home made wine there one Christmas Day. The local policeman on duty that day was Police Constable Greenleaf and he had gone to investigate after hearing the strains of carol singing coming from the well house. It was thought at first that drinks were being sold, but the story had a happy ending as they were found 'not guilty'. Eli Glasspool, who was Wally and Roger Trott's grandfather, was among this group of friends.

The *Shearers Arms* has always had a reputation for providing a warm welcome together with excellent repast for village clubs and societies who are celebrating special occasions. George Harfield when talking to Frank Williams in the 1960s remembered that the Oddfellows and the Foresters Clubs joined together annually for a dinner, which one year was at the *Shearers* and the next at the *Cricketers*. Preceding the dinner, George told Frank, '*we had a church parade with the Shawford and Compton band and two banners a flying and people come five or six miles to see it and the church packed out'*. Today, members of Owslebury's Senior Club sometimes go to the *Shearers* for a celebration lunch before Christmas.

Today's landlords are Christine and Raymond Sutherden who came to Owslebury with their young family, Neil, Kara, Martin and Jason, in the 1980s. Their youngest daughter, Kelly, was born in the village.

THE FORGE

Just past the *Shearers Arms* is *The Forge*, a modern building with a bungalow alongside where the farrier serving the horse-riding population of the parish today plies his trade. Alan and Rosemary Povey live in the bungalow and Alan continues to work *The Forge* together with son, David.

OWSLEBURY BOTTOM COTTAGES

Continuing down the hill from the *Shearers Arms Inn* one reaches the last houses in this corner of Owslebury. Nestling at the foot of the valley here and known appropriately as Owslebury Bottom, are two cottages numbered rather strangely as Numbers 42 and 43. Where are numbers 1 – 41 you might ask? Evidently, the numbers refer to the many cottages on the old Longwood Estate.

Owslebury Bottom Cottages looking towards Crabbes Hill *(DR)*

Owslebury Bottom Cottages with brothers, Roger *(on the left)* and Walter Trott *(EH)*

houses were rented by Walter and Daisy Trott in 1941. The rent at this time was £39 per year. Although they had spent their married life until then in Portsmouth, it was almost like coming home for them to be back in Owslebury. Daisy's parents, Agnes and Eli Glasspool had lived in *Rose Cottage*, Baybridge, now *Coach Cottage*, and Walter and Daisy had often been back with their young family for visits and holidays. This cottage, together with the one next door, was finally bought by Walter's and Daisy's sons, Walter and Roger, in 1972 when the Longwood Estate was being split up and sold.

Cottage Number 43 looks the same as it has

Number 42 is a low lying cottage with a thatched roof. It is the third and last of the remaining thatched cottages in the village today. It was built of brick and flint with timber framing and at the time of the sale the roof was half-thatch and half-corrugated iron. This was originally three cottages, although the sale schedule described the eastern end as having *'only been used as a workshop with storage room over'*, prior to the sale. Next door, Number 43 is situated on the corner of the little crossroads at the dip in the road before Jackman's Hill goes up to Morestead. This also is built of brick and flint but the roof is tiled. The

View of Longwood Road looking towards the Morestead-Corhampton crossroads *(DR)*

always looked from the front although it has been extended at the rear. It is here that Walter lives. He married his wife, Patricia, in the village church and brought up his son, David, here. Next door lives Walter's brother, Roger, and his wife, Joyce. Sons, Andrew and Jonathon, grew up in the village and the cousins all attended the village school.

Early each year, the bank opposite the cottage is carpeted with snowdrops. These heralds of springtime were planted there many years ago by Daisy Trott.

LONGWOOD ROAD

When travelling out of the main village past the Cricket Down towards the junction crossing the Morestead to Corhampton main road, the street changes its name to Longwood Road. On most maps of the area the Cricket Down is named as the 'recreation ground' but it is nearly always referred to by villagers today as the Cricket Down. The left-hand side of the road is bordered by open fields. These are part of an area known as Owslebury Down, which extends from the corner of Crabbes Hill, over the crossroads and on to Longwood. On the right hand side of the road, beyond the Cricket Down, are ten more houses and bungalows which mark the end of Owslebury Village. Many of these houses were built to replace buildings from a bygone era which were no longer habitable.

At the beginning of the last century the land at this end of the village was open downland, (part of Owslebury Down) but within the first ten years, small pockets of it were being sold and properties were being built. They were very primitive and makeshift properties by today's standards, for these first houses were made of corrugated iron. They included *Hillcrest, Homelands, Sunnyside* and *Hill View.*

HILLCREST

Hillcrest today is tucked away in a corner of the Cricket Down and approached from Baybridge Lane. Keith and Mary Taylor had this house rebuilt in the 1970s and their daughters, Anna and Sara, were born there.

HOMELANDS

Homelands has been home to the Harfield family since 1928. Harold and Gertrude Harfield became the second owners of *Homelands* when they moved in after their marriage. Alan Harfield was born here. During the Second World War it became a private nursing home when Gertrude took in evacuees and maternity cases. When Gertrude died in 1977, Alan had the old corrugated house rebuilt as a comfortable and modern home and moved here from *Nestledown,* on the other side of the Cricket Down, with his wife, Betty, and young sons, Richard and David, who both went to the village school.

SUNNYSIDE

Sunnyside is home today to Margaret and Gordon Jefferies who moved here in 1970. Their two young children, Andrew and Sally, grew up here and went to the village school. Before this however, Margaret had a link with the village going back many years. In 1910, her great Aunt Maud Mariana Bradley (née Glasspool) with husband John, purchased the land where today

Homelands alongside the Cricket Down, pre 1977 (BH)

Homelands, 2000 *(DR)*

Sunnyside when it was a corrugated iron 'Catalogue' bungalow, with owner, Maud Bradley (MJ)

stand three properties, *Sunnyside, Hillview and Kimmeridge.* Margaret tells how her aunt was reputed to have earned the £35.0.0 with which she bought this land, by collecting flints from the fields! A pair of semi-detached corrugated iron bungalows, known as 'Catalogue Bungalows', were built on the plot. Mrs Bradley and her husband lived in the one on the *Sunnyside* site and the other was rented out. John Bradley died in 1937 but Maud remained in the property until her own death twenty-nine years later in 1966. Some time before this, she had sold the land on which *Kimmeridge* now stands. Following Mrs Bradley's death the two properties were then sold and planning permission granted to build a three-bedroomed bungalow on the *Sunnyside* site. The bungalow on the *Hillview* site remained as it was for several more years. The three-bedroomed bungalow became home to Margaret and Gordon and their family. During the next thirty years they were to make several changes and improvements to their home. In the 1970s they added a new dining room and cloakroom and had the kitchen enlarged; in the 1980s an upper floor was added and in the 1990s a conservatory was erected at the rear of the property.

HILL VIEW

Hill View was transformed from its corrugated state in 1985 when villager, Eddie Emery bought it and rebuilt it as it is seen today. It is home now to John Stewart, our village veterinarian.

GREENACRES

Between *Homelands* and *Sunnyside* is *Greenacres*. This plot was originally owned by Bill Bunney but he sold it to Len Lampard from Twyford who had the house built here for his daughter.

KIMMERIDGE

Next door to *Hill View* is *Kimmeridge*. This house is the original one built on the land that Maud Bradley had sold. Today it is home to the village blacksmith, David Povey. David's father owns *The Forge* at Owslebury Bottom.

TREE TOPS

Originally on this site there was a small qualcast square bungalow owned by Mr Dovey. He kept a market garden here, which extended over the next two plots of land as well, and from which he sold fresh fruit and vegetables to villagers. After Mr Dovey's death, two more houses, *Arden* and *Hazeldene* were built here. Steve and Olive Jeffs were to purchase Mr Dovey's house. They moved in with sons, Philip and Christopher, and changed the name to *Avellino*. They operated a small nursery in the garden at the rear and many village gardens have plants and flowers now which came from this nursery. After Steve's death the property was sold, knocked down and rebuilt as the present house, now called *Tree Tops*. This is home to Professor Andrew Sansome, his wife, Petra, and two small children, Abbi and Tom.

PUFFINS

The last house in the row also began life as a qualcast bungalow built in the 1920s. It was inhabited then by David Livingstone and family, the brother to Raymond from *Old Barn Cottage*. Later Mr Davis ran a deep litter chicken holding here. The next owners were a Mr and Mrs Broome who gave it the name *Gwithian*. It was sold next to a Mr Spencer who changed its name again to *Eastacre*. Finally, to see out the twentieth century, this house became home to Brenda and Roger

Hilly Close, 2000 *(DR)*

Beech Grove, 1964 – Elsie Evans in the foreground, Erica Williams in the pushchair with sister, Claire next to her. (WI Scrapbook)

TWENTIETH CENTURY HOUSES

During the last century the village of Owslebury saw the building of many new houses. Spaces in certain areas of the village became filled with new homes for the new people who started to move into the village. As well as various individual properties, three areas came to be designated for the building of council houses, namely Hilly Close, Gorse Down and Beech Grove.

The first six such houses were built in 1928 in Hilly Close. At the time they had no provision for running water, bathrooms or electricity. Most residents had to wait until 1949, another 21 years for these modern comforts to become a reality for them. It was just after the end of the Second World War that seven more houses comprising Gorse Down were built on the opposite side of the road. These were the first houses in the village that were built with pipes installed for running water and with flush

Warson and their young daughters, Emma, Jennifer and Beth. They decided to make another name change and called their home *Puffins*.

HAZELDENE AND ARDEN

These two houses next door to each other are the original houses for these sites. John and Eileen Alford in *Arden* bought their house as first owners and Maggie and Malcolm Hayward are the third owners of *Hazeldene*.

Gorse Down, 2000 *(EH)*

toilets, although the first residents had to wait several months after moving in before they could actually enjoy these 'luxuries'. Pearl Hatt, who was one of these first residents, remembers that while the work was being completed, blocks were placed across the chimney tops so that fires could not be lit below, thus causing the then empty water boilers located behind the fireplaces to explode. Once the water was actually running through the pipes, a fire could be lit which would heat the water behind as well as the oven on top. Water tanks were at this time positioned in the front gardens of the houses and families filled buckets from

Beech Grove, 2000 *(DR)*

these. Pearl Hatt remembers inviting her neighbour, Mrs Palmer, from *Ivy Cottage* to fill her bucket from the tank rather than struggling up to the standpipe at Sawyer's shop. People's lives must have been totally transformed when this arduous chore was no longer part of their daily routine.

In 1952 the building of the Beech Grove houses began and this was done with the specific intention of housing people who worked outside the village. Bungalows suitable for more elderly folk were later built in both Beech Grove and Hilly Close.

Many of the council houses on both sides of the main street enjoy

Our red telephone box in Beech Grove *(EH)*

wonderful views across open countryside behind them. It is in these areas of the village that some of the neatest and prettiest gardens can be found. During the latter years of the twentieth century many changes have taken place to the original council properties. A considerable number are now privately owned and have had new windows and doors fitted, small extensions added and driveways opened up so that cars can be parked. Many folk who live in this area are long-standing residents from either before the Second World War or just after. It is they who have witnessed the many changes in the village first hand and have seen it fill up too with a variety of incomers not dreamed of in their youth. Arthur Thatcher has lived in his present house in Hilly Close with its beautiful garden for 67 years! Sheila and Ray Norgate, villagers for 41 years, live in a small extension built onto their original house where daughter, Marie, now lives with her husband, Robin Butcher, and children, Laura and Sam, who go to the village school, just as their mother did before them.

It is in Beech Grove that our village telephone box can be found. We are the proud possessors of one of the few remaining red boxes, designed by Giles Gilbert Scott in the 1920s. Over the years they became instantly recognisable features of the British landscape and many ordinary folk felt much distress when the idea for a new design was first announced. Luckily, Owslebury village, '*unknown to history*', escaped from the changeover and we still have our lovely red box!

Just behind Hilly Close a grassy area has been turned into a small children's playground with swings, a slide and climbing frame. This is a most welcome area for parents and grandparents to while away the hours during fine afternoons.

Opposite Beech Grove and Hilly Close in the main street is a row of modern houses and bungalows, most of which were built in the 1960s and 70s. These include *Merryways, which* used to be *Lynlea, Underacre, Amberleigh, Newlands, Longstone, Pipers Croft, Tayinloan, Merlecroft, Chaumine* and *Ashiana*.

Turning down Pitcot Lane are more newer houses and bungalows. These include, *Downlands, Long Ash, Pitcot House, Underdown Farmhouse,* and *Shadracks Paddock*. Some of these have been built to replace other older buildings. Where *Pitcot House* now stands there was once a wooden bungalow. Fred and Phyllis Merritt lived there briefly at the start of their married life. John Seabrook remembers a farmer, Mr Amor, living there in the 1950s. A field belonging to Mr Amor was later sold to a Chandlers Ford builder who built a number of bungalows fronting the main street through the village. The fact that Mr Amor's address was in the then named Church Lane is another reason given for these new bungalows situated in the main street, also having their address as Church Lane!

In the 1950s land towards the top of Pitcot Lane was owned by Richard Corbett from *Owslebury Farm*. The Hatts, who were another village family of several generations, rented land here then. Ownership passed from Dick Corbett to Mr Mitchell from Twyford Moors, of Spitfire fame, before Chris Hatt finally bought some of the land and built *Pitcot House* in 1959. Later, in 1976, Chris also built the bungalow *Long Ash* where

referring to the Plan	LANDS AND PREMISES	CULTIVATION	STATUTE MEASURE	PAYABLE TO	PAYABLE
268	Plot	Arable	. . 39		
303	Mean Lands	Arable	6 1 .		1
269	Gorse Down	Arable	5 1 17		
270	New field	"	. 0 38		
277	"	"	11 3 23		
291	Hilly Close	"	3 . 1		
292	Beech Grove	Wood	5 . 16		
293	Grove Close	Arable	14 2 18		
294	Home field	"	9 2 29		
295	House Garden Yard and Buildings		1 . 6		
299	Down Paddock	Arable	1 2 39		
304	Long Crofts	"	6 0 1		
305	Hatchills	"	13 1 24		
306	Little Hatchills	"	7 1 8		
307	New Close	"	6 3 45		
308	Whitecott	"	5 0 45		
309	Hedge Row	Wood	1 1 17		
312	Green Lane Close	Arable	6 . 44		
			99 . 24	. . .	

A page from the Tithe Book of 1840 where the names Beech Grove, Hilly Close and Gorse Down are recorded *(EH)*

Pearl lives today. Chris sadly died the following year and so never lived there himself. He had lived in the village all his life. He was born at *Longwood Dean Farm*, lived as a child at *Lower Farm Cottages*, received his education at the village school and was married in the village church. Chris' grandchildren, Kevin and Louise, who are Malcolm's children, are the third generation of Hatts to go to the village school.

The first bungalow on the left as one enters the lane, was built by Pearl's parents, Lily and Arthur Pritchard, after they sold *Chestnut House* in 1962. Many years later it was modernised by the Kill family.

Underdown Farm where Brian Emery today runs his egg farm, was actually a poultry farm many years previously. It was then owned by Albert Lush. He sold it to Sam White who in turn sold it to Brian Emery.

At the top of Pitcot Lane John Seabrook remembers there being a garage where Jack Churchill used to keep his car.

At the top of Whites Hill, there are four properties which were originally built as homes for the families of those who worked on the battery chicken farms. These are *Highfields, Springways, Downsview and Fourwinds*. Further down the track is a large modern house called *Longfields*.

Near *Lower Farm House*, several barn conversions have occurred in recent years, namely *Orchard House, Orchard Lodge* and *Orchard Barn*. Close by are *Ararat, Westering* and *Lower Cottage*.

Another property to be built during the last century is *Bottom Cottage*, on the right hand side of Crabbes Hill approaching Owslebury Bottom. This bungalow is surrounded by paddocks and stables and backs onto open fields. At the bottom of the hill, just past *The Forge*, is *Meadowcroft* another newer property.

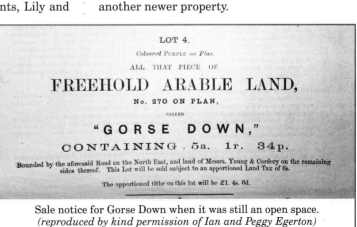

LOT 4.

Coloured PURPLE *on Plan.*

ALL THAT PIECE OF

FREEHOLD ARABLE LAND,

No. 270 ON PLAN,

CALLED

"GORSE DOWN,"

CONTAINING 5a. 1r. 34p.

Bounded by the aforesaid Road on the North East, and land of Messrs. Young & Cordery on the remaining sides thereof. This Lot will be sold subject to an apportioned Land Tax of 6s.

The apportioned tithe on this lot will be £1. 4s. 6d.

Sale notice for Gorse Down when it was still an open space. *(reproduced by kind permission of Ian and Peggy Egerton)*

When researching for this book it was fascinating to discover that the names given to some of these new areas were in fact very old names which existed long before any housing estates were dreamed of. On the Tithe Schedule of 1841 found in the church, the areas of land which we know today as Beech Grove, Hilly Close and Gorse Down were named as such then. The schedule informs us that these pieces of land were owned by Henry Cordery and occupied by William White. Another name that sprang from the page was Little Jagged Woods owned then by John Trigwell and occupied by James Mariner. Today *Jagged Woods* is the name of a bungalow originally built by Geoff and Joan Weeks who moved there from Beech Grove with children, David and Robin. Today it is home for Nigel and Carole Drew who came to the village with their sons Robert and Graham in 1989. The origins of the names Pitcot Lane and Crabbes Hill remain a mystery. Where these came from, even Betty Harfield does not know!

Many of the delivery firms coming to the village today have considerable difficulty finding some of our houses, not only because of the confusion concerning the naming of the main street, but also because all of the properties, barring those on the original council estates, are known by name rather than by number.

VILLAGE PONDS

Although Owslebury Village has no river, it has in the past known many ponds which have been formed from underground springs. Many of these have now disappeared but some of our older residents remember them well and have recorded their memories in past Newsletters. One such person is Arthur Thatcher who has lived all his life in the village. He wrote thus:

'There used to be when I went to school, opposite the Parish Hall entrance, a small paddock. The village blacksmith used a small pond where his house cow used to drink, where Merryways stands now. Also I have been told by a very old village resident, now deceased, of a pond on the recreation ground (the Cricket Down) where the water now runs across the road into a recently dug soak-away in the field. To go a little further afield, there was a pond at Lower Whiteflood, at Longwood Dean Farm, Lancing Farm, Lane End and New Warren Farm – wherever it was convenient for the steam engine to fill up'.

Arthur has recently noted that the pond at Lancing Farm has been relined and filled with water once again.

There have been other ponds recorded throughout the parish in the following places:

Morestead Ponds: Morestead crossroads – still there.

Manor Farm, Morestead: an ornamental pond now.

Bottom Pond Farm: This was concreted over to build milking parlours. The exceptional rain at the end of 2000 and the body of a fox which had got stuck in the soak-away, caused flooding here for the first time since the 1950s.

Stags Lane: normally now gone, but reappeared in the floods of December 2000.

Pond Cottage: replaced now by a garage.

Boyes Farm: inside gates – now concreted over.

Great Hunts: on roadway – outside of boundary line.

Document of court case concerning ownership of Boyes Farm Pond, 1859
(reproduced by kind permission of Ian and Peggy Egerton)

Whaddon Farm: in the field opposite.

Bottom Farm: inside the farmyard.

Marwell: left of *Hurst Cottages* – near car park.

Marwell Woods: somewhere in the middle of this area.

Greenhill: along bridleway on Mr Trigg's land

Coney Park: somewhere in woods.

Whiteflood Farm: a large one – immediately opposite the house.

Elm Farm: This used to be known as Baybridge Pond. When Cliff Percy owned it he had the top clay dug out to deepen it. It fills naturally from either side and always has water in it but the excessive rainfall at the end of the millennium year filled it to overflowing.

Frank Williams was given information in the past of yet another pond near *Yew Tree Cottage* in Baybridge. He was also told of the sad demise of the many ponds in the area and the reason was given as follows: *'There may be many a reason for this tale of woe but one at least is certain, the ponds were never cleaned out; indeed they were used as rubbish tips, and being so neglected it is as if they felt that the struggle was too much and they just faded away, unused, unwanted'.*

There is one more pond that is part of our village history, that was evidently of some significance back in 1859. At least it was of significance to **two** villagers of that time. They even went to court in order to settle their differences concerning this pond! The two gentlemen in question were Benjamin Boyes and Caleb Owton. Both were land owners in the village and the pond at the heart of the dispute was opposite where *Boyes Farm* is today. Peggy and Ian Egerton have old documents that tell the tale. Evidently there was

'Agreement made between Caleb Owton of Owslebury . . . Yeoman . . . and Benjamin Boyes of the same place, Yeoman . . . reciting that an action had recently been commenced in Her Majesty's Court of Queen's Bench by the same Benjamin Boyes against the said Caleb Owton for an alleged trespass on a certain Pond situate in the said Parish of Owslebury, contiguous to the land

opposite the Dwellinghouse of the said Benjamin Boyes being separated therefrom by the Highway leading from the village of Owslebury to Marwell'.

The document tells that the outcome was as follows:

'I do award and finally determine First that the said Pond is the property of the said Benjamin Boyes. Secondly that the boundary between the said pond and the land of the said Caleb Owton is the natural bank there now covered with brambles and old roots and that the said Bank is the property of the said Caleb Owton. And lastly I do award order and determine that the said Caleb Owton shall and do pay the said Benjamin Boyes within the space of One Calendar month from the day of the date hereof the sum of Thirty nine pounds, fourteen shillings and four pence for and towards the cost of the said Action and reference'.

It seems that Benjamin Boyes would have left the court with a smile on his face having proved that the pond was his and that Caleb had trespassed. Owning the bramble and root- covered bank hadn't counted for much for Caleb Owton that day!

Owslebury's Vital Statistics

In the early years of the 1990s, some very interesting statistics concerning the parish of Owslebury were published by Terry Russell in the village Newsletter. They were based on findings from the 1991 census and made fascinating reading, particularly as Terry also gave comparison figures for Winchester and Great Britain. They are reproduced here.

	Owslebury	Winchester	Great Britain
Number of residents	848	96,386	54 million
Persons per hectare	0.3%	1.5%	2.4%
Aged under 16	22%	19%	20%
Pensioners under 75	11%	12%	12%
Aged 75 and over	5%	8%	7%
People with long term illness	6%	10%	13%
Movers in previous year	12%	12%	10%
Women working	63%	66%	63%
Number of households	292	37,533	22 million
Owner occupied (inc buying)	71%	70%	66%
Renting from council	15%	16%	21%
Pensioner only households	22%	27%	25%
One parent families	1%	2%	4%
Without a car	11%	19%	33%
With two or more cars	60%	39%	23%

Terry went on to explain further:

'Obviously Owslebury isn't very different in most respects from the rest of Winchester or even the rest of Great Britain. We have more breathing space at 0.3 persons per hectare, but several other wards in Hampshire are even less densely populated. We compare well with two wards in Portsmouth with over 100 people to the hectare. We have slightly fewer old people, perhaps because there is no old people's home in the parish, but we do seem to be healthier than most. I think we have fewer one-person households because few young persons live alone compared with towns and cities.'

High numbers of owner-occupiers and ownership of cars is usually taken as a sign of affluence – but we need our cars so perhaps we are only moderately well off!

One aspect where Owslebury is slightly different, which is not shown above, is the sex ratio, which for us is 0.99 men to 1 woman; in Winchester it is 1 man to 1.06 women and in Great Britain it is 1 to 1.07'.

NB – a hectare is 2.471 acres or 100 sq. metres.

The Owslebury Millenium Tapestry

The items surrounding St Andrew's Church include the serpent, the font, the Mothers' Union motif, the wooden chest, the bells, the silver chalice, the church clock, the old organ and the War Memorials. The tapestry was stitched by almost three hundred villagers over a two year period and was dedicated and hung in the church during the Patronal Festival in November, 2000 *(EH)*

4: OTHER AREAS OF THE PARISH

The Parish of Owslebury extends a considerable distance round the village in each direction. Many areas are tiny hamlets or isolated homesteads which have remained much the same through several centuries. People have always gathered socially in the actual village of Owslebury as it is here where the church, the school, the parish hall and the shops in the past, have been found. Morestead alone has its own church and at one time it had a little schoolroom also. Although isolated, people of the parish have always felt an affinity one with another and this remains the same today as we approach the new millennium.

Let us now take a walk through other areas of the parish.

DOWNSTEAD

MAPLEDOWN FARM

This house, originally called *Endown,* was built in 1930 by Mr Tutt, as a gardener's cottage for his estate at *Downstead House*. The lane was a grass track and it was tarmacked by Italian prisoners of war in the 1940s. The old name of this road, which stretches from *Downstead House* to Owslebury Bottom is Warley Lane.

In 1955 *Endown* was bought by Major Childs and his Canadian wife and they changed the name to *Maple Den*. Major Childs had an agricultural business and they grew strawberries, asparagus and fruit trees. The Childs made many changes to the property, one being the filling in of a 260 foot deep well. The capped top is now in the dining room. An underground stream runs very near to the house and has been a very visible feature of the flooded land at Owslebury Bottom during the 2000 heavy rainfall.

Duncan, May, Margaret and Fiona Pollock-Gore moved into the house in 1960 and Rowena and Anthony were born there. Mr Pollock-Gore

Mapledown Farm (DPG)

continued with the growing of strawberries and changed the farm to an agricultural holding. For many years they sold cream from their herd of Guernseys, but now they rear beef cattle. Mrs Pollock-Gore has always bred and shown Dalmation dogs, but now they have just two which are kept as family pets.

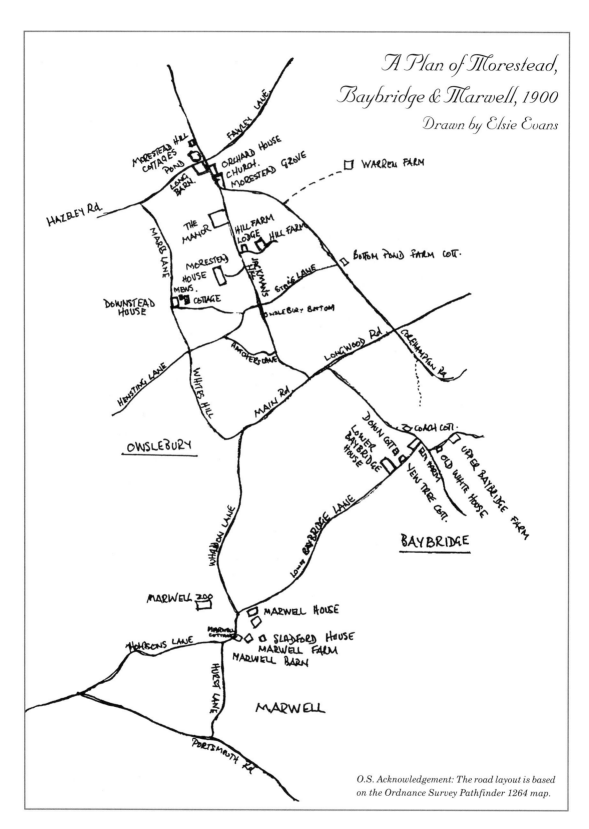

A Plan of Morestead,
Baybridge & Marwell, 1900

Drawn by Elsie Evans

FAWLEY LANE

MORESTEAD HILL COTTAGES
POND
ORCHARD HOUSE
CHURCH.
LONG BARN.
MORESTEAD GROVE
WARREN FARM

HAZELEY Rd.

MARLE LANE

THE MANOR

HILL FARM LODGE
HILL FARM

MORESTEAD HOUSE
MEWS.
COTTAGE
JACKMANS
STAG LANE
BOTTOM POND FARM COTT.

DOWNSTEAD HOUSE
OWSLEBURY BOTTOM

HINTON LANE
HACKERS LANE
LONGWOOD Rd.
COLENHAMPTON Rd.

HENSTING LANE
WHITES HILL
MAIN Rd.

OWSLEBURY

COACH COTT.
DOWN GATE
LOWER BAYBRIDGE HOUSE
ELM FARM
OLD WHITE HOUSE
UPPER BAYBRIDGE FARM
YEW TREE COTT.

WHADDON LANE

LOWER BAYBRIDGE LANE

BAYBRIDGE

MARWELL ZOO
MARWELL HOUSE
MARWELL COTTAGE
SLADFORD HOUSE
HOBBSONS LANE
MARWELL FARM
MARWELL BARN
HURST LANE

MARWELL

PORTSMOUTH Rd.

*O.S. Acknowledgement: The road layout is based
on the Ordnance Survey Pathfinder 1264 map.*

122

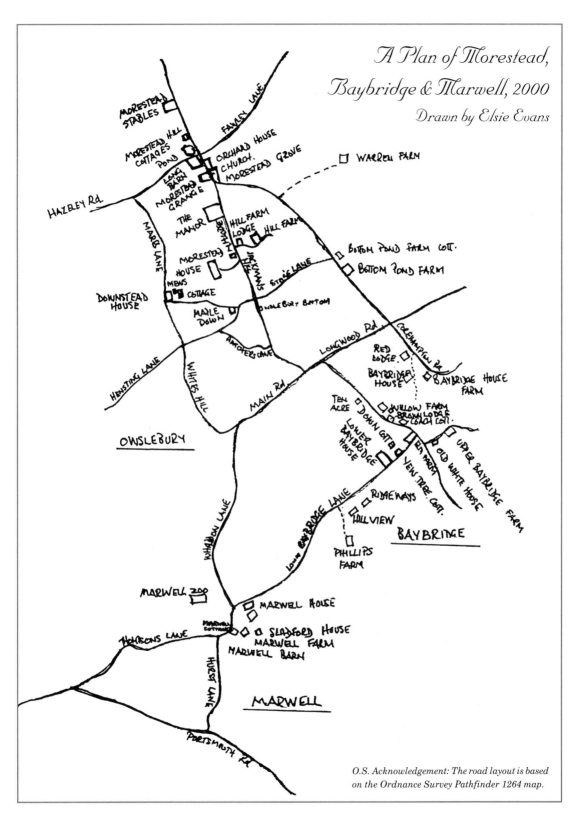

A Plan of Morestead,
Baybridge & Marwell, 2000
Drawn by Elsie Evans

MORESTEAD STABLES

FAWLEY LANE

MORESTEAD HILL COTTAGES

MORESTEAD POND

ORCHARD HOUSE

CHURCH.

MORESTEAD GROVE

WARREN FARM

LONG BARN

MORESTEAD GRANGE

HAZLEY Rd.

THE MANOR

MOORE LANE

HILL FARM LODGE

HILL FARM

BOTTOM POND FARM COTT.

MARLE LANE

MORESTEAD HOUSE

JACKMANS

STOKE LANE

BOTTOM POND FARM

MEWS

COTTAGE

DOWNSTEAD HOUSE

MARLE DOWN

OWSLEBURY BOTTOM

LONGWOOD Rd.

COLENHAMPTON Rd.

AMOYERS LANE

WHITES HILL

MAIN Rd.

RED LODGE

BAYBRIDGE HOUSE

BAYBRIDGE HOUSE FARM

HENSTING LANE

TEN ACRE

WILLOW FARM

BROWN LODGE

COACH COTT.

OWSLEBURY

DOWN COTT.

LOWER BAYBRIDGE HOUSE

ELM COTT.

YEW TREE COTT.

OLD WHITE HOUSE

UPPER BAYBRIDGE FARM

WHADDON LANE

LOWER BAYBRIDGE LANE

RIDGEWAYS

HILLVIEW

BAYBRIDGE

PHILLIPS FARM

MARWELL ZOO

MARWELL HOUSE

HOBSONS LANE

MARWELL COTTAGES

SLADFORD HOUSE

MARWELL FARM

MARWELL BARN

HURST LANE

MARWELL

PORTSMOUTH Rd.

O.S. Acknowledgement: The road layout is based
on the Ordnance Survey Pathfinder 1264 map.

DOWNSTEAD HOUSE

Downstead House was built in the late 1880s when it was known as *The Pines*. Some old records also name the house then as *The Firs*. It was home to William Shenton, a solicitor in Winchester who was twice Mayor of the city. William paid personally for the stone surface to be laid to the lane leading from his house to Hazeley Road, known as Mare Lane. The area of land which encompasses the main house, *Downstead Cottage,* and the stables, which are now named *Downstead Mews,* was once known as No Mans Land because it was neither in the parish of Owslebury nor Twyford. At a later date a boundary was drawn. This went up the drive and placed *Downstead House* in Twyford and the other two properties in Owslebury. Today after another boundary change, the house comes into the Owslebury civil parish.

In 1920 the estate was bought by Mr Tutt, a Winchester veterinarian. When Mrs Tutt was tragically killed in a hunting accident in 1953, she left the house to a relative, Captain Wilson.

Rear Admiral Gervaise Cooke bought the house in 1963 and moved in with his wife, Helen, and their children, Jonathan, who was at that time serving in the Royal Navy, Roderick, Paul and Georgina.

In 1992, Mrs Cooke moved into the renovated *Mews Cottage* and Captain Jonathan Cooke (Rtd), his wife, Henrietta, and their children, Arabella, Serena and Hugo made *Downstead House* their home.

Downstead House *(EE)*

Downstead Mews *(EE)*

DOWNSTEAD MEWS

The stables were built in 1878 and consisted of a harness room, two loose boxes and a three-roomed groom's flat above. When Mr Tutt lived in the main house, he used the flat as his surgery. He is still remembered by older residents of the parish for his generosity when treating their small domestic animals, rarely charging any fees.

When the Cooke family came to live at Downstead, the flat had been lived in by a stable girl and the facilities were very basic. There was no heating, hot water or sanitation. The cottage was renovated in 1965 and then let until 1992. The last tenant was John Alexander, the architect, who designed the new Owslebury Parish Hall. He also designed the extension on the side of the cottage which Mrs Cooke made her home, in October, 1992.

DOWNSTEAD COTTAGE

This cottage was built before the main house, known then as *The Pines*, and as *Downstead House* today. It was included in the estate and was used as a gardener's cottage. Mr Albert Berrill was the resident gardener from 1930 until 1951 and his son, Arthur, also worked in the gardens after that date. The cottage was once a coaching inn serving

Downstead Cottage (SL)

the Southampton to London route. In those days it had five bedrooms, a kitchen with a small serving hatch, an outside bell to alert the landlord of new arrivals, two large cellars for beer and food storage, and a well from which water was drawn just outside the west end of the building. The well was later covered with a wooden shed and this also housed the generator for electricity. The generator was later changed for a wind pump.

To enter the area the stagecoaches went through an arch into the stable yard at the back. This arched area is now the kitchen and the end building once housed an oat-crushing machine on the first floor. The route out of Downstead went back to the Morestead crossroads and up Fawley Lane, still referred to as the 'straight road to London'.

Extensive renovations have changed the original inn to a large family house and it is now the home of Hans and Sharon Lodder.

MORESTEAD

The small parish of Morestead lies to the south east of Winchester on the route of the Roman Road and at the crossroads from Twyford to Fawley Lane, which was, in years gone by, the stagecoach route to London. The road from Corhampton to Winchester, which follows part of the Roman road, is now a busy throughway for traffic heading to Winchester and the M3 motorway, overwhelming the tiny hamlet with vehicles during the morning and evening rush hours. Jackman's Hill provides a safer link road through Owslebury Bottom to the village.

Owslebury and Morestead are one civil parish and the links between the two villages are strengthened by their partnership in the Owslebury and Morestead Community Association as well as by a shared vicar, the Revd Mark Bailey.

MORESTEAD WATER SUPPLIES

Morestead residents' water supply is not part of the Owslebury system. Some houses are on line from Twyford, some have private bore holes and others get their water from Longwood, The Longwood bore hole is in the valley between the road and *Honeyman's Farm*. From there the water is pumped up to a reservoir on the left hand side of the road next to the trig point which marks the highest land position in the area, before the Lane End crossing.

MORESTEAD CHURCH

Morestead was one of the eight sub manors of Chilcomb mentioned in the Domesday Book. At Domesday, Chilcomb had nine churches and Morestead may have been one of these.

This ancient church, high on the bank surrounded by yew trees and a flint wall, is not easily seen by motorists travelling on the busy road that leads from Winchester to Corhampton. The church is unusual in that it has no known dedication. In 1958 the Revd. C H Gilson made enquiries at the British Museum's Department of Manuscripts and was informed that *'all records refer to it simply as the Parish Church of Morestead'*.

In 1921 the church was amalgamated with St Andrew's Church in Owslebury and the Revd Albert Briggs became rector of Morestead and vicar of Owslebury. The Bishop of Winchester, in

Morestead Church, c1910 (SS)

a letter to parishioners, explained his reasons for the joining of the incumbencies; namely, the saving of manpower and money.

Eleven years after the ecclesiastical amalgamation, a Local Government Act made alterations to the boundaries of parishes and Morestead was joined with Owslebury as one civil parish.

The last rector of the single parish of Morestead was Revd Edward Flower. He served the church from 1909 until his retirement in 1920. He moved from the rectory then and lived in *Orchard House* until his death in 1929. The rectory was sold and became a private residence. The name changed to *Morestead Grove*.

In 1975 the benefices of the joint parishes were added to St Mary's Parish Church in Twyford. The present priest in charge is Revd Mark Bailey who was inducted and collated in Twyford on 6 March, 2000.

The church maintenance costs for the care of this fragile and ancient building are met purely by the residents of the parish, with bequests, covenants and giving being the main sources of income. Income from savings accounts is re-invested.

In 1927 a large double door iron safe was purchased from the house sale of Captain Eden Richardson when he sold *Morestead House*. Mr New arranged the transport of the safe to the church, but on the day chosen there was a heavy snowfall and the safe was put onto a sledge and towed into the churchyard by a group of men. The safe was required to store parish registers and church plate.

The original registers, that date back to 1549, are now kept in the Hampshire Record Office in Winchester. Commander Guy Eddis photocopied the register beginning with entries in 1813 and continuing until 1989 and that is kept in the safe for people who visit in search of information on family history. The new registers from 1989 are also kept in the safe. The last baptism recorded was Rory Patrick William Mountain, the grandson to Sir Dennis Mountain, on 21st March, 1999. The last wedding was that of Rowena Pollock Gore and Michael Quinlan on 4th April, 1987. The last burial was for Mrs

Rector's Room, west side of the church *(EE)*

Nessie Margaret Grey Brinton, who was mother to Penny Bowes from *Lower Farm*, Owslebury, on 4th April, 2000.

The old Rector's room on the west side was joined to the church with an oak door in November, 1929 and is now used as a vestry. This room had formerly been used as the village school until the time when children went to schools in Owslebury and Twyford. In earlier days the rectory stood here but it was pulled down about 1835 and rebuilt as the school room. The cost of the work came to £35.17.0.

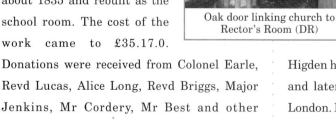

Oak door linking church to Rector's Room (DR)

Donations were received from Colonel Earle, Revd Lucas, Alice Long, Revd Briggs, Major Jenkins, Mr Cordery, Mr Best and other anonymous donors. A grant from church funds

of £3.6.6. completed the payment.

The following year in 1930 Revd Lucas of *Morestead Grange* presented a pair of oak entrance gates with paving and steps, to take the place of gates which had been erected to commemorate the Jubilee of Queen Victoria in 1897. These gates too have been replaced by wrought iron gates donated by Colonel Earle in 1969.

A tortoise stove was placed near the west wall of the church and a smaller one in the Rector's room. These were the only source of heating until electricity was connected in 1955.

To celebrate the coronation of King George V in 1911, oil lamps were bought by subscription, four lamps hanging in the nave, two on the chancel arch and one on the pulpit. These remained in use until 1955.

The present bell turret was erected by Revd William Jones to take the place of a larger one that had become unstable. The single bell bears the inscription, I.H. 1620, and was, like St Andrew's bells, cast by John Higden. Higden had worked for Joseph Carter of Reading and later at the Whitechapel Bell Foundry in London. In 1956 the bell went back to the foundry for repairs costing £48.0.0.

A drawing of Morestead Church as it was almost two hundred years ago with the bell turret, by W. Hamper, 1805. (Reproduced by kind permission of Morestead church wardens)

parishioners embroidered woollen covers for the church kneelers. In June 1969, the candlesticks were stolen from the altar. A few months later, St Thomas' Church in Southgate Street, Winchester was closed, and they gave their candlesticks to Morestead together with a credence table which is now by the altar.

The population of Morestead has always been very small and not many men were eligible for service in HM forces in the First World War. Sadly two sons of Mr Arthur Roots, the parish clerk, both lost their lives. John was killed in action in October, 1914 and his brother, William, died of his wounds in January, 1918. Five Morestead men lost their lives in World War Two. They were

> *Thomas Jeffrey Earle, RNVR*
> *Aubrey Louis Edwards, RA.*
> *Arthur Andrew Metcalf, RA.*
> *John Victor Williams, RN.*
> *Albert Charles Skeets, RE.*

The money for the repair of the bell, for new cassocks, a carpet and the installation of electricity was raised by holding regular whist drives in the Rector's room. The driver of the last Greyfriar's bus of the day (10 p.m.) would come inside the church and wait until his Winchester-bound passengers had finished their game and refreshments!

The communion plate is relatively new when compared to that of St Andrew's. The silver flagon, chalice and paten were assayed in London in 1871 and 1872 and bear the maker's marks FC and EC. What became of the plate that was used prior to this date is a mystery.

The Revd Gilson (1945 – 1962) and his

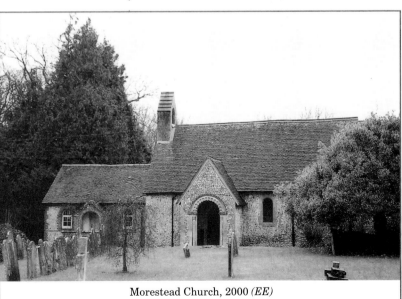

Morestead Church, 2000 *(EE)*

Miss Betty New of *Morestead Hill Cottages* took over as churchwarden from her father. Between them, they have served for over 60 years. Mr New received Maundy money from the Queen in 1979 for his services to the church. Miss New is also leader of the flower arranging team. Commander Guy Eddis is the other churchwarden. He has taken on the task of caring for the beautiful churchyard. Visitors to the church should not miss the carpet of snowdrops in early February.

MORESTEAD GROVE

The old Rectory House stood on the site of the Rector's room at the west end of the church. When Revd William Jones was appointed Rector in 1833, he described the house in a letter to the treasurer of Queen Anne's Bounty, as '*a mere cottage in a very dilapidated condition fit only for the residence of a labourer and in which the clerk of the Parish now resides and has done so for many years prior to the present incumbency, while the present Rector and his family are living in lodgings within the parish'.* Queen Anne's Bounty was a fund established in 1704 by Queen Anne to supplement the income of poorer Anglican clergy. The fund ceased in 1948 when it was amalgamated with the Ecclesiastical Commission to become the Church Commission for England.

Steps were then taken to build a new Rectory and after much correspondence between Revd Jones, the Bishop of Winchester and Queen Anne's Bounty, the building commenced in 1835. In 1869 Revd A B Burnett enlarged the house at a cost of £400 borrowed from Queen Anne's Bounty.

In 1910 additional land was given by Lord Northesk in exchange for the Rector's garden that then became part of the churchyard. In 1921 the

Morestead Grove (TS)

expedition of 1924. The General was a keen ornithologist and recorded a comprehensive list of birds in and around the *Grove* garden.

Since 1987 *Morestead Grove* has been the home of Tony and Katherine Sellon and their children, James, Edward and Louisa, relatives of General Norton. The Sellons have converted the servants' quarters and included them in the main house.

ORCHARD HOUSE

This house was originally two cottages built in 1883 and lived in by people who worked for the church. On his retirement Revd Flower (Rector of Morestead 1909 –1921) moved into *Orchard House* when Major Jenkins bought the *Rectory* (now *Morestead Grove*). He lived there with his brother and sister, Annie, until his death in 1929. Miss Flower's cousin, Miss Hilda Marie Ashley, came to live and work in a bungalow in the garden.

Miss Ashley was an artist and gained national recognition. One of her most published pictures was of an ascending angel wearing thick socks. The caption underneath read, '*Wolsley socks, fit*

benefices of Morestead and Owslebury were amalgamated and the Rectory was sold to Major A Jenkins. The name now changed to *Morestead Grove*. In 1945 General Norton bought the house. As Colonel Norton he led two major Everest expeditions in the 1920s, one being the Mallory

Orchard House, 2000 (RM)

Orchard House 1927 drawn by Hilda Marie Ashley
(reproduced by kind permission of Betty New)

for the Gods'. This was published in many newspapers and advertising posters of the times. Some of her more traditional pictures of the surrounding countryside are owned by private collectors in the village. The bungalow/studio in

the garden became apple sheds. The large apples were sold, mainly to Winchester College.

In the 1970s *Orchard House* was used as the set for a remake of Noel Coward's film 'Brief Encounter', starring Sophia Loren and Richard Burton.

Orchard House is now the home of Dr and Mrs Moreton and their children, Sukie, Becca, James and Kate.

N°s. 1 and 2 Morestead Hill Cottages

The two cottages were built in the early 1820s and became part of the *Morestead House* estate. The New family has lived in the cottages for one hundred years. Miss Betty New's father was born there in 1904. The family has given years of

The crossroads at Morestead with Orchard House on the left, c1910 (SS)

Morestead Hill Cottages, No 1 near the road (BN)

devoted and practical service to the parish church and continue to do so to this day. Miss New has worked from home as a dressmaker, her reputation for detail and excellence being well known, but sadly for her clients she has now retired.

The brick and flint cottages lie very close to the busy Winchester road. Interestingly at the opposite end of the property in the garden, lies the evidence of the **old** Roman Road to Winchester.

The cottages remain as two separate units for the purpose of government and local taxes, electricity and even television licenses, but internal doors link the two cottages.

During renovations in No.2, a bread oven was discovered in the deep chimney wall. There is every reason to believe that there is a similar oven yet to be revealed in No.1. The second resident of the cottages is Mr Arthur Berrill who has lived and worked in the parish for many years. He uses his gardening skills to great effect on the large sloping garden of his home.

MORESTEAD STABLES

The stables were built in 1920 for a trainer and lads, and apart from the war years, when the whole area was taken over by the military, they have been associated with the training of race horses. Mr Harry Willis, who died in February, 2000, having retired and moved to a cottage in Hazeley Road, worked there for thirty-five years. He began life as a foundling, an abandoned baby, but ended up being respected internationally in the horse-riding world. Following his experience as a jockey he became a well-known trainer, someone with incredible patience and understanding in coaching the art of horsemanship. He also was an expert in bringing back to health broken down horses.

The present trainer is Mr Brendon Powell and he has renovated the stables to pristine condition. He is well known as a successful ex-jockey, one of his many wins being the 1988 Grand National on Rhyme 'N' Reason. Mrs Powell has also worked in the racing industry and she too has associations with the National, having led the 1990 winner,

Brendon and Rachel Powell at Morestead Stables *(EE)*

Mr Frisk, into the winner's enclosure.

Rachel and Brendon Powell live in the bungalow with their children, Brendon and Jenney, and with Mrs Powell's brother, John.

A Greyfriars bus on a special outing to Bournemouth in 1941– *standing back left*, Des Rogers, Arthur New (father of Betty), William Oliver wearing a trilby hat (father of Wendy Wilson and Walter), unknown, Jack Thatcher (father of Arthur and Peggy Smith); *seated front left*, Mary Berrill and her sons, Arthur and Bill, Edith Oliver with Wendy and Walter peeping over his sister's shoulder. Walter Oliver was born on the day war was declared with Germany, 3 September, 1939 (BN)

LONG BARN

Contributed by Kate and Bob Bennett

The redundant farmyard at Morestead became known as *Long Barn* when Kate and Bob Bennett arrived in 1980. However, the site has been closely associated with farming for much longer with the

As the Second World War approached, the site which by now had been isolated from the adjoining farm land, was commandeered by the military and turned into an ammunition store which was guarded by three naval ratings quartered in an old cart shed. It was at this time that the remains of the old thatched roof were removed, a simple 4ft x 2ft frame added to the decaying roof timbers, and a new corrugated iron roof built. Part of the conversion to an ammunition store was the installation of two huge pot-bellied stoves with stack pipe

The stables at Long Barn, 1982 (RB)

original buildings dating back to about 1650 and more recent building on the site dated 1817 and 1820.

The farmhouse was demolished at some time between the first and second World Wars and after that the farmyard fell into decline. A

The cottage, Long Barn, 2000 – previously the stables (RB)

revival of fortune came when the yard was used as a game farm for the production of young game birds.

chimneys which protruded through the new roof. Just before the D-Day landings, the entire stock of ammunition was transported to the docks for shipment to France and the site fell silent again.

For at least the next forty years the brambles and nettles took over and the old cattle pond dried up. Kate and Bob Bennet found on arrival, a site that showed every sign of total neglect with only the old cart shed having a nearly watertight roof. The next five years were spent renovating the buildings, planting 250 young trees and starting a masons' yard for which planning permission was granted. The enterprise slowly took shape and *The Lime Centre* as we know it today developed.

Morestead is now on the international map as a centre of excellence when considering the repair of historic buildings. The training courses here have attracted visitors from America, Australia, Sweden, France, Italy, Canada and the U.K. The enterprise has been sufficiently successful that there is now a Scottish Lime Centre working in close co-operation with Morestead.

Future plans include the restoration of the old farm pond and improvements to the garden, including the conservation of wildlife areas such as nettles and unmanaged land that supports the beehives and butterflies.

MORESTEAD GRANGE

Morestead Grange was built in 1910 and is alleged to be of the 'school of Lutyens' in style, but no evidence has been found to support this premise. In 1919 the house was bought by a retired priest, Revd F G L Lucas. When the Morestead and Owslebury churches were amalgamated in 1921, he became honorary curate and offered to take two services every Sunday. This meant that Morestead Church had three services every Sunday until the Second World War. Revd Lucas often wore his hunting clothes beneath his cassock. After his death in August, 1939, Mr Arthur Berrill, now living at *Morestead Hill Cottages*, was employed to service the carbide lamps and to stoke up the boiler in the house, twice a day, seven days a week.

Morestead Grange was bought in 1961 by the present owners, Guy and Mary Eddis, and they brought up their five daughters there.

THE MANOR

The Queen Anne Manor at the bottom of Jackman's Hill was awarded Grade 2 listed status because of its original and impressive staircase. Sir Dennis and Lady Fleur Mountain have extended the manor house with a complete wing and have converted the dairy farm yard and

Morestead Grange (GE)

The Manor *(EE)*

Jackman held the land where *Hill Farm* now stands; hence the name of the lane.

The original part of the house was an open hall built in 1560. Victorian additions were added to either side. The landowner in the nineteenth century was the Rt Hon. the Earl of Northesk and one of his tenants was James Goggs (1838 – 1928). Mr Goggs was mainly responsible for the enclosure of Longwood Warren where he employed a warrener. The rabbits of Morestead were celebrated for their peculiarly delicate flavour and were an important food source. When the church held fund-raising events in the 1950s, a rabbit was one of the raffle prizes. Farmers and gardeners now look on them as pests.

Mr Goggs was the clerk to the court for the famous Titchborne trial in 1874. The Tichborne

buildings into a large turning circle around a restored pond and granary and staff accommodation.

On the roadside wall next to the gate is a Victorian post box which is still in regular use.

Sir Dennis farms 700 acres and his 200 Holstein-Friesian herd is now at *Warren Farm* on the road to Corhampton. The remainder of the farm is arable and he grows wheat, barley, maize and oilseed rape.

Farm workers live in the cottages at *Warren Farm*. Trevor and Tracey Dicks with children Stephen, Christopher and James live at Number 1, and Steve Townsend, the herdsman, lives in Number 2 with his wife, Debbie, and their children, Sophie and Tom.

HILL FARM

Hill Farm is situated at the highest point of Jackman's Hill. In 1426 there were nine tenant farmers in the parish of Morestead and Richard

Warren Farm Cottages *(EE)*

Family has owned the estate near Cheriton since Anglo Saxon times. The family is especially famous for both the Tichborne Dole, which dates back to 1150 and for the trial in 1879 when Arthur Orton claimed to be Sir Roger Tichborne, the heir who was previously drowned at sea. The case cost nearly £100.000 and lasted for 100 days in a blaze of publicity. Films, stage and television dramas have been made, re-enacting this amazing story which proved Arthur Orton to be an imposter.

During his youth, Roger Tichborne used to ride over to Owslebury three times a week for lessons with the Revd Charles Maberley, the first resident incumbent of Owslebury Church. His visits must have made an impression on the vicar's oldest daughter because she recorded her memories of this event when writing about her childhood in the village, as an old lady of eighty.

In the nineteenth century, *Hill Farm* was one of the last venues where there was a prosecution for cock fighting, apparently held in the attic.

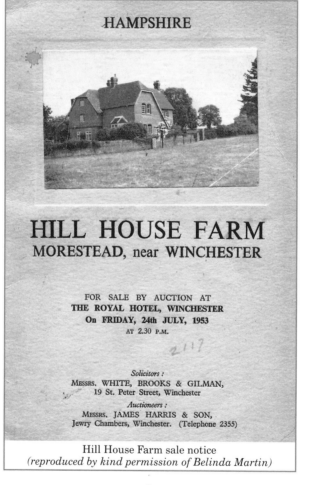

HAMPSHIRE

HILL HOUSE FARM
MORESTEAD, near WINCHESTER

FOR SALE BY AUCTION AT
THE ROYAL HOTEL, WINCHESTER
On FRIDAY, 24th JULY, 1953
AT 2.30 P.M.

Solicitors :
MESSRS. WHITE, BROOKS & GILMAN,
19 St. Peter Street, Winchester

Auctioneers :
MESSRS. JAMES HARRIS & SON,
Jewry Chambers, Winchester. (Telephone 2355)

Hill House Farm sale notice
(reproduced by kind permission of Belinda Martin)

In 1953 Mr and Mrs Wallace bought the house from Mr Applethwaite who lived there with his faded chorus girl companion. Before renovations could begin on the house and garden, the new owners had to dispose of hundreds of empty gin bottles.

Mrs Wallace was an enthusiastic and talented gardener and she visited many well known and established gardens around the country. On one of her frequent visits to Sissinghurst Castle in Kent she met Vita Sackville-West who had established one of the finest gardens in the country. Mrs Sackville-West presented her with a rose cutting for the new *Hill Farm* garden and this rose flourishes today in the exquisite garden. Mrs Wallace's daughter, Belinda, continues her mother's skilled care and opens her home and garden to visiting gardening enthusiasts. When Mr and Mrs Wallace retired to the *Lodge House* in 1982, Belinda and Will Martin and their children, James, Nichola and Rebecca took over *Hill Farm*.

Hill Farm, 2000 *(BM)*

HILL FARM LODGE

The *Lodge* was originally a farm worker's cottage and part of *Hill Farm*. In 1982 Mr and Mrs Wallace moved from *Hill Farm* into the extended and renovated property. Mr Michael Jackson, his wife, Diana, and their children, Katherine, Alice and James live there now.

MORESTEAD HOUSE

Morestead House was built in 1900 for Captain R Eden and Mrs Katherine Richardson as a game farm where pheasants were reared. Captain Richardson was born in Carmarthenshire and Mrs Richardson was the daughter of Walter Long of the *Holt* in Upham and the sister of Walter Vansittart Cambell-Wyndham-Long of *Corhampton House*. Their first daughter, Doris, died in infancy and they donated a large birdbath from their garden to the churchyard in memory of her.

Colonel and Mrs Earle bought the house and estate in 1927. The Colonel always invited the older residents to celebrate his birthday with tea in the garden. When King George V1 was crowned on May 12th, 1937, he hosted a celebration party for everyone after a Holy Communion service at the church. During the Second World War the house was used as a boarding school by the boys of Acton County Secondary School who were first evacuated to Weymouth and then to

Hill Farm Lodge, 2000 *(EE)*

Morestead House *(EE)*

Owslebury Primary School while living here.

During the Second World War a few bombs were dropped in Morestead. One fell in the paddock but did not explode; another bomb which did explode nearby was the probable cause of damage to a west nave window in the church.

In 1963 Colonel Earle divided *Morestead House* into two parts. He continued to live in the east section made up of the main reception rooms, and converted the western part into three flats that were let.

The present owners, Bob and Maureen Niddrie, bought the house in 1972. They are only the third family to have lived there in the hundred years since it was built. Occasionally they

Morestead House in November, 1940. Some took an active part in the church. Dr Ernest Balls, the science master, became the Rector's warden until January, 1944 and the boys formed a small choir. The boys moved out in September, 1943 and Portsmouth Northern Secondary School used *Morestead House* then as a hostel for girls attending school in Winchester. Those

Captain Eden Richardson   Mrs Katherine Richardson
(BMN)

children who went to church attended Sunday School in Owslebury. The school returned to Portsmouth in November, 1944 and from early in 1945 the house was used as a children's hostel by The Salvation Army. The children attended

are visited by ex-schoolboy residents from the war years and they are happy to give their visitors access to the house and gardens.

WEST MORESTEAD HOUSE

When Colonel Earle lived in *Morestead House*, in the 1960s, *West Morestead House* was three separate flats. After the Colonel's death in 1970 many of the farm buildings and land were sold and a developer reconverted the three flats back into one house. This house is now the family home of

Claire and Harry Criswell in the garden at West Morestead House *(EE)*

John, Claire, Jamie, Harry and Millie Criswell.

THE LODGE AT MORESTEAD HOUSE

The Lodge at the entrance of the drive to *Morestead House*, was built in 1920 for Colonel Earle's chauffeur. The timber house of this time was built from prefabricated huts made for troops of the Boer War. Mr Bridger, a local farmer, used the house for his staff and then moved into it himself. He had the exterior faced with brick and made other improvements.

The *Lodge* is now the home of Stephen Rendall and Alison Niddrie. Alison is the daughter of Mr and Mrs Niddrie at *Morestead House.*

BOTTOM POND FARM

The timber farmhouse known as *Bottom Pond Farm* was built in 1927 for Mr Cordery, the agent for Lord Eldon of Longwood. Lord Eldon, an ex-Indian civil servant, was at that

The Lodge *(EE)*

Bottom Pond Farmhouse *(EE)*

Mr Hellard and his sons collected pieces of pottery and flint from the fields around the farm. A neighbour, Mr A R Edwardson of *Red Lodge*, also collected flint instruments and recorded some earthworks.

In the autumn of 1961, Mr Peter Dicks made a spectacular discovery when deep ploughing at the farm, when he disturbed a cremation site. Mr Hellard reported it to the Winchester Museum Service who investigated this exciting discovery. The following spring further deep ploughing revealed

time, a Lord-in-waiting to King George V. Mr Cordery is remembered on a memorial plaque in Owslebury Church.

Mr Philip Hellard moved into the farm in 1940 and his wife, Mary, came in 1943. For some years

Haymaking at Bottom Pond Farm, c1910 –
from left to right, Mrs Warren, Mrs Stone, Mrs Dyke, Mrs Laurence, Mrs Norgate (BN)

a corn drying oven and this was followed by trial trenching the land and aerial reconnaissance. Excavations continued on the farm until 1971. Students who were majoring in archaeology came from all over the world and set up tented camps at the farm. Many people in Owslebury offered them the use of their bathrooms and some gave short term lodging to any student who became unwell.

The dig was managed by Miss Capstick of the Winchester Museum Service together with John Collis who was head boy at Peter Symonds School and who later became professor of archaeology at Sheffield University. Some of the pottery excavated is now on display at the British Museum in London. The skeleton of a Belgic or pre-Roman tribesman was a major discovery; the grave goods found alongside the body were those of a warrior, - a leaf-shaped iron spearhead, bronze sheeting, a heavy iron sword with remnants of a scabbard and a bronze shield boss. Warrior burials were common on the continent but distinctly rare in this country.

Some of the artefacts found at *Bottom Pond Farm* are now on display at the Museum of the Iron Age in Andover and the warrior skeleton is kept at *Chilcombe House* in Winchester.

BOTTOM POND COTTAGES

The two *Bottom Pond Cottages* are a part of the *Bottom Pond Farm* estate and were built by the Earl of Northesk in 1858. A plaque on the front wall bearing the initials EN and the date 1858, is typical of many of the cottages built for workers on the Longwood estate at that time. *Pond Cottage* in Owslebury has a similar plaque.

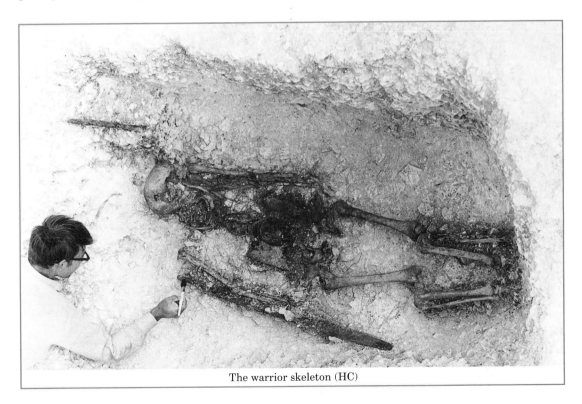

The warrior skeleton (HC)

Cottages at Bottom Pond Farm *(EE)*

BAYBRIDGE HOUSE

Baybridge House is reached from a driveway on the hill, off the Morestead to Corhampton Road, southeast of the Longwood crossroads. A lane now used as a private bridleway for Anna and Felicity Coutts Donald, linked *Red Lodge* on the Corhampton Road with *Brown Lodge* on Baybridge Lane, close to *Willow Farm*.

The house was built in 1911 by Edward Macdonald Lucas and his French countess wife. The southern French style house set around a courtyard was designed specifically for entertaining guests. The only room on the first floor had a glass roof, a full size billiard table and a stage. Downstairs there was another stage off a large reception room. This stage was 4ft. high and had a removable partition. In later years this room was used as a study. Around the room were curtained alcoves, most probably used as dressing rooms for the entertainers. All five bedrooms also had dressing rooms attached.

Edmund Jack Macdonaid Lucas, the eldest son, was killed in the Second World War. After the war his brother, Duncan, returned to Baybridge and lived in the family-owned *Elm Farm*. He sold the farm in 1950 and went to Rhodesia. Some years

Mr Peter Dicks, the ploughman who discovered the cremation site on *Bottom Pond Farm*, lives in one cottage and Mr George Foot and his son live next door. Near the cottages and the granary which stands alongside, is a milestone giving distances to Bishops Waltham, six miles and to Winchester, four miles. Unfortunately the facing plaque on the stone has been lost, probably as a result of roadside maintenance.

BAYBRIDGE

The tiny hamlet of Baybridge lies about a mile southeast of Owslebury and is made up of farms, cottages and a deconsecrated Primitive Methodist Chapel. One hundred years ago the first house reached from Owslebury village beyond the Cricket Down was *Coach Cottage,* then named *Rose Cottage*, opposite the Methodist Chapel. It remains a quiet enclave and the lanes that lead to it from the Longwood Road, Marwell and

Baybridge House *(EE)*

later a Rhodesian mechanic on the Holt estate in Upham told Mr Les Gould, who was living in the house at that time, that the Macdonald Lucas family were his ex-neighbours in Africa.

During the Second World War the house was requisitioned by the army who manned a searchlight unit. British and American soldiers were resident there at that time. Edward Macdonald Lucas never returned and Mrs Annie Jane Gould bought the house in 1947 and moved in with her nine-year-old grandson, Leslie. She often spoke of her time helping her mother in their Windsor shop and of how she met Buffalo Bill and Sitting Bull there who were on a tour of Europe with their circus.

In the late 1940s a 50,000 gallon reservoir was built on the land. The water source was Otterbourne Water Works and it was piped to Baybridge via Compton, Shawford and Twyford Pumping Station. This system is still in use today and supplies all the water for Owslebury and Baybridge. Before the connection to mains water there were large rain water tanks close to the house. Mrs Gould would have to strain the debris and insects through a muslin cloth before using the water in the house.

Annie Gould gave the house to her grandson, Leslie, in 1964. She died in 1968 aged 91 years.

Les and his wife, Thelma, began farming pigs and then changed to pheasant-rearing in 1974. They continued with this until 1997 when they sold to William and Priscilla Coutts Donald. Thelma and Les moved to a farm in Dorset, but their second son, Andrew, still works as a carpenter from one of his father's farm buildings.

The 16 acre garden was first laid out as park land with ornamental gardens. Over the years the land has been divided into smaller properties and industrial units.

Baybridge House Farm, *centre left*, Red Lodge, *lower right* (JB)

BAYBRIDGE HOUSE FARM

The 1970-built house faces *Red Lodge* on the drive leading to the industrial units and eventually to *Baybridge House*. Neil and Jane Briercliffe came as tenants to farm pigs and lived in a wing of the big house. They later built the farmhouse and moved in with their children Timothy, Katie, Simon and Philip. Neil's mother Mrs Edith Briercliffe lived in an attached 'granny annexe'. Since Mrs Briercliffe's death in July 2000, the annexe has been home to Jane's mother, Ruth Piper.

The pig farm ceased working in 1991 and the farm buildings were converted into five industrial units.

RED LODGE

The old lodge at the entrance to *Baybridge House* on the Corhampton Road was renovated and extended by Gary and Sandra Wheeler in 1979. The new owners are Stan and Ann Elliott.

BROWN LODGE

The *Lodge* on Baybridge Lane has fallen into disrepair. Some of the last tenants were Mr and Mrs Cox, parents of Eileen Sankey, Pat Rudgley and their brother, Norman. Mrs Violet Cox and daughters, Eileen and Pat, today all live in Owslebury Village. The last tenants were Mr George Doe and his family. Mr Doe was a prolific writer of letters to local newspapers, especially the Hampshire Chronicle. He moved when he bought ten acres of land in Baybridge Lane.

The present owner of the *Lodge* is Andrew Gould, the second son of Les and Thelma. He is the fourth generation of Goulds to have owned the property.

Willow Farm and Willow Farm Cottage, *centre right* (DE)

WILLOW FARM

Halfway down Baybridge Lane between the Cricket Down field and *Coach Cottage* is the 100 acre *Willow Farm* owned by David and Adele Emmans. The family moved to Baybridge in 1977 from Townhill near Southampton. Their farm here was compulsorily purchased for housing development following the government's Land Community Bill in 1977 and they were given twelve months to vacate their home and farm business. Eleven months into the year's notice they had built the farmhouse and outbuildings in Baybridge and were, therefore, able to continue their pig-breeding livelihood. Over the years since their arrival they have bought more land to make it the farm it is today. The 100 acres are purely arable and the resulting harvests are made into 600 tons of pellets for feeding the animals and this accounts for over half of their requirements.

The land is fertilised by manure from the hundred sows. One sow and her progeny are sufficient to fertilise one acre of land.

David's and Adele's son, Harry, lives with his wife, Michelle, in a cottage on the farm. They are expecting a baby in February, 2001 and this child will be the youngest Baybridge inhabitant then. Harry works on the farm with his brother, Oliver, who lives in the farmhouse with his parents.

TEN ACRE FARM

Mr George Doe moved to the ten acre plot from *Brown Lodge* and lived in a mobile home for the time it took to build his house here. He and his family lived there from 1953 until he sold the house to James and Jean Green in 1983. Some years before he sold the house, he had sold eight of the ten acres to the Ventham family. They built a house on the land and began pig farming there.

John and Andrea Kennedy moved into *Ten Acre Farm* in September 1994 and converted the farm buildings to stabling. They bought a further 4 acres from Mr Jim Pritchard bringing their total to 12 acres. It is now a thriving riding school and livery stable called The Owslebury Equestrian Centre. John and Andrea have three small children, Alex, Harry and baby Todd, born in 2000.

TEN ACRE COTTAGE

James and Jean Green now live in the house that George Doe built in 1953. They retained two acres of garden and have created an interesting and unusual garden, using topiary as the main feature on the hedges.

When the Greens arrived they found themselves the owners of an old railway carriage in the garden. Since it was much too heavy to move they built a shed over it. The Greens finally decided they wanted to get rid of the carriage and contacted the Watercress Line at Alresford for their advice. A representative came to look at it. Through him they discovered they owned a very rare Banana Carriage which had been preserved wonderfully under Jim's shed! In September, 1994 they arranged for Gerry Tull from Owslebury to

Gerry Tull delivers the Banana carriage to Ropley in September 1994. The old timber crane lorry belongs to Roger Davy (GT)

transport it to Alresford. Today the carriage is being used as a signal and telephone store and can be seen alongside the signal box at Alton Station.

An extension has been put onto the house

Coach Cottage, once Rose Cottage, with Primitive Methodist Chapel on the left *(DR)*

making a separate unit for Jim's and Jean's son, Kevin, his wife, Paula, and their baby daughter Maria, born in February, 2000, Baybridge's first millennium baby.

COACH COTTAGE

Coach Cottage was originally two thatched, brick and flint cottages built in the 1800s. One was known then as *Rose Cottage* and both were homes for farm labourers. They were converted to one cottage about 1950. For a good part of the last half of the previous century it was home to Jimmy and Catherine Phillips. Baybridge Lane runs close to the front door and an unusual feature is the fact that the main garden is on the other side of the road.

Overlooking the garden is the Baybridge Primitive Methodist Chapel which dates from 1861. It has for many years been used as a garage and storeroom. Emma and Robert Mitchell who moved into Coach Cottage in 1998, are now converting it into a playroom for their two small boys, Harry and Theo. The old garage door is being closed up and the original Chapel door leading into the garden, is being reinstated to make a perfect link from playroom to garden. The chapel was deconsecrated one hundred years after it opened and the last minister was Revd Peter Woodward. The deeds of the Chapel state that there were restrictions on the use of the building; *'there must be no alcohol sold on the premises, neither must gambling take place'*.

The cottage was, like many small houses in the parish, a part of the Marwell Estate. Before the last war the landlord was Mr Pery Standish. Eli and Agnes Glasspool were tenants in *Rose*

149

Cottage. When Eli died, their youngest son, George, and his wife, Mabel, took on the tenancy and brought up their sons, Peter and Barry, there. Encouraged by Squire Standish, George bought the property for £90, paying the Marwell Estate weekly rental until he achieved the selling price. Then the Squire gave him the deeds. When George became ill, he and his wife moved to Winchester. Mabel Glasspool, now 91 years old, lives in Devonshire House, part of the St John's Almshouses.

George Glasspool used the garden opposite the house to grow vegetables. In the late 1940s, Duncan Macdonald Lucas, owner of *Baybridge House* and resident at that time in his other property, *Elm Farm*, disagreed with the use of the land as he believed it belonged to him. He arrived one morning and drove a vehicle over the vegetables. When he had gone, Mabel Glasspool discovered a sign in the garden which stated *'This land is the property of Baybridge House and Trespassers will be Prosecuted'*. She pulled up the sign, chopped it up and threw it on the fire. The local policeman was called and the outcome was settled amicably. The garden, was in fact, common land. George and Mabel , from this time on, paid five shillings a year rent.

Eli Glasspool 1857-1924 wearing his Hampshire Volunteer Force uniform. He was grandfather to Roger and Walter Trott from Owslebury Bottom (WT)

George and Mabel Glasspool's son, Peter, now living in Port Solent, was a keen cyclist in his youth. He began his competitive cycling career by winning all the local County Championships. He then went on to ride in the Milk Race Tour of Britain in 1958 and 1959, finishing in 8th position in 1958. He held the record for pursuit racing at the Southampton track for many years. His favourite claim to fame in the cycle racing world was when he beat Peter Brotherton, the World Champion Silver Medallist in the invitation pursuit race. Peter was awarded the BEM for his services to trade unionism.

During the Second World War, British and American soldiers, based in Longwood, came to Baybridge each morning to dump swill which they transported on Bren gun carriers, at a farm in

The Old White House (AH)

Harfield), later bought the house, which now was called *White Lilacs* and earned their living rearing and selling turkeys.

The Old White House today is the home of Adrian and Suzanne Hardman.

UPPER BAYBRIDGE FARM

Brian, Angela and Jayne Powell's two hundred year old farmhouse is set in 32 acres of land. When Mr and Mrs Powell began farming there forty-two years ago they concentrated on dairy farming. After twelve years they changed to arable farming and grew mainly barley. Today 50 per cent of the land is 'set aside' land.

Before and during the Second World War, John (Jacky) Dovedon and his mother lived at *Upper*

Lower Baybridge Lane. On their return from the farm they would give children a lift to school and Peter remembers gifts of candy to eat on the ride.

THE OLD WHITE HOUSE

This house which was once three cottages, dates from the 17th century. One of the cottages was a pub called *The Flowerpot*. The land adjacent to the property was a malt house where the beer was brewed. This was condemned in 1958 and demolished in 1959.

The cottages were rented early in the twentieth century by William and Selina Harfield who lived there with their eighteen children. Jack and Lily Plowman (née

Upper Baybridge Farm *(EE)*

Elm Farm 1928 with Baybridge Farm, *centre*, Old White House, *on the skyline*, and the Malthouse, *on the left* (LL)

Elm Farm, 2000, with Baybridge Farm and the Old White House, and the Methodist Chapel, *on the left (EE)*

Baybridge Farm. Mrs Dovedon bred retriever dogs that were sold as puppies to be trained as gun dogs. They employed a kennel maid called Phyllis who lived on the farm. She preferred to dress in men's clothing and always wore her trilby hat and smoked a pipe! She used to ride her bike most nights down to the *Ship Inn* where she drank pints and played darts. During an altercation in the pub one night, she hit her opponent with such a punch that he was laid low.

Jacky served in the RAF throughout the war and was sadly killed a few weeks after VE Day when his bomber aircraft crashed when returning to England from the Berlin airlift. Because he died after the war ended, he was not included on the memorial in St Andrew's Church.

ELM FARM

This brick and flint farmhouse and the flint barn were both built round about 1850. For some years prior to its sale in 1950, *Elm Farm* had been owned by the Macdonald Lucas family of *Baybridge House* and the tenant farmer was Mr G Jeans.

Elm Farm was always a dairy farm and the last farmer to operate it in this manner was Mr H T Rigg who bought the 37 acre farm in 1956. He moved to *Hillview Farm* in Hensting Lane in September, 1968. Mr Rigg kept a herd of Jersey and Guernsey cows at *Elm Farm* and retained a small acreage of barley. The flint barn was used as storage for the hay and brewers' grains. Mr Rigg's son, Andrew, remembers the wonderful smell of the grain and said that the cows loved it too.

Clifford and Gina Percy bought the property in 1968 and began the development of the stables. During this time some land was sold off to neighbouring farmers. Mrs Percy was Gina Campbell before her marriage, daughter of Donald Campbell who died in 1967 on Coniston Water in the Lake District after a water speed record attempt in his boat, Bluebird. Mrs Percy broke the women's world speed water record in 1984.

The farm is now owned by the Lambert family who have further developed the stables and continued renovations to the house and garden.

YEW TREE COTTAGE

Yew Tree Cottage, built behind *Down Cottage* and at about the same time during the seventeenth century, was part of the Marwell Estate. This Grade II listed Jacobean cottage has been renovated and extended over the years and still retains its original charm. The well that once provided water for both *Down* and *Yew Tree Cottages* is now under the kitchen floor.

The typically English country garden has been an outstanding feature of the property in years gone by and past gardeners who have treasured it are Mrs Scully, mother of Pat Scully in *Down Cottage,* and Mrs June Marjorie Coombs who continued the care of the garden and made it famous.

When Sheron, Joseph and William Wylie-Modro bought the cottage, they found that the garden had become overgrown and many of the plants were missing. The garden had been popular with writers and photographers in the past and using their publications, Sheron was able to restore the garden to what it had once been. She was able to identify the roses from colour photographs and these were then replanted. Today it is once again a nationally recognised example of the traditional English country garden and has featured in recent books such as the cover of the 1998 *Gardening Year Book*, '*English Cottage Gardens*' and '*Great English Gardens*' by Andrew Lawson and Jane Taylor.

DOWN COTTAGE

This brick and thatch cottage is another Marwell Estate cottage and the deeds go back to the seventeenth century. It is now a listed building. The large inglenook fireplace has a recessed salt box in the back wall.

An ancient right of way existed through to

Yew Tree Cottage, Baybridge *(DR)*

153

Down Cottage *(DR)*

nearby *Yew Tree Cottage* so that tenants of *Down Cottage* could have access to the well there for water.

The house is now the family home of Pat and Daphne Scully and their children, Heather, who was born here, and Mark. The Scully family moved to *Down Cottage* in 1947.

LOWER BAYBRIDGE HOUSE

The present *Lower Baybridge House* used to be a number of separate cottages, Numbers 1 – 5 Lower Baybridge Lane, and these were then farm workers' dwellings. The two acre plot was used by each cottager to grow vegetables for his family. Their water came from a deep well found in a small gap between cottages Numbers 3 and 4. This was filled in when mains water supplies came to Baybridge.

The last person to move out of the end cottage was Mrs Eva Vidler. She was then 97 years old and for many years she made a weekly contribution to the Owslebury Newsletter. She found most of her inspiration from magazines, especially *The Peoples' Friend*.

As people moved out, the cottages were bought and joined on to each other. The gap between Numbers 3 and 4 was built over. The well is now

Lower Baybridge House *(DR)*

under the present drawing room floor.

Sir John and Lady Sylvia Rix moved to *Lower Baybridge House* in August 1977 and have created a stunning garden covering the two acres. They have also made a small vegetable plot.

OTHER HOUSES ON LOWER BAYBRIDGE LANE

Halfway between *Marwell House* and *Lower Baybridge House* on Lower Baybridge Lane are three more houses in a group up on a bank. These are bungalows built in 1936 as smallholdings. Over the years two of them, *Hill View* and *Ridgeways,* have been altered and made into substantial properties. *Phillips Farm House* remains as it was. A well-walked bridleway runs through the land around *Phillips Farm House* and the Roman Road is very close to this house. *Hill View* is the home of Celia and Sean Thompson.

Their children, Toby and Naomi, grew up here and attended the village school. Celia is well known throughout the parish as the Owslebury village postmistress. *Ridgeways* is now lived in by Chris and Sarah Haddock.

Mr Dick Lush, a retired farmer, lives in *Whaddon Farmhouse* which lies nearer to the centre of the hamlet.

MARWELL

Marwell is another significant area of the parish lying to the southwest of Owslebury Village. *Marwell Cottages, Marwell Barn, Sladford House* and *Marwell Farmhouse* were all part of the *Marwell House Estate* until 1986. Originally all the land here had been part of the *Marwell Hall Estate*, with *Marwell House*, formerly *Marwell Lodge*, being the Dower House. For many

Aerial view of Marwell, 1964 (AS)

centuries, much of this land was owned by Corpus Christi College in Oxford.

This 1964 aerial photograph shows the working farm with the sixteenth century barn, now *Marwell Barn* at the bottom left. *Marwell Farmhouse* is in the centre and *Sladford House*, once a pair of cottages, is to the right. At the top of the photograph are the outbuildings, tennis court and orchard of *Marwell House*.

MARWELL HALL – NOW MARWELL ZOOLOGICAL PARK

Today the name Marwell, to most people, means Marwell Zoological Park, a world famous conservation centre of excellence. The beautiful old house in the centre of the park, originally built between 1315 and 1325, was once *Marwell Hall* and has been home to several famous families in the past, among them the Seymours in the 1500s, the Mildmays in the 1600s, the Dacres in the 1700s and the Longs in the 1800s. It was William Long who in 1816 extensively refurbished the house, rebuilding much of it but keeping to the original architectural style. At the beginning of the 1900s it was home to the Standish family. Major William Pery Standish married his wife, Evelyn Cecilia Phipps, in 1901 and their five children grew up at Marwell. Major Standish died suddenly of a stroke when returning home from a day's hunting in November, 1922. In his obituary he was described as a '*soldier, sportsman and county gentleman*', and also as being '*a*

Marwell Hall (GW)

kindly, genial personality'. He took a very active role in public life and gained his OBE following his work as Assistant Commandant of the Romsey Remount Depot from 1915 until almost the end of the war. In Owslebury, so the obituary tells us, *'he was one of the Church wardens ... and was beloved as the "Squire" by all classes; he was the President of every village organisation and the universal friend'*. Mrs Standish was also much loved in the parish and it was with great sadness that villagers noted her moving away from *Marwell Hall* after the marriage of her eldest son, 'Mr Teddy'. He was the third generation to be 'Squire' at the *Hall* but was later tragically killed in a road accident in 1933.

This historic house has been a significant part of the parish of Owslebury through the centuries and much of the village's history and legend is associated with the Marwell Estate. Stories of tragedy and ghostly hauntings have been passed down through generations, and they are a rich part of the area's legacy.

A poem entitled *'The Mistletoe Bough'* by Thomas Haynes Bayly recounts the tale of a young bride who on the night of her Christmas wedding hid in an old oak chest which closed on her with a spring lock, only to be found many

Marwell Hall (AE)

years later. It is said that around 11 pm on the night after Boxing Day, the sounds of young wedding guests can be heard rushing along the corridors of the *Hall*.

Another ghostly lady is said to be Ann Boleyn who haunts the yew tree walk that leads from the *Hall* to Whaddon Lane. Her ghost is said to have made straight for *Marwell Hall* following her execution in London, on the day her former husband, King Henry VIII, married Jane Seymour at the house. The story of the marriage at *Marwell Hall* is pure local legend because it is a fact that the king's marriage took place at Hampton Court on 20th May, 1536.

A few slightly more peaceful centuries later, Mr John Knowles bought *Marwell Hall* and 417 acres of land in September, 1969. He made it his home until 1980 when the house was made over to offices for the zoological park.

Mr Knowles faced fierce opposition to his planned zoo from the residents of Owslebury. They feared excess traffic through the village and were extremely worried that animals might escape. A meeting was held in the Parish Hall in June, 1969 when people voiced their objections. Just 21 people voted in favour and 130 were vehemently opposed to the plan. A public enquiry in Winchester was convened three months later, but the final decision was eventually made by the Minister of the Environment who approved the planning application in May, 1971.

Marwell Zoological Park first opened its doors to the public in May, 1972 and Sam White from *Chalk Dale*, Whaddon Lane was the first person to buy an entrance ticket.

Since those early days the park has developed into a major tourist attraction and has continued to extend its valuable contribution to the world's conservation programme. Relationships with the village have improved considerably and during the last 30 years, people from the area have found employment there and children from the school have adopted a succession of animals. Traffic to the park has been directed through other routes and the only escapees have been four parakeets, who made their flight for freedom on the night of the great storm in October, 1987, and two scarlet macaws who tried to do the same in March, 1994. The macaws were actually caught later by members of the public.

MARWELL HOUSE

This house was once the Dower House for *Marwell Hall* and at one time was known as *Marwell Lodge*. This was another property that was owned by Corpus Christi College in Oxford and one of the last to be sold. The sale was finalised in March, 1960 when it was conveyed to Dorothea, Viscountess Kelburn of *Marwell Farm*. Lady Kelburn came to live here in 1948 and farmed the 280 acre farm surrounding the house

Aerial view of Marwell House, 1964 (LK)

until 1986 when it was divided into five separate properties.

Lady Kelburn is a very well known figure in the parish and has been much involved in village life over the years. She was particularly associated with the Owslebury and Morestead Horticultural Society. She still lives at *Marwell House* which has retained 30 acres of woodland and paddocks around it.

MARWELL FARMHOUSE

The *Farmhouse* is one of the five properties that was separated from *Marwell House* in 1986. It was originally built round about 1600 and additions were made in the eighteenth and nineteenth centuries. Today it is a Grade II listed building.

In the original part of the house there is a large inglenook fireplace and many old oak beams. The eighteenth century single storey addition retains the original brick fireplace, bread oven and copper. This section also has a boarded over deep well that was used for farm animals as well as the house until mains water became available in the 1950s.

Until 1986 the house was occupied by tenant farmers. At this time the extensive farm buildings were demolished and the *Farmhouse,* along with 12 acres of land, was separated from the estate. The present occupants are Vivienne and Andrew Sturt and their two children, John and Victoria.

Marwell Farmhouse (AS)

MARWELL BARN

Marwell Barn is a sixteenth century construction with a timber frame. It had been used as a traditional farm barn on what was known then as *Marwell Farm* until 1986 when it became one of the five separated properties. Permission was granted then to convert it to a dwelling. Great care was taken with the conversion and it has made a magnificent house with an intriguing Garden Room at the western

Marwell Barn (AS)

Sladford House (AS)

end. It is a Grade II listed building.

The present occupants are Tony and Wendy Stevens, with Wendy's daughter, Annette, her husband, John Harris, and their children, James and Danielle.

SLADFORD HOUSE

This elegant house was originally a pair of farm workers' cottages. They had dirt floors and no sanitation when they were purchased as part of the *Marwell Farm Estate* by Lady Kelburn in 1948. When she decided to sell in 1986, they were converted to one dwelling with 10 acres of land.

Rodney and Gloria Tabor lived here until 2000. The house was then bought and extensively remodelled by James and Rosie Hoare who live there today with Rosie's two sons, John and Alex.

MARWELL COTTAGES

These two cottages were built around 1900 for estate workers. Today one cottage is still retained by Lady Kelburn, the owner of *Marwell House* and the other has been sold and extended. This is currently occupied by Paul Baron.

Estate cottages for Marwell House *(EE)*

5: SOCIAL ENCOUNTERS
VILLAGE ORGANISATIONS

OWSLEBURY PARISH COUNCIL

Contributed by Dr Jane Dawson, Chairman Owslebury Parish Council, 2000

"Local self-government is the life-blood of liberty". J L.Malley, 1853

When Matley wrote these words, local government had recently undergone a major development in its legal status, management and responsibilities, which reflected the change in society brought about by the industrial revolution of 19th century.

What was local government like before this period? Where did parish councils originate? In medieval England, for ecclesiastical purposes, the country was divided up into parishes which had some of the functions that later became the responsibility of local government. When in 1274-5 Edward 1st surveyed the "Hundreds" (an area of local administration), the bailiff of the Hundred, acting for the Sheriff, was responsible for justice, law, military defence, land tenure and taxation. Owslebury is shown on an early map to be part of the Hundred of Winchester. An important piece of legislation was the Poor Law of 1611, which gave parishes the responsibility to punish 'sturdy beggars', but to provide for the needy poor by levying a rate on households, a forerunner of the Community Charge! By 1723, parishes were able to build workhouses, appoint constables and repair roads.

The civil and ecclesiastical responsibilities of parishes were effectively separated in 1834, when parishes were grouped together into Unions for the administration of the Poor Law. The Municipal Corporations Act of 1835 and the Local Government Act of 1834 established local government bodies, including parish councils, in a more modern format and enshrined in statute the principle of elections to councils and for meetings to be open to the public. But whereas county, district and borough councils have been considerably altered since then, and are still changing, parish councils have remained substantially the same for over a hundred years. Unlike these higher levels of government, parish councils are rarely political; that is, policy and decisions are not dictated by specific political parties or allegiances.

What can parish councils do in the twenty first century? A textbook on local government gives an amazing variety of functions and responsibilities. It lists allotments, bus-shelters, cemeteries, clocks, footpaths, recreation facilities, rights of way, planning, village greens and tombstones as amongst the things with which parish councils can concern themselves. Parish councils represent the voice of local residents in decisions taken by district and county councils. They are a channel for gauging and communicating the opinion of residents on a wide variety of issues and can alert other agencies to matters of concern, whether these be traffic calming, planning violations or threats to the natural and local environment.

Parish councils no longer levy a rate for Poor Relief, but they do set a rate, or precept, for other purposes. In fact, the precept is dictated largely by the district council (Winchester) and an amount is returned to the parish council calculated on the size of the population. For 2000 - 2001 the precept for Owslebury and Morestead was set at £13,000. This has to cover everything; administration, grass cutting, grants to local voluntary organisations, subscriptions to various organisations and any other work, such as tree planting, which the parish council decides to undertake. In recent years the parish council has given money to the Cricket Club to upgrade the changing rooms, made a loan to the Parish Hall Committee, has supported a number of millennium activities and is currently re-furbishing the children's play area. It is also paying part of the cost of traffic calming measures.

There are seven parish councillors, elected every four years. They then elect a chairman. Parish councils are supported by a paid parish clerk, who deals with all the day-to-day administration and book-keeping. They usually meet once a month, though they may form sub-groups or working parties to consider specific issues. However, all decisions have to be agreed at a full meeting of the council, at which members of the public are present.

The Parish of Owslebury extends to and includes Morestead, Marwell, Baybridge and part of Hensting.

The current members of Owslebury Parish Council are:

Chairman Dr Jane Dawson – Dr Dawson has been a councillor for three years and chairman for two years. She originally trained as a nurse, then worked in the National Health Service in a variety of roles. Dr Dawson came to Owslebury 28 years ago.

Councillor Howard Adams – Councillor Adams is a farmer. He has served on the council for 18 years, having moved into the parish 23 years ago, though he has lived in the area for 50 years.

Councillor Mollic Bailey – Councillor Bailey has lived in Owslebury for 40 years. She has served as a parish councillor for 16 years and has been vice-chairman at various times. Councillor Bailey is the Rights of Way representative for the parish.

Councillor Alan Hobbis – Councillor Hobbis designed and tested computers for IBM until his retirement and has lived in Owslebury for 22 years. He has been a member of the council for three years and was chairman for a year.

Councillor Keiron Norris – Councillor Norris is a Sales Manager. He has lived in Owslebury for 11 years and has served on the council for three years. Councillor Norris is the Owslebury Parish Council representative as a School Governor.

Councillor John Seabrook – Before retirement Councillor Seabrook was an engineer. He has lived in Owslebury since 1960 but before that lived in nearby Whiteflood. Councillor Seabrook served on the council for 16 years, then resigned, but rejoined three years ago.

Councillor Trish Le Voi – Councillor Le Voi has been a councillor for three years and is vice-chairman. She now works as an Office Manager but was at one time a parish clerk to a neighbouring parish. She has lived in Owslebury for six years.

Clerk – Mrs Virginia Sherwood

Unfortunately, many people do not see the work of councils as relevant to them and it is increasingly difficult to persuade people to stand for election to the council. This is of concern to all who value democratic institutions and the right of people to be properly represented.

OWSLEBURY AND MORESTEAD COMMUNITY ASSOCIATION – OMCA

The Owslebury and Morestead Community Association was formed in 1977, the year of the Queen's Silver Jubilee. It was set up at this time in order to co-ordinate all the village organisations and areas, when arranging a carnival and various other celebrations to mark this occasion. Rather than closing down at the end of that year, OMCA continued and has since then played a significant part in village life. The committee still consists of representatives of village organisations and areas and it is now a platform where people can meet to air their views on events that occur and also to synchronise fund-raising activities. It meets on a regular basis, and holds an AGM in the Parish Hall, which is open to all who are interested. OMCA funds are available to any organisation that wishes to apply to support a worthwhile activity; for example, the church, the school, and individual projects such as the Raleigh Project. OMCA also makes a point of remembering individual villagers when celebrating a special birthday or anniversary or

when a sad occasion occurs. At such times all receive a gift from the organisation. This is an OMCA role which gives real pleasure and is a unique feature of our village life.

Those so ably serving our community in the year 2000 are as follows: Ann Boston (chairperson), Gwyn Evans (hon. secretary), Barbara Holden (treasurer), Gwen Barney, Philip Bayley, Jennifer Bayley, Penny Bowes, Barbara Crabbe, Guy Eddis, Adrian Hardman, Betty Harfield, Simon Purnell, Vivienne Sturt, Trish Le Voi and David White.

PAROCHIAL CHURCH COUNCIL

Contributed by Barbara Crabbe – Church Warden, 2000

The Parochial Church Council is an elected body, voted for by those villagers who are on the church electoral roll. There are about 50 such people in Owslebury and the election takes place at the AGM. The aim of the PCC is to help the smooth running of the church and to maintain the fabric. They represent all parishioners whether or not they are on the electoral roll. There are usually three or four meetings held each year when the running and maintenance of the church is discussed. The PCC is also the link, through the wardens, to the diocese. This becomes particularly important when a new vicar is to be appointed and there is an interregnum. No one is paid to be a member of the PCC or a warden.

Members of the St Andrew's Parochial Church Council in 2000 are the following people.

Chairman Revd Mark Bailey – the priest in charge

Wardens	Barbara Crabbe and Adrian Hardman
Secretary	vacant post – currently being performed by Adrian Hardman
Treasurer	Philip Bayley
Members	Ann Boston (parish electoral roll)
	Penny Bowes
	Paul Bowes
	Betty Harfield (organist)
	Caroline Perry (organises covenant and tax efficient giving)
	Vivienne Sturt
	Andrew Sturt (organises lesson readers)
	Gwen Barney (verger)

Contributed by Evelyn Houghton

Philip Bayley, treasurer for the PCC, has commented on the ongoing problem of financing the church as we enter the new millennium. It costs approximately £800 **each month** to maintain our church! Because the fabric of the building has been well looked after during the previous century, we are not facing any huge bills at this moment in time. However, costs are ongoing. Recently when preparing the wall for the hanging of the Millennium Tapestry, an area of damp had to be remedied at a cost of £1400. Every five years the church has to undergo a structural survey and then to comply with the findings, whatever the cost. Some income is generated from special services; from marriages £142.00, from funerals £68.00, from burials £123.00. Regular weekly giving by parishioners is of huge importance. A way of topping up private giving is the Gift Aid system which provides a means of a bonus for the church through reclaimed income tax. This means of giving, which brings in more income with reduced paper work, is a highly beneficial way forward for the future.

NEIGHBOURHOOD WATCH

The village has been involved in a Neighbourhood Watch scheme for almost ten years. The idea for such a scheme was first announced in the Newsletter and the subsequent meeting in the Parish Hall was attended by a large number of enthusiastic villagers who filled the hall almost to capacity. The police explained what would be involved and how much it would cost to put up the signs. After agreement that the village would benefit from such a scheme, volunteers were asked to represent different areas of the neighbourhood.

Since the scheme has been operating the village has reaped the benefit. We are fortunate to have one of the lowest crime rate areas in the country. Significant happenings are reported in the Newsletter and this reminds us all of the need to ever keep a watchful eye open for any suspicious activities.

Our volunteer Neighbourhood Watch co-ordinators as we begin the new millennium are the following people:

Paul Bowes, Gwyn Evans, Ann Boston, Gwen Barney, Vera Bampton, Gerry Sanderson, Liz Porteous, Betty Harfield, Jean Green, Duncan Pollock Gore, Guy Eddis and Ray Lampard.

THE NEWSLETTER

The *Newsletter* is a weekly publication unique to the village of Owslebury. Newcomers moving into the village are usually amazed and delighted to read a little message of welcome on the front page of the publication in the early weeks after their arrival and then to realise that it is due to totally **voluntary** effort that it arrives through their letterbox week after week.

It all began back in 1959. A Youth Club was being set up in the village by Jo Williams and Commander Tower and funds were urgently needed in order to do this. The idea for a newsletter was born, initially so that the aims and programme for the club could be advertised. It was decided that the editor should be one of the young folk who would liaise with Jo to make final decisions about what should be included. When the first edition was published on 5th September, 1959 it was entitled *The Owslebury Youth Club News*. Robert Gray was the editor and it was sold at 1d a copy. It was printed in Winchester by the firm of Balfour Barrow, and the first deliveries were done by the youth club children.

As time went on and it became obvious that the *Newsletter* had become a much enjoyed and permanent fixture of village life, a Gestetner printing machine was purchased, which did away with the journey into Winchester each week. Other changes were taking place too. Deliveries

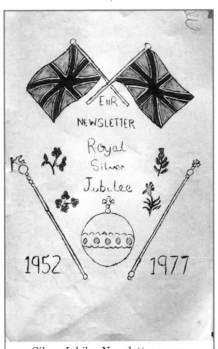

Silver Jubilee Newsletter cover. The covers were designed and then coloured by hand by Jo Williams and family for this special edition *(EH)*

were now undertaken by Paddy Boyle along with his newspapers and then later by Paul White, along with his milk bottles. By 1965 the editor was now an adult and it had changed its name to the *Scouts and Guides Newsletter*. It was in 1977 that it became simply the *Owslebury Newsletter,* as it is known to this day.

As we entered the new millennium the village was publishing edition number 1756 and each copy now costs 8p. There is a team of volunteers who do the typing, photocopying and the delivery each week and it is photocopied at Quilver Business Services in the village. As well as an editor, the team now has an assistant editor and a treasurer. Each week two hundred copies are delivered round the parish of Owslebury.

Over the years *Owslebury Newsletter* has been a mine of information on village happenings and village history; it has provided a medium for airing views and opinions, albeit sometimes contentious ones; it has given 'hatched, matched and dispatched' details; it gives a diary of coming events including church services; it offers recipes, poems, weather reports, hints and tips; it gives details of forthcoming planning applications and advertises items for sale, as well as being a medium for local businesses and trades to advertise their services.

All in all the *Newsletter* offers a wonderful way of keeping in touch with each other, of being entertained, and of keeping us all up to date about what is going on in village life. It would be hugely missed if our volunteers didn't keep on volunteering.

The 2000 team consists of the following people:

Editor Petra Sansome

Assistant editor Cynthia Mariner

Treasurer Hazel Crowsley

Typists Carole Drew, Sandy Emery, Karen Marsh, Graham Oakley, Sheena Passfield, Katherine Sellon, Miranda Sprot, Mary Taylor, Trish Le Voi.

Photocopiers Georgie Grace, Jill Hancock, Barbara Holden, Cynthia Mariner, Graham Oakley, Margaret Rigg, Nichola Snudden, Celia Thompson, Brenda Warson, Jo Williams

Deliverers Jennifer Bayley, Phil Bayley, Marie Butcher, Jill Chase, Barbara Crabbe Edith Crockford, Guy Eddis, Adrian Hardman, Betty Harfield, Pearl Hatt, Evelyn Houghton, David Marsh, Sheila Norgate, Kieron Norris, Caroline Perry, Daphne Rogers, Terry Russell, Gerald Sanderson, Trish Le Voi, Simon Wakefield, Gwen Windebank.

CRICKET CLUB

The Cricket Club plays a very significant part in village life today and has done for almost two whole centuries. All through the years, apart from closure during two world wars, the club has played at least once a week. It is a familiar sight on summer evenings and weekends to see the white-clad figures involved in a game on the Cricket Down.

In days gone by the village was fortunate in being central to the two large estates of Marwell and Longwood which both had their own cricket pitches. The owners of the two mansions on each estate, joined frequently with their house guests to play cricket in the village. In the 1900s a generous landowner (thought to be the Earl of Northesk from Longwood) donated the present ground for cricket. The club members of the time prepared the ground and in 1909 a tender of £44.15.00 was accepted to build the pavilion. A year later, in 1910, after much fund-raising by the cricketers, the new pavilion with a tin roof, was

Thatched cricket pavilion, 1958 – *from left to right,* Tom Knowles, Bill Berrill, Bert Derrick, Arthur Thatcher, Bill Jennings, Arthur Rogers, Stephen Pike, Doug Rogers, Alan Harfield, Colin Trow and Barry Glasspool (BH)

Owslebury Cricket Club, 1940s – *standing from left to right*, Tommy Lee, John Purnell, Bert Derrick, Bill Jennings, Dot Davis (scorer), Alan Harfield, David Pike, George Elliott, *kneeling*, Arthur (Digger) Moon, Arthur Rogers, Doug Rogers and John Burchmore (© E A Sollars)

Owslebury cricketers, 1996 – winners of the Igglesdon Cup –
standing from left to right, Alan Harfield, Jim Barker, Peter Cledwyn, George Rees, Tony Wilson, David Harfield, David Buckett, Tim Richman, *kneeling*, James Conick, Ken Windebank, Adrian Heath (captain), Clive Mansell, Richard Harfield and Mark Egerton (scorer) (HC)

built and paid for. Ten years later, in 1920 it was decided to accept a tender of £2.10.00 in order to have the pavilion roof thatched. Villager Mont

Spectators by the pavilion, 1998 *(DR)*

Rogers, father to Doug Rogers and Margaret Moon, used another of his many skills and did the thatching. This thatch lasted until 1977 and when a new estimate was sought in order to repair it, it was something of a shock to discover that the cost now of thatching the roof was £1,620! This was way beyond the club means and so sadly, the decision was made to have the roof tiled for the sum of £400.

For many, many years the club prided itself on being a true village team with only local village lads belonging to it. The rules today have had to be relaxed slightly due to lack of available village lads, but the majority of club members are still villagers, and young men who have moved on, still

creep back home for cricket. Over the years notable century scorers have been Ted Harfield, Doug Rogers and Bumper (Brian) Lush.

George Pierce, the son of George Pierce, who was headmaster of the village school in the early years of the twentieth century, wrote of his very fond memories of village cricket at the time when he was growing up in Owslebury. He remembers the pride and affection and communal efforts

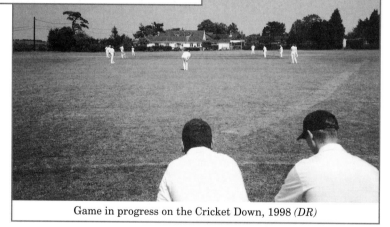

Game in progress on the Cricket Down, 1998 *(DR)*

of villagers contributing to the game. He remembers too significant differences in the game in the early 1900s which are hard to imagine now. Then, it was just the table itself that was mown and the outfield grass grew long. Skylarks and partridges would nest in this long grass and a fielder walking backwards is reputed to have fallen over a sow and her piglets lying hidden in the grass near the boundary! Before an important

Once upon a time Owslebury had a ladies' team too! (BH)

match a farmer might be persuaded to graze his sheep on the field for a few days beforehand. It is possible to be instantly transported back to these bygone days when reading George's concluding words. He describes a cricket tea provided by wives and daughters as a *'serious sit-down job'*. He tells us that, *'strawberry jam, wasps and honey, homely smiling faces and brown arms, swifts screaming and whirling over the thatch and round the elms, the church clock striking, the scent of hay and lime blossom, the sun-drenched summer field where the 'run stealers flicker to and fro', these are the unchanging, unforgettable things that have always made the very essence and enchantment of our Hampshire village cricket'.*

For most of the last century, the fact that the club continued to play on an excellent pitch was due in no short measure, to the Harfield family. Alan Harfield was presented with an award for 'Service to Sport' and has been a familiar village figure who waved cheerily to passers-by as he lovingly tended the green during the cricket season. Alan followed in his father, Harold's, footsteps in being responsible for the care of the ground and recently, Richard has taken over from Alan and is keeping up the family tradition in order that cricket may continue to flourish in the village.

FOOTBALL CLUB

Sport has always played a major part in the life of this village, and football has been played here for almost as long as cricket; namely, close on two hundred years. Before the First World War the

Owslebury football team outside the Cricketers Inn, c1910 – *back row from left to right*: Mr Cordery, Harold Harfield, Monty Lavington, Jim Heath, Mont Rogers; *centre row*: Charlie Anstey, Tom Read, unknown; *front row:* unknown, George Pierce, unknown, Frederick Read, unknown.

team would play on a pitch opposite the *Cricketers Inn* which is now *Northwood House,* but later transferred to the Cricket Down in the main village. Early in this century, there were enough local young men for three village teams. Nowadays, the club has to rely largely on people from outside the village to make up the teams, although there are still three of them – one which plays on a Saturday and two on a Sunday.

During the Second World War the club was disbanded and then another decade was to pass before a new team was formed. Play restarted then due to the enthusiasm of Edmund Harfield.

Football matches are played today on the pitch at the Cricket Down. During the new millennium season the club had the benefit of floodlighting so that play could continue for longer on dark winter evenings. The ground obviously suffers from a great deal of wear and tear which demands a lot of tender loving care before a new cricket season can commence on the same ground.

KEEP FIT GROUP – SUE'S FITNESS WORKOUT

This group came into being fifteen years ago in 1975. It began in order to provide an outlet for folk to keep fit. The group was started by Sue Arney who lived not far from the village and who agreed to come on a weekly basis for an hour's session to put people through their paces in a fun way, with aerobic exercises set to music. The sessions took place in the Parish Hall and at the beginning had some male members as well as female!

Today the group is all female and they have their own logo-printed tee shirts and sweatshirts showing a little koala bear and the words "Sue's Fitness Workout". When the new Parish Hall was being designed the group did a can-can along the length of the village in order to help raise funds to provide a wooden, rather than a concrete floor in the hall. The floor in the old hall was wooden but very splintery. Today the new floor is a wonderful base for the group's keep fit endeavours.

THE SPORTS CLUB

The Sports Club came into being after the closure of the Working Mens' Club in 1948. It meets each week during the winter months in the Parish Hall. Nowadays, as when it began, it is there to provide an evening out for youngsters in the village. It used to be a club for all ages but is now recognised as a youth organisation with both boys and girls attending. Table tennis, pool and bar billiards are all provided and youngsters can join the club when in their last year at the village school. A committee of adults oversees the proceedings and looks after the equipment. This is chaired by Terry Russell who has done the job since the early 1960s. He is ably assisted by Gordon Jefferies and Trevor Dicks. Pete Dicks is also available to help out if he is needed.

In the days when the club met in the old Parish Hall, there was a full size billiard table permanently in position for play. Unfortunately this restricted the use of the Hall for other users and particularly the size of the Drama Club's audiences. At some time during the 1980s the decision was made to sell the table; it was sold for more than it originally cost! The proceeds from the sale were invested and the interest from these plus normal subscription fees, have funded the club and continue to do so today.

In a village where evening public transport to activities anywhere outside the village is non-existent, a club such as the Sports Club provides an invaluable opportunity for young folk to meet together and have fun somewhere safe and close at hand.

SENIOR CLUB

The Senior Club meets in the Parish Hall once a month. Such afternoons provide an opportunity for senior members of the village community to get together for a chat and to catch up with all the latest happenings. Edie Crockford heads the committee and Phyl Merritt is the treasurer. Phyl and sister, Irene Bliss, are known as the 'chief tea ladies' and never fail to provide delicious plates of sandwiches, biscuits and cakes as well as endless cups of tea. Irene bakes all the cakes and scones herself while Phyl does the sandwich fillings. Daisy Gray organises a Bring and Buy each month and there is always a draw, which is so planned to ensure that everyone has a small prize. At the same time this makes a small amount of money for club funds. Sometimes a speaker is invited to address the meetings. The club holds coffee mornings twice a year to help raise money and they also organise half-day outings and theatre trips. They enjoy a special Christmas lunch each year, sometimes at the *Shearers Arms* in the village and sometimes going further afield.

OWSLEBURY AND MORESTEAD WOMEN'S INSTITUTE

The Owslebury and Morestead Women's Institute came into being in 1921. The first committee meeting took place in the Parish Hall on 21st November of that year. Mrs Evelyn Standish from *Marwell Hall* was the first president. For many years the monthly meetings of the organisation were popular with the village ladies who took a keen interest in matters of national importance as well as those affecting local people. During the

years of the Second World War the group met regularly at Marwell where they were involved amongst other things in making over 700lbs of jam and knitting numerous pairs of socks and other garments to be sent to men folk fighting overseas.

The regular monthly meetings often had an interesting speaker and there was always a little competition in which members could participate, which would involve something cooked or sewn or knitted or grown, or maybe a household hint or a holiday souvenir. They would organise outings and social occasions too. During the year of their golden jubilee the Women's Institute put together an interesting scrapbook about the village.

JERUSALEM
—
And did those feet in ancient time
Walk upon England's mountains green ?
And was the Holy Lamb of God
On England's pleasant pastures seen ?
And did the countenance divine
Shine forth upon our clouded hills ?
And was Jerusalem builded here
Among these dark satanic mills ?

Bring me my bow of burning gold !
Bring me my arrows of desire !
Bring me my spear ! O clouds unfold !
Bring me my chariot of fire !
I will not cease from mental fight,
Nor shall my sword sleep in my hand,
Till we have built Jerusalem
In England's green and pleasant land.

(W. Blake)

OWSLEBURY and MORESTEAD WOMEN'S INSTITUTE
OFFICERS AND COMMITTEE 1973
President: Miss FOWLER
Vice-President: Miss WAYMENT
Secretary: Mrs. DEWDNEY
Treasurer: Mrs. TROW

Committee
The above Officers and Mesdames Berrill, Bailey, Giles-Clark, Maddock, E. Harfield, D. Harfield and Russell

Press Correspondent	-	Mrs. RUSSELL
Competition	-	Mrs. MADDOCK
Lucky Parcel	-	Mrs. GILES-CLARK
"Bring and Buy"	-	Mrs. BERRILL
Social Secretary	-	Miss E. HARFIELD

PROGRAMME 1973
Meetings take place in the Parish Hall the Second Thursday in the month at 7.30 p.m.
Annual Subscription - 50p
All Meetings begin with Business
"Bring and Buy" and Trading Stall each month

Hostesses: Mesdames Maddocks, J. Herrett, Dee

APRIL 12th	
Speaker:	Mr. ANDREWS - "Care of Furniture"
Competition:	Handy household hint
Hostesses:	Mesdames D. Harfield, Edwards, Boston

MAY 10th	
Speaker:	V.C.O. - Resolutions for A.G.M.
Competition:	Spring posy, 3 inches across
Hostesses:	Mesdames Peachey, Trow, Russell

NE 14th
. F. WILLCOCKS - "Simple dry"
s Walker, Nicholls, Weeks

LY 12th
S' MEETING

MBER 13th
ASE - "W.I. Markets"
s Shaw, Mulder, Messinger

BER 11th
ACHEY - "Thread of n"
Competition: Dressed doll
Hostesses: Mesdames Sharp, M. Lush, B. Lush

NOVEMBER 8th
ANNUAL GENERAL MEETING
Competition: Four rock cakes
Hostesses: Mesdames Wayment, Bungay, Hellard

DECEMBER 13th
BIRTHDAY MEETING
Competition: Home-made Christmas card
Hostesses: Mesdames E. Harfield, White, Bailey

As the Women's Institute entered the last decade of the twentieth century, Barbara Holden was president. Sadly it became her task to close the Institute in 1998 when there was no longer enough support to keep it going.

MOTHERS' UNION

The Mothers' Union is another village organisation that sadly has no part in village life today. In the church can be found the Mothers' Union banner, a reminder of its significance in Owslebury throughout most of the last century.

Old record books give details of Mothers' Union members for Owslebury and Morestead as far back as 1912. Meetings were held monthly either in members' homes, in the Parish Hall or in the

Mothers' Union outing – from back to front, Phyl Merritt and Dorothy Berrill, Evelyn Merritt and Gladys Bradshaw, unknown and unknown, Honor Dewdney and Queenie Maddocks (BH)

church. In the early days the subscription for members was 6d and as well as special church services at intervals throughout the year, members enjoyed a variety of interesting speakers, films and outings. They also organised fund raising events such as whist drives, bring and buy stalls and supported many good causes.

One of the last major events organised by the Mothers' Union was an exchange visit with a London group from Hornsey in 1988. Owslebury entertained 'the city' in 'the country', and Hornsey entertained 'the country' in 'the city'!

The Mothers' Union was always closely connected with the Church and in the early days it was usually vicar's wives who were leaders. Later this role was more often taken by leading church members. The very first president of the Owslebury and Morestead Mothers' Union in 1912 was Mrs Glasspool. Evelyn Merritt was president for many years and it was Honor Dewdney whose responsibility it became to close the Union down.

OWSLEBURY AND MORESTEAD HORTICULTURAL SOCIETY

An eagerly anticipated day in the parish in times past was the annual Owslebury and Morestead Horticultural Show. For many years this took place at *Owslebury Farm*. As the result of Dick and Ann Boston's kindness, the barns and grounds alongside the house were taken over for several days while stalls were erected, judging took place and prizes awarded. It was one of the highlights of the village year and one in which many villagers from oldest to youngest participated. There were classes for vegetables, flowers, jams and pickles, cakes and bread, knitting, embroidery, flower arranging and special classes for children. To win a cup for the 'best of – ' was everyone's ambition. There was a Beauty

Lady Kelburn opening a Horticultural Show in the 1960s (HC)

The Silver Jubilee Horticultural Show, 1977 –
from left to right, Jennie Bailey, John Pike, Tracey Matthews and Marie Bevis (HC)

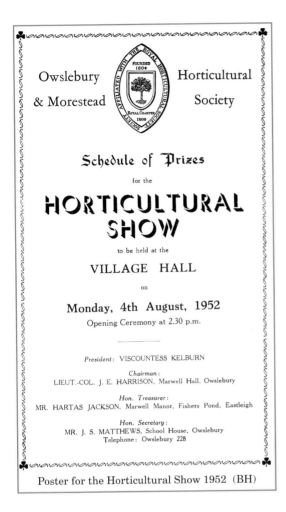

Owslebury Horticultural
& Morestead Society

Schedule of Prizes

for the

HORTICULTURAL
SHOW

to be held at the

VILLAGE HALL

on

Monday, 4th August, 1952

Opening Ceremony at 2.30 p.m.

President: VISCOUNTESS KELBURN

Chairman:
LIEUT.-COL. J. E. HARRISON, Marwell Hall, Owslebury

Hon. Treasurer:
MR. HARTAS JACKSON, Marwell Manor, Fishers Pond, Eastleigh

Hon. Secretary:
MR. J. S. MATTHEWS, School House, Owslebury
Telephone: Owslebury 228

Poster for the Horticultural Show 1952 (BH)

Queen for the day and great fun was had by all.

The Horticultural Society was started after the war in November, 1945 when the first AGM was held in the old school. Dorothea, Viscountess Kelburn, was elected president and she continued to hold this office for as long as the society existed. In 1978 the village show was given extensive coverage by the Hampshire Chronicle newspaper. It took place as usual in the grounds and barns of *Owslebury Farm*. They reported that John Pike was the show secretary and Jimmy Philips from Baybridge was chairman. Honor Dewdney was treasurer and Julie Molden was much involved

in organising all of the sideshows. Marilyn Bishop from *Bottom Farm* organised and judged the dog show and Mrs Lutyens from *Chestnut House* presented all of the trophies. The Chronicle reported that after the award ceremony '*she received a memento of the occasion from the Misses Nicola and Melanie Lush*'. At the end of the day there was an auction to sell off all the first class produce and the auctioneer was George Molden.

Sadly this is an institution that has now gone from village life. The last show took place in 1984. Hume and Charmian Jones were chairman and secretary respectively then, and organised a quality show right to the end. They managed to arrange for Mary O'Hara, the singing nun, to open the occasion one year, and for Erica Rowe, famed for her streaking, to do the same another year. No singing or streaking, however, was done in Owslebury!

Several years later Cynthia Mariner and Pat Payne made a valiant effort to revive the Horticultural Show and after a lot of hard work, one more took place in September, 1990, but the response was very disappointing. There has never been another.

DRAMA CLUB

Many people who have lived in the village for some time have very fond memories of the Owslebury Drama Club. Sadly this is another village institution that has not survived to see in the twenty-first century.

The Drama Club first came into being during the years of the Second World War and must have brought a welcome relief from the worries, restrictions and hardships of that time. The first

175

The newly formed Drama Club, c1944 – *from left to right*, unknown, Myrtle Jennings (née Davis), Aileen Hunter (née Sawyer), Alan Harfield and Barry Glasspool (BH)

production was a one-act comedy entitled *"The Colonel's Consent"* and the performance took place in the Parish Hall on 8th December, 1944 at the annual St Andrew's Sale.

It is the pantomimes of the 1980s for which the society is most remembered, although other productions continued to be performed. So many people became involved in the pantomimes, either in the producing or acting, prompting, costume making, stage managing, lighting, tea making, ticket selling, backcloth painting, programme printing or as an audience. Both young and old and people from all walks of life, spent many winter evenings happily involved in planning and preparing for the annual pantomime performances. Actors will relate how the

rehearsals gave them as much fun and pleasure as the actual performances.

Barbara Holden was a key figure in drama productions for many years, masterly producing memorable performances. Shirley Ball, during her years at the *Old School House*, painted the most professional backcloths which enhanced productions wonderfully.

CUBS AND SCOUTS

Today in Owslebury it is a sad fact that there are no cubs or scouts.

Lads growing up in the village in the 60s and 70s were luckier because then, first Frank Williams and then Fred Merritt were scout masters. Frank was actually inducted at Twyford

A Drama Club pantomime, 1982 *(EH)*

and then began as leader of the Owslebury scouts. He continued with this for the next six years before leaving to take over duties as Assistant District Commissioner for Activities in Winchester. Fred began his involvement with the cubs but then took over as scout leader as well when Frank gave this up. Both were dedicated to the task of upholding Lord Baden Powell's ideals for village lads through the scout movement. In his forward to 'Scouting for Boys' in 1932, Lord Baden Powell had written, '*A true scout is looked up to by other boys and by grown ups as a fellow who can be trusted, a fellow who will not fail to do his duty however risky and dangerous it may be*'. Fred instilled in his boys a pride in what they were doing and a respect for others that many grown 'lads' of his remember with gratitude to this day.

It was Fred whose idea it was to have some permanent scout premises where the boys could meet, rather than using the Parish Hall where it was impossible to store all the equipment. When working one day at his Hampshire County Council job in Winchester, he spied through the window, where the new Law Courts now are, two wooden huts which Fred knew instantly would fit the bill perfectly for his dream of permanent premises. He managed to negotiate a deal whereby the huts cost nothing as long as he would arrange to have them dismantled and moved to their new site. Bill Gough from the village provided the transport and so in 1967, it was a proud day when the Jubilee Hut was duly opened as the village Scout Headquarters by Lady Kelburn. Many a brownie pack was to camp here during summer months and this helped to raise funds that were constantly needed to maintain the hut.

Fred received much support from a committee that was responsible for raising funds. Lady Kelburn was president until the early 1980s when Ann Boston then took over. Betty Harfield was

Scouts at camp – in the front row Fred Merritt is on the left next to Frank Williams (PM)

treasurer for 13 years.

As well as running the weekly pack meetings Fred took the boys away camping. They were encouraged to make camp blankets for themselves decorated with badges and other suitable motifs and these were worn when they were sitting round the camp fire, singing songs and drinking mugs of hot cocoa. Fred himself had a beautiful blanket, patiently stitched by his wife, Phyllis. There are so many badges stitched on it that it is hard to see the actual fabric of the blanket.

In the late 1970s, Fred became ill and had to have a leg amputated. It was shortly after this that he felt he must give up as he could no longer do justice to the job and continue to do it the way he wished. The company continued for a short time longer with the village policeman, Bill Holmes, taking over and being assisted by Michael Houghton. Early in the 1990s Sheila Conway Miller took over the cub pack and was also involved in setting up the newly formed Beaver group, which was for boys too young to become cubs. Her husband, Terry, was a willing helper and daughter, Jolene, was one of the first girl scouts in the Winchester area. By the mid-nineties the Jubilee Hut was facing a huge bill for maintenance and repair. This proved to be the last straw and shortly afterwards the cubs were disbanded and the sad decision was made to demolish the Hut. Gerry Tull undertook this task in 1997. The Scout Hut had served the village well for thirty long years.

Phyl Merritt with the camp blanket stitched for scout master, Fred (EH)

BROWNIES AND GUIDES

A Brownie pack was started in the village 38 years ago in 1962. Pat Emery began it, holding meetings in her own home, the bungalow at the poultry farm down Pitcot Lane. Pat was Brown Owl and Wendy Wilson her assistant, Tawny Owl. Wendy later took over as Brown Owl and Peggy Egerton came to help. Stella Jones was to take over from Peggy and Wendy's oldest daughter, Dawn, also helped. Wendy was to serve for fifteen years before handing over to Stella, who led our last few Owslebury brownies, assisted by Girl Guide Elizabeth Houghton, before the pack sadly closed down in March, 1982.

During the Brownies' hey day, Wendy remembers that they were much supported and helped by 'some wonderful mums and a wonderful committee'. On the committee were Peggy Derrick, Evelyn Merritt and Doris Harfield. They worked tirelessly to raise the ever much needed money. This included the cost of all the badges that the brownies earned as well as their enrolment badges which were an ongoing expense. Jo Williams and Marian Trow were particularly supportive mums who were always on hand to provide transport and as testers for the brownie badges.

Mary Norgate started the Girl Guide Company, ably assisted by Kath Alden and Myrtle Jennings. They used to join with the Brownies for parades on Thinking Day and St George's Day each year and also went with them on their annual outing to Sandbanks in the

Brownies – Rosemary Richman, Tina Light (with pennant) and Sally Trow (WW)

Guide leader, Mary Norgate,
with daughters Jane and Anne (WW)

to help carry and supervise and then enjoy a sunshine-filled day on the beach. Wendy remembers that they were somehow always lucky with the weather.

The Guide Company closed down in 1979 and Owslebury girls then had to go to Twyford to join the company there. Mary Norgate is now in Australia with her family. Wendy is still very much part of village life and still lives in Owslebury. She has actually lived here since she was two years old. She started at the village school the same day as Dot Davis began there as infant teacher. As a child Wendy lived at the bottom of Whites Hill with parents, William and Edith Oliver (nee Guy). Wendy's grandparents were George and Georgina Guy and her grandfather had worked as a coach driver for the Schwartz family at Longwood. Today, Wendy's granddaughter, Georgia, who is her daughter Paula's daughter, is the fourth generation of the family to go to the village school.

summer. For the outing they used to hire a coach, pack an enormous bag of food, coerce husbands

Brownies and Guides together – leaders, Wendy Wilson and Anne Jennings, *on the right* (WW)

SUNDAY SCHOOL

Going to Sunday School each week used to be a significant aspect of village life and this is something else that has changed hugely in recent times. It was during the Second World War that the Children's Corner was established in the church. Florence Lush was a Sunday school teacher at the time, a time when she had just lost her only son in the war. When Revd John Pringle was vicar (1967 – 1973) he used to organise a rota of drivers who were willing to collect children from outlying areas of the village. Johnny Jones was one of these willing folk and his wife, Stella, remembers how he used to keep a few sweets in his pockets to tempt the more reluctant attenders!

Going to Sunday School remained a weekly event into the 1970s. The younger children then would meet in the vestry and they would be given a stamp to stick in a little book to record their attendance.

As the last century drew to its close, Sunday School became Sunday Club and was a monthly occurrence. Revd Mark Bailey, who joined the parish early in 2000, hopes to organise a monthly gathering of children from Twyford, Morestead and Owslebury together, starting early in 2001.

MOTOR CROSS EVENTS

Woodham Hill, rising up from the valley between Owslebury and Baybridge, has for a number of years played host to Winchester Motor Cycle Club three or four times a year for their 'scrambles'. On such days the noise of the bikes can be heard for some miles around, depending

The scramble track on Woodham Hill as seen from the church tower *(EH)*

on which way the wind is blowing. Other sounds affecting the village in the same way are those of guns on 'shoot days' and animals at Marwell Zoo. The scrambles provide a rare opportunity in an isolated village for an activity in which local youngsters can be involved. Luke Lush is one such lad who has become an expert rider and who also travels to venues all over England in order to pursue his hobby. The Cycle Club advertises in the village Newsletter to give plenty of warning concerning dates for future events. They always make a donation to the village as a 'thank you' for the use of the site.

HANDBELL RINGERS

Owslebury Church possesses a very old but very fine set of handbells, which until recently have hardly ever been used. It is believed that they were originally purchased so that bell ringers could practise in the warmth and comfort of their own homes or in the pub during winter evenings when the church would be freezing. Back in the 1930s Doug Rogers' father, Mont, trained a bell ringing team which included Doug along with Tom Marchant, Cecil Ford and Bert Derrick, an all male team. Today's team is all ladies and includes Gill Bostrom, Jill Chase, Carol Hall, Fiona Nash, Melanie Norris and Celia Thompson. Their musical director is Lizzi McAndrew who is a professional solo handbell ringer. When the group was first formed, the church paid quite a large sum of money to have the bells re-set. Determination and hard work on the part of the ringers, who have opened their gardens, held craft sales and organised coffee mornings, has enabled them to repay the loan. Their new-found skills have been much enjoyed when they played during a Christmas carol service and they have so far in the middle of the year 2000 had one small public performance. It is good to know that the village can look forward to many more such performances.

In July 2000 Lizzi, Celia and Jill participated in the ninth International Handbell Symposium in Birmingham. Here they played with 850 other ringers from Japan, Korea, Australia, Canada, U.S.A. and Great Britain.

Back in the 1950s when groups of villagers would walk round the parish carol singing each December, Michael and Brian Lush, as members of the Young Farmers' Club, remember the handbells being used to accompany the singers then. Peggy Smith (née Merritt) also remembers such times, carol singing with other villagers, with the handbells as an accompaniment, and particularly she remembers visiting *Morestead House*. There used to be a beautiful Christmas tree in the hall there and after being invited in by Colonel Earle, the carol singers would enjoy this while eating the mince pies kindly offered to them.

6: Trades and Services to the Village

When the new century dawned in 1900 the village of Owslebury was a virtually self-sufficient community. There was no reason to leave the village as everything needed to sustain daily living was all provided by villagers for villagers. There were several dairy farms and people kept their own pigs and hens. Wheat was grown, the flour milled and then baked into bread. Anyone not baking their own could buy it from one of the shops. The village had its own blacksmiths, wheelwrights, thatchers, wall builders, carpenters, sawyers, flint gatherers, carriers, shopkeepers, teachers, farmers, agricultural labourers, publicans, as well as its shoe maker and cobbler, vet, nurse, vicar, postman and undertaker.

Gradually the village began to see changes. Cars became a means of transport and road surfaces were improved to cater for this. The state of the roads at the beginning of the last century made a lasting impression on villagers living here then. Bill Bridle told Frank Williams, *'it was all flint and stone roads then you see, never steamrolled in or anything'*. Roadmen used to break up the larger stones, but Bill related how sheep used to run on the roads, pick up stones in their feet and end up in an awful state. When riding a bicycle, he remembered little pieces of broken flint coming up *'like knives'*. George Pierce, the village Headmaster's son, remembered how the flints would gradually become crushed by the steel-rimmed wheels of farm wagons and carts. Side roads were little more than tracks, deeply rutted where cartwheels ran and bare in the middle where horses' hooves pounded down the stones. Dust was another problem on these roads of old. Bill told Frank, *'on the Longwood road, if you see anybody coming down with a horse and trap or anything there was enough dust there coming you couldn't see; it was worse than a smoke screen in the army'*. He explained too that *'if anything went along, clouds of dust would come in – you never had your windows open'*.

During the floods at the end of 2000, road surfaces were badly damaged and often washed away leaving huge potholes and sharp edges, causing flints underneath the tarmac to re-appear.

In the early years of the 1900s the village carrier would leave Owslebury about twice a week to make contact with the outside world. The journey to Winchester would take about two hours. Peter Hewett when writing 'Owslebury Bottom', remembered the carrier from his childhood days wearing a high crowned black bowler hat. He would let down a round metal step for his passengers to climb aboard and they would sit on low seats which ran along each side of the trap, facing each other. There was a tailboard behind to be secured to prevent any item from falling off. The trap listed backwards and the whole ride would become something of an adventure. There were constant stops to collect and deliver items on route and whenever a hill was to be climbed, and there were plenty of those between Owslebury and Winchester, all the passengers and even the carrier had to get out and walk because the inclines were too steep for the horse to pull a loaded trap. The journey was bumpy, as well as long, and Peter Hewett's sister, Joan, was sick before reaching the city. The carrier's horse was often old and didn't last long at the job, but whenever one died, villagers would club together to buy another one. George Pierce remembered Jack Knight, Will Lee and Bob Bunney, all being village carriers in the early years of the 1900s.

A motorised bus service began in Owslebury in the late 1920s when Mr Dovey invested in a vehicle in which he took village folk to town once a week. This old bus, which used to be kept in the garden of *Avellino,* has since become famous. It travelled to several shows, appeared on television and even went to America before finally coming to rest in a museum. During the Second World War the bus service increased tremendously and six to eight buses travelled in and out of Owslebury daily. At this time the drivers didn't just drive the bus but acted as paper boys, butchers, postmen, - anything, and people would wait by their gates to collect the goods as the bus came by. A private company called Greyfriars and owned by Mr Matthews operated this service. Later when Mr Matthews retired the company was taken over by Chisnells who ran the old King Alfred buses. Just after the Second World War a bus even went into Winchester on a Saturday evening so that villagers could go to the cinema. As more and more people began to own their own cars, so the bus service to the village became less and less. Today there is a limited service operating during weekdays and on a Saturday, but it is impossible to travel from the village by bus either in the evenings or on a Sunday.

Irene Bliss well remembers a bus driver in the 1950s called Mr Scorey. He would drop people off with their shopping right by their houses. He would carry radio accumulators to get them recharged. At the end of a journey he would take his bus up to the Bank Tree and stop there to have a cup of tea with Mrs Millie Bliss in *Yew Tree Cottages.* In those days the bus would be absolutely full and the fare to Winchester was 1/9d return! Today the same journey costs £2 90. Pearl Hatt also has memories of this kindly bus driver. She would phone up Mr Barlow, the butcher, in Winchester to order a piece of beef. Mr Barlow would pop the parcel of beef onto the bus and Mr Scorey would deliver it to Pearl's door!

As we approach the new millennium, traffic is an ongoing problem for the village, the quantity of it, the size of it and the speed of it! Traffic surveys have been carried out locally and indicate what a problem traffic now is. Commuters have discovered that Owslebury is a convenient short cut. Cars travelling to the school are also much increased in number because so many of the children now come from areas outside the village. The main road through the village is narrow and has no pavements. Consequently it can be quite hazardous for pedestrians, particularly when drivers ignore the 30 mph speed limit. The size of some of the lorries and tractors can be quite frightening too. Half a century ago such problems were never dreamed of. In the 1950s it was bicycles that caused the traffic jams! Michael and Brian Lush remember the road at Longwood *'being choked with bikes when people came home*

The 1960s Library Van (WI scrapbook)

newspaper deliveries, logs and tree surgery and we have a chiropodist, a garage repair and breakdown service, builders, ground maintenance and fence makers, a farrier and blacksmith. Businesses operating from village premises include orchid growers, egg farms, and a printing and photocopying company. There are still two working farms in the village and we have a resident vet.

Back in the 1860s Owslebury had a 'vet', then described as 'a horse and cow doctor'. His name was Caleb Owton and he lived at *Lower Farm*. Gravestones revealing his family's history can be seen in the churchyard today.

from the sawmills there'.

During the second half of the last century, both milk and newspaper deliveries would arrive daily on our doorsteps without fail, due to the

The 1990s Library Van
with Peggy Smith (née Thatcher) *(DR)*

commitment of villager, Paul White, who was ably assisted by his wife, Marion, and sons, Andrew, Richard, Robert and Christopher. The family was very involved in village life and left a gap when they decided it was time to move.

As we enter the new millennium several services are still available within the village itself but most now come from further afield. These include milk and postal deliveries, the library van, the fruit and vegetable van, window cleaners, hairdressers and a laundry and dry-cleaning service. From within the village community itself we are still provided with

Choosing a book, 1999 –
Mrs Ashton with librarian, Brian Giles *(DR)*

He was a real village character in his time and Alfred Young when writing of these times, revealed that folk had felt a bit afraid of him as he shouted his welcome or his order, from the back of a black cob. Alfred used a very effective recipe of Caleb's to cure fret in horses. This was a wineglass of turpentine added to a pint of linseed oil. Perhaps John Stewart, our vet of today, might be tempted to try this recipe next time he meets a case of horse fret!

We have never had our own resident doctor in the village, although we have doctors among our community but in the days prior to the Second World War, we did have a nurse, who was a well-known and much loved person. Even on her gravestone she is remembered as 'Nurse'. Her 'other' name was Gertrude Harfield (née Mabbit).

Alan Harfield wrote about his mother for an edition of the Parish Magazine. He described the area she worked in as being *'extensive and scattered: Fishers Pond, Hensting, Marwell, Baybridge, Owslebury, Longwood and Lane End – all in those early days covered by bicycle (no gears either!) and always with her a good supply of puncture outfits'*. Occasionally she would be given a lift – what a relief this must have been. Once when she had delivered a baby at Silkstead, beyond Otterbourne, a horse and cart arrived to take her to the next baby arriving at Lane End. Her bicycle was strapped on the cart and she was given a lift – a great luxury, particularly as it was winter and the middle of the night. The overall length of her journey would have been about eighteen miles.

After her arduous cycle ride to outlying districts, there were no 'mod cons' as Alan said, to help her bring new babies into the world. It was just *'a well to draw water, a kitchen range or oil stove to heat the water, candles, oil or Tilley lamps to work by'*.

Villager Walter Trott belongs to a family that came under her ministrations, for his sister, Vera, born when they lived in Baybridge, was brought into the world by Nurse Harfield.

During the Second World War, Alan remembers that their house *Homelands*, alongside the Cricket Down where he himself had been born, became a small private nursing home. He would

Nurse Harfield, c1920 (BH)

wake in the morning to find himself in a different bed and a baby crying somewhere!

Nurse Harfield was given a reference by Dr George Marsden Roberts from Twyford in 1924 and his words describe her perfectly. *'She has carried out her duties most conscientiously in this extensive district. Often going seven miles or more* from one case to another, her work has been of a most arduous nature. She is a capable midwife and very popular with her patients'.

Electricity and running water are commodities that would have made life considerably easier for Nurse Harfield but she and other villagers had to wait until after the Second World War for these aspects of life which today we take for granted. Water mains were laid in 1948 covering Owslebury Village, Baybridge and those parts of Morestead south of *Hill Farm* but it was not until August in the following year that the supply was available to consumers. Two years later an extension was added to the system to cover Hensting Lane and early the following year, in 1952, folk here could also, at last, turn on their taps. Our water supply is piped here from Yew Hill Reservoir in Otterbourne.

Electricity for villagers also arrived gradually depending on where one lived. The main village had its first supplies in October, 1949. Owslebury Bottom and Baybridge had to wait until 1956 and Hensting until 1957. Even towards the end of the last century, when power cuts occurred, as during the storms of 1987, there was no consistency in the reconnection of the power supplies. Some areas of the village had to stay without their electricity for much longer than others. In 1999 new overhead strengthened cables were installed in the village which should mean that we are less prone to power cuts in times of future severe weather.

When the village first had access to this 'miracle' power, Frank Williams remembers that some villagers were caught unawares and had no light bulbs ready in order to light up their houses!

OWSLEBURY POSTAL SERVICE – THEN

In 1961 Frank Williams from *Shepherds Cottage* chatted to Miss Walker who had been postmistress at Twyford for many years. She revealed to him some fascinating details concerning the job of a postman at the turn of the century. Frank recorded these details.

Owslebury's mail was then brought to Twyford from Winchester by Mr Court of Hursley who was literally 'up with the lark' in order to unload the mail sacks in Twyford between four and five in the morning.

The letters had to be sub-sorted by 5.30 am when one of the two Twyford postmen, Mr Alfred Turton, known as old Alfie, or Mr Burner who covered the Owslebury district alternate weeks, would be starting out on his bicycle for the Morestead crossroads. Here he would meet the Owslebury postman, Mr Bert Hutchings, sort out his mail, unofficially in the porch at Morestead Church and then cycle on up the Bishop's Waltham Road. At the Longwood crossroads he would turn right to cover the bungalows this side of the Cricket Down, then retrace his route to call at *Longwood House, Honeymans Farm* and *New Warren Farm*. This would be the completion of his morning round and he would then return to the post office hut on the Longwood Estate and have breakfast.

During the day he would do some gardening as a part time job, and then in the evening, about 5 o'clock, he would start out again on his rounds. Back first he would go to the post box at Lane End, on to *Longwood House*, where, if there had been a successful shoot, he might be loaded up with game, on to the Longwood crossroads, past

Today's postman, Goff Prentice, outside what was the Post Office, 2000 *(EH)*

OWSLEBURY POSTMEN

The Owslebury postman, having collected his mail from his colleague at Morestead would then start off on his round. First he would go to *Manor Farm* at Morestead then up past *Hill Farm* and down the steep slope to Owslebury Bottom. Having enjoyed the run down to these cottages, he would now have to make the steep climb up Crabbes Hill to Owslebury Top. In the village post office, at *Restholm,* he would sort out the remaining mail and then travel on through the village to deliver to *Marwell Hall , Marwell Lodge,* now called *Marwell House,* Hurst Farm Baybridge, Whiteflood and Lane End. On average the daily mail would amount to only some 50 or 60 letters but the distance involved in delivering these was considerable.

A midday mail was brought out in those days from Morestead, by among others, Mr Rumbold, and then delivery of this

the bungalows to the Cricket Down and then along Baybridge Road to clear the second post box in the hamlet itself. Next he would go along Baybridge Lane to the post box at Marwell, decorated with the Royal Cipher of Edward VII. From here he would have the long pull up to Owslebury village where he would be greeted by Miss Taylor with the village mail in a sealed bag. Then he would go down Crabbes Hill, to clear the fourth box at Owslebury Bottom, the fifth box at *Manor Farm,* Morestead, and after turning left along the Hazeley Road, the sixth post box at Mr Best's cottages. By this time the postman had been out nearly fourteen hours and it must have been a long mile and a half down the flint-surfaced road to Twyford with his sacks of mail perched in front on the carrier. Early in the last century the postmen endured long hours, all conditions of weather and terrible road surfaces for a bicycle, but it was seldom that the post was late.

Postman, c1930, with Maud Bradley outside Sunnyside (MJ)

would be made by the Owslebury postman in the village and Marwell districts only.

OWSLEBURY POSTAL SERVICE – NOW

Today, in the year 2000, our postman arrives in the village in a Royal Mail van rather than on a bike. His round starts in Hensting Lane at *Meadowview Farm*. He drives up Whites Hill into the village and after deliveries here, goes on to Downstead and the Morestead end of Hazeley Road. Rather than 50 to 60 letters to deliver, today's mailbag for our postman is up to 1000 letters a day as well as 20 to 30 packets. Parcels are a separate delivery altogether. In recent times there has been a slight drop in the number of personal letters being posted, due maybe to electronic communication through e-mails, but a huge increase in advertising mail. There is one delivery early each morning to each house, but two collections from the post boxes around the parish, including one on Sundays.

When sending a letter today, we can choose from either a first or second class service. The first class service costs 27p and should guarantee delivery on the following day. Second class postage cost 19p and takes a little longer.

Our village postman today is Goff Prentice. He is not a villager but he nevertherless has much interest in our little community and provides a caring, thorough and professional service for all of us. He seems like one of us as he gives a cheery wave and a smile to passers-by and we miss him when he is sick or on holiday.

Today's postmistress of 2000, Celia Thompson, serving villager Margaret Moon *(DR)*

SUCCESSION OF POSTMEN FOR OWSLEBURY VILLAGE

1910 approx   Mr Arthur Taylor (Miss Taylor's brother)

1913 – 1923   Mr Herbert Hutchings

1924   Mr Reginald Hawkins (who later transferred to Reading)

1925   Mr Bartlett who at one time lived in *Shepherds Cottage*.

1931   Mr Ledger

1939   Mrs Conduit

1940s   A three week roster was shared between:

     Mr Noble

     Mr Batchelor

     Mr Cole

1950s   Mrs Orchard

1960s-1970s   Mrs Furness, the last person to deliver post by bicycle

2000   Goff Prentice

SUCCESSION OF POSTMASTERS AND POSTMISTRESSES IN OWSLEBURY

1878-1889   Miss Fanny Hooker

c1890   Mrs Ellen Taylor, assisted by her daughter Miss Fanny Taylor

1911 – 1924   Mrs Lane, who later became Mrs Hayter

1924-1956   Mrs Hutchings

1956   Mrs Harvey

1950s   Mrs Ward

1960s   Mr John Purnell

1960s-1970s   Mrs Marjorie Blackman

1980s   Mrs Margaret Oakley

1990s   Mrs Celia Thompson

7: HIGH DAYS AND HOLIDAYS
OWSLEBURY CELEBRATIONS

When listening to stories told by villagers who have lived here a long time, and when reading accounts of village life in the past by those who have moved away, one thing is very obvious. They knew how to enjoy themselves, how to organise a celebration for the community. The smiles on their faces as they retell their tales today, confirm how much pleasure such activities brought.

Early in the century whenever a village organisation had a reason to celebrate, the rest of the community was very happy to join in. The Working Mens' Club, Football and Cricket Clubs together with societies such as the Foresters would have their annual parades and outings. George Pierce remembered being secretary of the Pig Club. '*This was a kind of Pig Insurance Club . . . if the pig died, they'd get the value of the pig out*'. When people gave up keeping their pigs, surplus money from the kitty was used to organise an outing. They travelled to Southampton and then by boat to Portsmouth with lunch at Lowmans on the way. George recounted how some men had never left the village before this!

It is noticeable when reading accounts of such activities early in the last century that they were

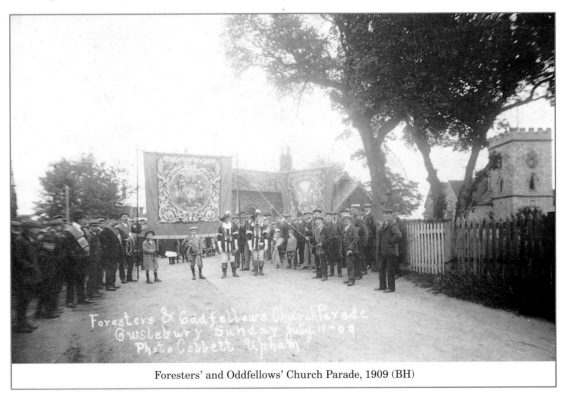

Foresters' and Oddfellows' Church Parade, 1909 (BH)

Juvenile Foresters and Oddfellows, 1909 (BH)

often only for men!

Outings have always been a happy feature of village life. In the 1950s, Michael and Brian Lush remember their Sunday School outing as being *'the highlight of the year'*. The vicar at the time had relatives in Bournemouth; consequently that is where they went. They remember too how the headmaster, Mr Matthews, used to take them for a wonderful day out to the Royal County Show. Peggy Smith (née Merritt) also remembers Sunday School outings to Bournemouth, in the days when two charabancs from Santoys of Fairoak were hired for the day. The outing was a real treat, looked forward to from one year to the next. It was the only time then that village children saw the sea.

As well as local reasons for celebrations, many

such occasions were prompted by a Royal happening, - a coronation, a wedding, a jubilee.

Three years before the close of the nineteenth century, Owslebury, together with the rest of the nation celebrated Queen Victoria's Diamond Jubilee. On 22nd June a huge bonfire was lit by Robert Bunney *'in the field well known as Old Windmill Field'*. A service was held in the church, and sports were enjoyed in the afternoon before 300 villagers sat down, in relays, to a tea in Mr Anstey's barn. Prizes were presented by Captain Standish from Marwell Hall. The church clock was bought to mark this special occasion.

Miss Maberley, the first resident vicar's daughter in the 1830s, actually remembered Queen Victoria's Coronation celebrations! She remembered too that the village had *'a fine flag*

Maypole dancing in the garden of the Old Vicarage, 1969 (BH)

staff, and such lovely flags which we hoisted on many occasions'. In recent years the only time Owslebury has seen a flag was after the tragedy of Princess Diana's death in 1997. The Union Jack then flew at half-mast above the church. To mark a happier annual event, the flag of St Andrew is raised above the church to mark the Saint's day each November.

In 1902 the village celebrated the Coronation of Edward VII. On August 11th they enjoyed a dinner, tea and sports, with 400 adults and 212 children from Owslebury, Morestead and Lane End participating. A planned bonfire had to be cancelled because the actual coronation had had to be postponed due to the King's appendicitis.

In the early 1900s, May Day and Empire Day were always causes for celebration. May Day was remembered by George Harfield as *'Garland Day, chimney sweeper's holiday'.* Jessie Norman (née Tuffs) recounts how children would dance round the maypole in the morning before having a holiday in the afternoon. Children would also go round the countryside gathering flowers to make garlands. They would then sing a little ditty and perhaps be given a penny or two.

The first of May is garland day
Chimney sweeps' holiday
Please ma'am, thank you ma'am,
What do you think of my fine garland?

Later in the same month, on 24th May, children had a half-day holiday to mark Empire Day. Jessie tells how *'we all marched to the school field and sang songs – "Land of Hope and Glory", "There'll Always be an England", and finished with a*

Pat Parsons with the Jubilee Queen after winning the competition for the best decorated house (HC)

open-air, floodlit dance in the evening. Everything ceased briefly at 9.00 pm so that the Queen's speech could be relayed. The dancing then continued until 1.00 am the following morning.

Twenty-five years later in 1977, the village organised another wonderful day to mark the Queen's Silver Jubilee. The copper beech tree

Owslebury Jubilee Queen, Tracey Matthews, with Ann Boston (HC)

Hymn and raising the Union Flag'.

In 1953 Owslebury and Morestead celebrated the Coronation of Queen Elizabeth II and the present church gates were then installed to mark this special occasion. A long day of activities was planned and Greyfriars buses were hired to bring folk from Hensting, Baybridge and Morestead. The day began with Holy Communion and then a church service at St Andrew's. Sports and a tea followed in the afternoon before the lighting of a bonfire and an

Shepherds Cottage – runners up (FW)

on the Glebe was planted to mark this occasion and a specially designed mug was produced for villagers to buy, alongside a mug of a different design which was given to all the village children. Senior Citizens were given a bottle of home-made wine.

Months of planning went into the organisation of the day's events and a special committee was set up. All village organisations were invited to participate by decorating a float. On the day itself individuals decorated their houses with banners and bunting and Pat

Eddie Emery as a majorette with Irene Bliss (IB)

Paul and Marion White with their float (IB)

Crowds in front of the church (AB)

Drama Group float depicting 'The Best of British' – *from left to right*, Sylvia Grace, Daisy Gray, Peggy Smith (née Merritt), Queenie Maddocks, Gwen Windebank and Kath Sharpe (HC)

Princesses-in-waiting Jennie Bailey and Marie Bevis with fancy dress winner, Michael Houghton *(EH)*

The Brownies as clowns *(EH)*

Alan Harfield starting the barbecue (IB)

Parsons from Hilly Close won the competition for the 'Best Decorated House'. Runners-up were Jo and Frank Williams from *Shepherds Cottage*. There was a Jubilee Queen, of course, eighteen year old Tracey Matthews, the daughter of Sally from the *Ship Inn*. Her princesses-in-waiting for the day were Jennie Bailey, aged fourteen, and Marie Bevis aged nine.

The village street became impassable to traffic for much of the day and in spite of the almost inevitable showers together with some hailstones, nothing could dampen the spirits of Owslebury villagers on that occasion. The procession of eleven floats was an amazing and impressive spectacle and seemed to go on for ever – we wanted it to go on for ever! Nearly all the children were in fancy dress of some sort and the sound of Dick Boston's fairground organ cheerfully played as a background to all the merriment. In the afternoon the children enjoyed a picnic tea.

The celebrations continued long into the evening and the early hours of the next morning, with a barbecue and dancing. Many villagers continued celebrating in their own homes well into the next day, reluctant to let go of the feelings of community and happiness that had marked the day. It was a wonderful occasion, remembered and talked about still as one of the Great Village Celebrations of the past.

8: THE WEATHER

Whether the weather be fine
Or whether the weather be not
Whether the weather be cold
Or whether the weather be hot –
We'll weather the weather
Whatever the weather
Whether we like it or not!

Anon

The weather is a daily topic of conversation nationwide. It is a significant feature of British life, often to the amusement of foreigners. It is something we all share in common and the one thing we can do nothing about! Records have been kept for centuries and nowadays weather forecasts on television and radio are made and listened to daily. Owslebury too has its fascination with the weather, and in recent times, villager Nick Perry has published interesting records annually in the Newsletter.

At the turn of the century in 1900, the weather was perhaps of more significance than it is now, often making its influence felt in the daily lives of ordinary folk. Owslebury was a predominantly farming community and what the weather did could make or break someone's livelihood. In the days when children often walked four miles or more to school, bad weather meant that they simply couldn't attend.

During the latter years of the 1800s a keen weather observer of the time made quite detailed records for Owslebury. In 1885 there was recorded

'a severe drought. In June, July, August, not enough rain fell to lay dust. In August fields in which turnips had been twice sewn were quite bare'. In the same year there had been a very severe snowstorm on 22nd March. The year 1886 began with a severe winter – frost lasted from 10th February until 18th March. In May that same year *'such severe thunderstorms, so much rain that the Church was flooded to chancel steps, water entering main entrance, having overflowed gratings at bottom steps. Ten stable buckets of water were baled out. Rain washed soil into lanes and roads to depth of 2ft in some places – potatoes newly planted were washed 200 yards away'.*

Entering the twentieth century, any strange or significant weather has often been noted in school logbooks and in the *Owslebury Newsletter*. There have been some happenings that have received national coverage too and certain years stand out in people's memories.

One such year was 1927 when on Christmas night a great storm blew up. George Pierce, the headmaster's son recorded that, *'by daybreak huge drifts filled sunken lanes, and roads and cottages were covered to a depth of 15ft. The blizzard continued all through the next day, and although downs and fields were almost bare, deep drifts lay against ricks and buildings. Many hamlets and villages were completely cut off from the nearest towns and food had to be dropped by aeroplane to isolated houses . . .It was not until February 6th that the last of the snow disappeared'.* The Betteridge family in Baybridge walked to Upham for bread and never once saw a hedge.

Three years later in January, 1930, during a severe storm, 3000 trees were blown down on the *Longwood Estate.*

Shortly following the end of the Second World War came the winter of 1947. Snow began to fall on Friday, 24th January, and the worst winter of the century had begun. Snow fell every day until March 16th. The observatory at Kew recorded no sunshine at all between February 2nd and 22nd. Snow crippled the roads and railways and the River Thames in London froze. Coal supplies were almost non-existent and the ground was so frozen that it was impossible even to bury the dead. The thaw, which eventually began in March, brought its own problems. Snow melted into torrents and the ground was then covered with floodwaters. It is unlikely that even the wonderful summer that was to follow would drive away the memory of that dreadful winter. In fact people still talk about it today.

1963 is another year remembered for its grim start. The snow began to fall on Boxing Day 1962 and virtually the whole of the British Isles remained as a white landscape until well into March 1963. The memory of the temperatures then over such a prolonged period of time, brings shivers to the spine even now!

The summer of 1976 is remembered for just the opposite reason. We had a heatwave when the sun shone and shone. The year 1990 saw similar hot and dry summer days. By September of that year the landscape was brown and parched with huge cracks in the ground and small trees were dying. There were anxious concerns about the drought conditions and huge placards appeared along major roadsides displaying urgent prayers for rain. The prayers were answered and the rainfall that particular autumn broke many previous records!

Thursday, 16th October, 1987 is another date that anyone living in the south of England will find hard to forget. Villagers in Owslebury have good reason to remember, for much of their local landscape was totally transformed and decimated by the hurricane that blew across the south during the dark hours of the night. Winds had blown across the land at 120 mph! As well as damage to property, huge trees had been uprooted by the storm, blocking roads and cutting off power supplies and telephone lines. The tree damage was devastating. The 'cathedral' of beeches on the road to Winchester was non-existent. Trees on the Longwood Estate, down at Marwell and along Jackman's Hill leading to Morestead lay prostrate on the ground, with huge root systems totally dwarfing mere humans coming to look at the storm damage. As well as beech trees being the main victims, ancient yews also were to fall under the power of this storm. A tree 400 years old at *Bottom Farm* had to be lifted by crane to clear the road. Yew trees close to *Boyes Farm* came down, but a reminder of these trees exists today

A snow-covered Ship Inn (BON)

A wintry Bank Tree, 1978 *(EH)*

A tree across Jackman's Hill, Morestead, January, 1990 *(EE)*

in some wooden bowls that were afterwards carved from them.

The village was cut off for several days while roads were slowly cleared. Candles and camping stoves were brought out of cupboards and had to suffice until power supplies were resumed. Life gradually returned to normal, but the landscape around our village, even with newly planted trees, will never be the same again for our generation.

Two years later in January, 1990 yet another hurricane type wind was to do dreadful damage in the south of England. Many of those trees weakened in the previous storm now fell and once again brought daily life to a halt. A beautiful old walnut tree in front of *The Cricketers* became a victim in this storm.

In the last decade of the twentieth century we have had several spells of very dry weather resulting in cracked soil and hosepipe bans. Rainfall in October, November and December 2000 more than made up for this and brought the worst floods within living memory. On October 30th we had 36mm rain overnight! This caused all trains in the south to stop running, but here in Owslebury village we were still blessed with our milk, postal and paper deliveries! Thereafter it just rained and rained and rained! Hensting Lane became a fast flowing river and Owslebury Bottom a lake, stretching almost as far as the eye could see. The road there became completely impassable for cars. The main road to Winchester was flooded at *Bottom Pond Farm* and at Morestead too, water flowed right across the road. *Bottom Pond Farm* has often been troubled by

FLOODS, 2000

Floods in Hensting Lane *(EH)*

Water flowing as a river in both directions *(EH)*

The 'lake' to the side of Hensting Lane
at Owslebury Bottom *(EH)*

The road at Owslebury Bottom with another
'lake' alongside Stags Lane *(EH)*

At Owslebury Bottom *(EH)*

flooding in the past because of the underground springs rising from *Honeymans* at Longwood. To help alleviate the problem, pipes to drain surplus water away were installed under the road. When checking these pipes after the recent floods, it was found that a fox had got stuck in the pipe thus preventing the water from flowing through! The flooding caused extensive damage to road surfaces throughout the parish, and as the water slowly receded huge potholes and sharp edges were revealed. Several families had to leave their homes, so bad was the flooding and damage.

On the wettest day during these months 48mm of rain fell! That was on 5th November. Somewhat surprisingly perhaps, our village 'meteorologist' Nick Perry recorded that April 2000 was actually the wettest month of the millennium year. That month recorded 190.6mm of rain. He told us in the Newsletter that '*over the last eight years the number of days on which there has been rain, however slight, has varied very little with an average of 157 days per year. However, the average volume of rain per day was up by one millimetre in AD2000 over previous years*'.

I guess that as we move forward into the twenty first century we'll continue to '*weather the weather, whatever the weather, whether we like it or not!*'

9: Significant Trees, Hedges And Footpaths

Contributed by Jill Hancock

Throughout the twentieth century special events or occasions within the village have often been marked by the planting of a tree. Plans are being made to plant some trees to mark the beginning of the new millennium. Such trees stand as a living heritage from one generation to another.

1911

The members of Owslebury Cricket Club passed a vote of thanks to Mr Lucas from Morestead for the gift of trees for the cricket ground given in memory of King Edward VII. We are still enjoying these, now huge Norwegian maples and whitebeams as they continue to grow and flourish on the Cricket Down.

1914 May 14th

Trees and shrubs were planted on the new playing field when the old school took over the ground; beech, horse chestnut, holly and silver birch. The trees have matured and given great pleasure to generations of children.

1920s

Limes alongside the village hall were planted by Gerald Bunney, uncle to Brian and Michael Lush.

1927 February 11th

The Bird and Tree Festival was held at 3 pm in the Parish Hall.

Mrs Pierce, the headmaster's wife, planted a horse chestnut tree in the school playing field to commemorate the school's success in the event.

Generations of children who have attended Owslebury School have had the great pleasure of collecting conkers from this tree each autumn.

1928

On the present school field along the border on the Beech Grove side, a holly and a silver birch, were planted by Edith Bunney as a schoolgirl, (Brian and Michael Lush's mother). They continue to flourish.

1940s (late)

Horse Chestnut trees were planted on the Cricket Down to commemorate the ending of the Second World War.

1971

The WI planted flowering trees and shrubs alongside the church path to commemorate 50 years of WI in Owslebury, 1921-1971.

1977

Richard Harfield, then aged 8, planted the horse chestnut tree, now growing near the school pond.

The copper beech on the Glebe was planted at

the time of the Queen's Silver Jubilee. It is known as the Jubilee Tree and was purchased with money donated by the Motor Cycle Scrambling Club.

1978

Three trees, (one for each class) were planted alongside the school netball pitch, to mark the Queen's Silver Jubilee. The alder and silver birch survived but the oak was replaced with a Norwegian maple. The alder also later died and so only two trees remain today.

1984

A hedge of indigenous trees and bushes was planted, with the help of the children, alongside the Beech Grove edge of the Owslebury School playing field. It was hoped that the children would watch with pleasure as the hedge matured. The hedge would complement trees previously planted here. It would provide food and shelter for birds and not least, give some shelter from the cold winter winds for all of the children while playing on the field.

THE BANK TREE

The magnificent sycamore standing on the bank outside the *Ship Inn*, is always referred to as the Bank Tree and appears to have been rather like Topsy and *'just grewed'*. It is known to have been here since at least the 1850s and is now a tall and stately landmark watching over our village.

Sadie Mills, who spent her childhood in

The Bank Tree *(EH)*

Owslebury early in the last century, was later to write after her marriage, when she accompanied her husband to the Himalayas, '*with the majestic view of Mt Everest from my bungalow window and the best of the East, my constant mirage was of my quiet, cool village and the bank tree in particular.*'

Peggy Smith (née Merritt) remembers singing gospel songs under the Bank Tree as a child.

Standing close by is the lime tree, which will eventually replace the sycamore and look just as magnificent at this entrance to the village.

FOOTPATHS

Owslebury villagers are blessed by having on their doorstep, a number of footpaths that lead away from the village and out across the surrounding countryside. They provide instant access to a means of being 'away from it all', in the peace and beauty of the landscape close by. They provide a link between all the villages and outlying hamlets.

The extensive range of footpaths can be seen on the Ordnance Survey map of the area on the following page.

(Reproduced from the 1993, Pathfinder 1264 Winchester (South) and Eastleigh 2½inch to 1 mile – 4C to 1km Ordnance Survey map by permission of Ordnance Survey on behalf of the Controller of Her Majesty's Stationery Office © Crown Copyright MC 100031686)

10: MILLENNIUM EVENTS AND HAPPENINGS

The village spent almost two years deciding upon the most fitting ways to mark the start of the third millennium. Many original and exciting ideas were suggested and then put into action. The first such happening was the lighting-up of our Christmas illuminations.

OWSLEBURY VILLAGE CHRISTMAS ILLUMINATIONS

Contributed by Evelyn Houghton

At 5 o'clock on the evening of 13th December, 1999, a little bit of magic happened upon the village of Owslebury. Suddenly, down the whole length of the darkened street, coloured lights twinkled into action, bathing the whole area in a soft coloured glow.

Owslebury village had its first Christmas illuminations!

The whole idea was the brainchild of Clive and Ali Mansell, landlords of the *Ship Inn*. They organised everything from the donation appeal to the fixing of wires and light bulbs. The latter were put into place during the preceding week, often in appalling weather conditions. Among those who braved the cold, rain and wind with Clive were Nigel Drew, Andy Gwynn, Ian McLeonards, Graham Oakley, Bob O'Neill, Lea Shipley, Rod Tabor, Gerry Tull and David Wilkie.

Two hours after the lights were switched on, people could be seen wending their way through the village towards the tree decorated with lights in front of the *Ship Inn*. Clive was already there, with a charcoal fire lit to mull the wine. It seemed as though the whole village had turned out. To complete this scene, Dave and Karen Edwards' white horses, Oliver and Polly, pulled a trap up and down the street giving a Dickensian touch to the scene. With glasses of mulled wine warming both hands and hearts, the carol singing began, voices of young and old filling the cold night air. In the pauses mince pies were much enjoyed.

When the singing was over, everyone joined in

Putting up the Christmas lights, 1999 *(EH)*

three heartfelt cheers for Clive and Ali, without whom none of this would have happened. People seemed reluctant to leave. The lights seemed to have lit up more than just the street and brought our little community together in a way that rarely happens nowadays. The lights will continue to be a pleasure for villagers for years to come through the new Millennium. That is a very good thought.

OWSLEBURY MILLENNIUM BASH

Contributed by Karen Marsh

The idea of a party started from a collection of small ideas. Our first idea was to hire a marquee and hold the party in somebody's garden but fortunately and unexpectedly the Parish Hall became available. Our garden party plan was dropped and planning began for The Millennium Bash.

It was then that the really hard work started. Many, many meetings for the committee took place, ideas and suggestions became working plans and final details were added. The committee wanted especially to welcome all the senior residents and they received special invitations.

The hall was beautifully decorated; masses of balloons complimented the silver 2000 signs. Tables laid with white cloths and napkins were individually decorated. The whole hall was transformed into a venue fit to welcome in the New Millennium. Needless to say the food was bounteous and the wine flowed.

Nick's Disco, run by Nick Holden, provided a real variety of music and everybody from youngest to oldest joined in the dancing.

At midnight the New Millennium was ushered in with the traditional singing of Auld Lang Syne, followed by You'll Never Walk Alone. A truly wonderful evening was had by all. The planning committee had excelled themselves. Members of the committee were as follows:

Jackie and David Crockford
Carol and Malcolm Hatt
Janet and Chris Hunt
Liz and Brian Kerswell
Karen and David Marsh

The party was a non-profit making event, but there was some money left over which was donated to Mencap and the Magpie Scanner Appeal.

THE DAWN OF THE NEW MILLENNIUM

Contributed by Evelyn Houghton

Saturday 1st January 2000 , a new day, a new year, a new century, a new millennium!

The village of Owslebury planned no huge celebration to mark this unique moment in time, but celebrate a great many folk did. The *Ship Inn* was actually closed but the Millennium Bash was organised in the *Parish Hall* for this last evening of the old year. Whilst some folk went to this celebration others stayed in their homes or marked the occasion in their own personal ways.

As midnight approached a light rain began to fall but this did not dampen the spirits of another group of villagers who, in the last minutes of the old year, made their way towards the Glebe, in order to see and hear the church clock strike midnight. The first surprise of the evening was that the church clock had stopped! The hands marked the time at ten to three. This has been beautifully recorded for posterity on the church

Tapestry. However a second surprise was the realization that Sandy and Eddie Emery had thoughtfully brought along a radio. Thus we were able to join with others nationwide in listening to the tones of Big Ben as twelve o'clock midnight rang out and marked the beginning of the new millennium. The sound of our own church bells, rung by Nigel Drew, David Houghton and Lea Shipley, then rang across the night air and everyone was exchanging hugs and kisses, even with people previously unknown! The champagne corks were popping and glasses filled to mark this special moment. Small groups joined hands to sing Auld Lang Syne. Yet another surprise was a beautiful cake, in fact four cakes baked together to form the number 2000, generously provided by Sandy and Eddie Emery, which was then cut and shared out.

Very soon fireworks began to go off from various points around the village and the sky became aglow with a display that was taking place in Southampton. The village Christmas lights had been left on and these lit up the main street. People's spirits were also lit up on that evening and for those who participated, there was a wonderful feeling of warmth, goodwill and optimism at this dawn of the new millennium.

At 12.00 noon on January 1st, 2000, the bells of St Andrew's Church rang out with others across the nation to celebrate this special moment in time. The day was a beautiful sunny one and the bells were a joyful sound to bring in this New Year. It was a team of bellringers from Twyford who made it possible for Owslebury to join in this national celebration. The Twyford ringers who so kindly came were John Denham (Captain of Bells), Paula Denham, David Little, Tony Norris, Jennie Richardson and Angela Wood.

OWSLEBURY MILLENNIUM CELEBRATION

Contributed by Jill Hancock

There was, of course, much nation-wide hype over the coming millennium, which led to a feeling that our move into the year 2000 must be marked in some special way. For many Christians, it underlined the beginning and continuing strength of their faith. With this in mind some villagers chose to celebrate the coming of the New Year in the splendour of Winchester Cathedral. Here the ancient building was filled with the glorious sounds of voice and brass. And at midnight, a fanfare and the bells rang out.

The village too, had its own special service to mark Jesus Christ's 2000th birthday.

On Sunday, 2nd January, 2000 at 3.00 pm St Andrew's Church was packed for a Service of Prayer and Dedication for the New Millennium.

The Revd Vivien Moffitt led the service. Mrs. Elizabeth Harfield played the organ. The service began with the welcome, then prayers and hymns followed.

The church echoed to the sound of the old favourite hymns, 'Praise my soul the King of Heaven', 'It came upon the midnight clear', and 'Now thank we all our God'.

The whole congregation joined in the special Prayer for the Third Millennium and then The Millennium Resolution:

Let there be

respect for the earth

peace for its people

love in our lives

delight in the good

forgiveness for past wrongs

and from now on a new start.

It was a happy and thoughtful service which ended with the Blessing.

THE MILLENNIUM TEA

Contributed by Jill Hancock

After the service everybody was invited to a very special tea in the Parish Hall. It was indeed a really scrumptious tea that the Friends of St Andrew's had prepared. There was much chatter in between all of the munching. The afternoon was a very happy village occasion.

During the gathering there was a presentation of a framed map of the village given by Betty Harfield and Jill Hancock. They had, by chance, become the village correspondents for The Hampshire Chronicle. The rate of remuneration paid by the newspaper was 10p a line. Each Friday the number of lines printed about events in Owslebury was added up to see how much money had been made.

It took almost a year to earn enough money to buy a copy of the beautifully restored hand coloured Map of Hampshire by Charles Smith, dated 1808.

Phillip Shewan of the Woody Card Co. produced this, and with the help of modern technology, it was possible to print a copy of the map centred on Owslebury. The map was then framed.

It was presented to Dr Jane Dawson, chairman of the Parish Council, who accepted it on behalf of the village.

Presentation by Betty Harfield to Dr Jane Dawson of the old map of Owslebury.
Onlookers are Melanie Norris, David Houghton, Revd Vivien Moffitt and Evelyn Houghton (BH)

Terry Russell and the Parish Hall committee very kindly hung the Millennium Map in the entrance of the Parish Hall

St Andrew's Church, Owslebury: Millennium Wall Hanging and Millennium Mug

Contributed by Nick Perry

The call in a late 1997 Newsletter for ideas to commemorate our entry into the third millennium spurred Caroline Perry to devise two projects within the Parish. One would be a fund-generating memento; the other a permanent and visible statement of community involvement. Thus the St. Andrew's Church Millennium Mug and Wall Hanging were conceived.

The designs of both carried two common features; a north western view of the church and the millennium logo designed by Jane Gillett of Alton. Prices' Candles had already used this logo on a candle to commemorate the '2000th Anniversary of the birth of Jesus Christ'. Jane offered the design to Caroline who first charted it as an embroidery item which The Tapestry Centre sold to raise money for charity.

The Millennium Mug was launched at the church summer fete of 1999.

In 1998 Caroline Perry was building visions of the proposed wall hanging by photographing various recognisable objects and aspects of our parish church which were soon to be translated into coloured sketches by Diana Snagge of Winchester. Members of the parish church council were unanimous in their support for the size, eventual positioning and most favoured design which Diana then hand-painted onto canvas for cross-stitch working with seven holes to one inch. Design costs and all the materials, including the fifty-six shades of Appleton Tapestry Wools, were donated by The Tapestry Centre, Alresford.

Initial needlework on the canvas was carried out by the earliest volunteers including The Rt Revd and Rt Hon. Donald Coggan Archbishop of Canterbury 1974 - 1980 and, in his retirement, an occasional visiting preacher at St. Andrew's Church. Our vicar from 1991 – 1999, the Revd Dr Peter Lippiett, chose and stitched the New Testament text from the Letter to the Hebrews, before taking up his new appointment as Warden of the Carlisle Diocesan Conference and Retreat Centre at Rydal Hall and Priest-in-Charge of St Mary's at Ambleside, Cumbria.

There were three public opportunities for people to add a stitch. By early May 1999 some 60 had responded to the invitation before the wall hanging started to be worked on by experienced volunteers.

The stature of the design began to be enhanced by a few subtle ongoing changes to the original wool shadings, Caroline's decision to use Jane Gillett's 2000 logo and the re-setting of the time to be shown by the Tower Clock in the side panel. Ten minutes to three o'clock had to recall the anticlimax of midnight on 31st December 1999 when the clock failed to chime in the Millennium Year.

With five months to go to Dedication Day, Sylvia Rix added vital impetus by taking over the reins and by having open house for those who had agreed to stitch chosen areas of the design. Altogether the completed work contained 129,200 stitches worked by nearly three hundred people

Caroline and Nick Perry introducing the Millennium Tapestry to headteacher David White and the schoolchildren *(EH)*

between the ages of two and ninety-five, including over eighty children of Owslebury School.

Caroline researched, designed and managed the final framing and hanging, which was mainly paid for by villagers and Owslebury & Morestead Community Association. Paul Davis expertly constructed the sapele wood cross-pieced frame

Dedication of the Millennium Tapestry with Lady Coggan and the Venerable John Guille *(EH)*

which unfortunately, but hopefully, will never be admired by anyone except the very few who helped in the final moments.

The unveiling by Lady Coggan and the dedication of the tapestry by the Archdeacon of Winchester, the Venerable John Guille, took place at the Patronal Festival of St Andrew's Church on Sunday, 26th November, 2000. The church was filled to capacity for the service and seventy-five people went to the Parish Hall afterwards for lunch given by the parish church council. This was to celebrate the completion of the St. Andrew's Church Millennium Wall Hanging project, about which more detail can be found in

Parish Lunch in the Parish Hall following the dedication of the Tapestry, November, 2000 *(EH)*

the scrapbook held in St Andrew's Church.

PARISH HALL MILLENNIUM WALL HANGING

Contributed by Margaret Jefferies

Encouraged by the success achieved in making a patchwork quilt for fund-raising purposes for the new Parish Hall in the 1990s, the suggestion was made by Jackie McLeonards in 1998 that a group should be formed to make an item for the Parish Hall to commemorate the millennium.

Several meetings took place culminating in a decision being made to make a pictorial wall hanging depicting various buildings, objects, businesses, flora and fauna which were existing in the village at the commencement of the new century. Mainly Elsie Evans took photographs and Heather Lush was enlisted to assist with sketches. By the end of 1998 and with the assistance of a small grant from OMCA we were able to purchase the necessary materials and make a start. Meetings were mainly held at *"Sunnyside"* where we have met and chosen materials and have been able to encourage each other in the progress of the work. As a result appliquéd blocks have been made of the Cricket Pavilion, Baybridge Chapel, Ship Inn, Shearers Arms, both the new and old schools, the Old Shop, the Farmhouse, St Andrew's Church, Chestnut House, the Parish Hall and Owslebury Farmhouse to name but a few. In addition, the wall hanging will be framed with smaller blocks depicting various businesses, flora, fauna, and signposts.

From the original group of nine ladies, numbers have decreased to six but we are confident that the end product will give future generations some idea of what Owslebury was like at the time of the millennium, at the same time enhancing a bare wall in the new Parish Hall. Progress has necessarily been slow because all the ladies involved lead very busy lives; it has been hard work at times but we have enjoyed the experience and meeting others whose paths we would not normally cross. It is hoped that the project will be finished by spring 2001.

The millennium appliqué wallhanging for the Parish Hall.
Planning the layout are, *from left to right*, Margaret Jefferies (project leader),
Jill Chase, Janet Bartlett, Jackie McLeonards, Evelyn Houghton and Jane Dawson *(DH)*

Those who participated were;

    Janet Bartlett from Bishopstoke

    Jill Chase

    Jane Dawson

    Evelyn Houghton

    Margaret Jefferies

    Jackie McLeonards

MILLENNIUM BULB PLANTING

Contributed by Elsie and Gwyn Evans

In the autumn of 1998 OMCA financed the purchase of blue and white crocus bulbs and snowdrops from Winchester Bulb Growers. They were then sold to people in the village who planted them near the road.

Evelyn Houghton planted 1032 snowdrops under the Bank Tree as part of this millennium project. The school and church also planted bulbs in their grounds. Over the coming years the bulbs should naturalise and be a colourful welcome to every New Year.

THE LIVING SUNDIAL

Contributed by Evelyn Houghton

Villager and horticultural student, Andrew Bailey, won a distinction for course work, for his design of a living sundial planted with yew and box. After a delay in approving a site for the

Evelyn Houghton planting 1032 snowdrop bulbs under the Bank Tree,
September, 1999 *(DH)*

sundial, it is hoped that the digging and planting for this will shortly commence in a corner of the Glebe Field. It will be a unique millennium project for the village of Owslebury today and for generations to come.

Owslebury Primary School

Contributed by David White, Headteacher of Owslebury School

The school marked the start of the new millennium with a special celebration, organised by the friends of Owslebury School, on Friday, 7th January, 2000.

The first event was the digging of a deep hole, not to bury the headteacher, but in which to place a time capsule. This contained an interesting variety of items which the children, staff and parents had collected to represent Owslebury, the school, and what life was like at the turn of the millennium. The local press turned up to capture the ceremony.

The afternoon continued with the pantomime 'Mother Goose' performed by a visiting theatre group in the school hall. This was great fun, full of all the usual traditional parts. We followed the pantomime with a party tea for all of the children and the presentation to each child of a unique millennium mug. This proved to be a super afternoon, one to treasure for many years to come.

The children enjoyed a special opportunity to actually work on the village Millennium Tapestry. Caroline and Nick Perry kindly arranged to take the unfinished tapestry into school.

Then each child was able to add some stitches of his or her own to help complete the needlework.

The school also received two sacks of daffodil bulbs as part of the Lord Lieutenant's Millennium Bulb project. Children and parents planted these in the school grounds. Near to the school gates the bulbs were planted in the form of a large number 2000. So each spring, this display of golden daffodils will remind the children, parents and visitors of this special year.

The Millennium Book

Contributed by Evelyn Houghton

The publishing of this book, *'Owslebury Then and Now'*, is the result of an idea originally discussed informally by a couple of villagers. This was later passed on to OMCA who gave it their support as a village millennium project.

The Pilgrims' Trail

Contributed by Jill Hancock

The Hampshire Millennium Pilgrims' Trail runs between Winchester and Portsmouth. It forms part of a long-distance walk following the old St Michael's Way. This was the route used by mediaeval pilgrims as they journeyed to Mont Saint Michel in Normandy. Here they stopped before walking on to Santiago de Compostela in Northern Spain. The cult of Saint Michael was widespread from the ninth century. By the time of the reformation in the sixteenth century there were more than six hundred churches in England dedicated to Saint Michael.

The trail aims to take walkers through today's landscape with the eyes of a pilgrim.

Leaving Winchester the trail runs through Owslebury, described as a pretty village with mediaeval origins through which pilgrims passed. The trail continues through the St Andrew's churchyard into Pitcot Lane. The signpost on the Glebe Field points the way for our modern day travellers, forward to Portsmouth or back to Winchester.

It is suggested that a stop for refreshments could be made at the *Ship Inn*. Owslebury walkers could, perhaps, begin their journey with a stop at the *Ship Inn!*

The walk can be done in a series of separate shorter distances and a card can be signed at recognised checkpoints, as a record of the trail achieved.

A challenge for the New Millennium is to walk the 28 miles of the Pilgrims' Trail from Winchester to Portsmouth.

With acknowledgements to Hampshire County Council Information Centre.

11: IN LOVING MEMORY

Scattered around the village of Owslebury are several items that have been given over the years in loving memory of relatives who had lived here before their deaths. These remain as lasting memorials to loved ones and give pleasure and benefit to folk who live in the village today. Many such memorials are to be found in the church.

John and Henry Cordery; A bell was added to the bell tower at the beginning of the twentieth century by James Cordery in memory of his brothers, John and Henry.

James, John, Henry and another brother, Arthur, were almost certainly sons of John Cordery who is commemorated on a plaque on the church wall alongside the altar. He is described as being *'of this parish near which he also was born and passed his boyhood and for which he retained throughout his life a vivid and warm affection'*.

The family continued to have strong links with the village throughout the next generation. James Cordery, the giver of the bell, died on 26th October, 1919, in his 85th year.

Olive Gill; The altar cloth was given in loving memory of Olive Muriel Gill, by her son and daughter. Olive lived with her husband, Maurice, and children at *Marwell Lodge*. She was remembered as a great lady who did so much good for other people. Olive died on November 23rd, 1956, and is buried in the churchyard alongside her husband, Maurice, who died just two months after her.

Arthur Sylwood Lush; The font cover was given in memory of Arthur Sylwood Lush in 1946. Arthur was one of three young men from

Owslebury who gave their lives for this country during the Second World War. He is named with two others on a plaque on the church wall. He was the only son of Florence and Albert Lush and was just 22 years old when he died. He served in the RAF and was shot down and killed over Germany in 1942. Prior to the war he had been a sidesman in the church for two years.

Alice May Gurman; Two oak candlesticks were given to the church in memory of this much-loved infant teacher who had spent all her teaching years at the village school. She was always known as Daisy and is buried in a corner of the churchyard.

Revd Charles Buston; The pulpit crucifix was presented to the church in memory of Revd Charles Buston. He was vicar of St Andrew's Church at the turn of the last century. He served fifteen years of his ministry here from 1896 until 1911, and died in 1920, aged 64.

Major William Standish; There is a beautiful stained glass window installed in the south wall of the church which was placed there to commemorate the life of Major William Pery Standish. He had lived at *Marwell Hall* with his wife and six children and was always regarded as the squire of the village, being much loved as such. He was Master of the Hambledon Hunt and it was while returning with his daughter from a day's hunting in 1922 that he suddenly collapsed and died. He was aged 62 years. The window was placed in the church six years later in 1928. As well as the Standish Arms and crest the window depicts the figures of three saints; St George, the patron saint of England, St Hubert, Bishop of Liège and patron of hunting, and St Martin, Confessor and Bishop of Tours.

Richard Tryner Boston; The church organ  was given in loving memory of Richard Tryner Boston who died on 21st March, 1985. The brass plaque on the side of the organ tells us that it was *'the gift of the Boston family of Owslebury Farm; installed by the generosity of family and friends and dedicated on 28 July 1987 by Rev Anthony Caesar, Chaplain Chapel Royal'*.

When Dick moved to *Owslebury Farm* in 1966 the organ in the church was hand blown, and Dick decided it was time to electrify it. He was able to do this because he was a skilled organ builder. When he was a schoolboy he had been an organ pupil and as such automatically became involved in helping the school organ builder with maintenance. This started a life long interest. Although unbeknown to him at the time, this was maybe due in part to his genetic inheritance, for his ancestors had been involved in the firm of

organ builders, named *Wren and Boston*. Dick served in the Fleet Air Arm during the war and when he was demobbed, did a Rural Industries course before achieving his life-long ambition to work full time as a craftsman organ builder. He was actually working on the organ now installed in St Andrew's Church when he died. It is thought that some of the pipes actually came from the firm of *Wren and Boston* in Preston. Martin Neary, who at the time was organist in Winchester Cathedral, played the organ at the dedication service.

During his years in Owslebury, Dick played an active part in village life, serving as a manager of the school, as president of the Cricket Club, a committee member for the Horticultural Society and he was also involved with local Conservatives.

Countess of Northesk; **Lady Margaret Carnegie**; **Alice Long**; Inside the Church are also to be found other memorials to three families associated with Owslebury back in the nineteenth century. These include stained glass windows placed in memory of Georgina, Countess of Northesk, who died on 23rd February, 1874 and Lady Margaret Carnegie who died 27th September, 1871. The window behind the altar was given *'To the Glory of God and in memory of Alice Long of Marwell who died 18 September 1840 aged 81 years. She provided for the poor and needy'*.

Samuel Montague Lavington; In the vestry there is a leather bound book , 'The Order for the Administration of the Lord's Supper or Holy Communion'. On the flyleaf of the book the inscription tells us;

'Given for use in Owslebury Church by Mr and Mrs Lavington in Memory of their son Samuel Montague Lavington, September 14th 1920.'

The Lavingtons were a well-known village family who had lived for several generations at *Bottom Farm* when it was still run as a working farm. Samuel was the son of James and Alice Lavington. He was born on 14th September, 1906, and died on 30th July, 1920, when aged just thirteen years. The book was given to the church on the day that would have been his fourteenth birthday.

WAR MEMORIALS

Also to be found within the church are memorials to those men from Owslebury who gave their lives in the two World Wars of the last century.

> *They shall not grow old, as we that are left*
> *grow old:*
> *Age shall not weary them, nor the years*
> *condemn.*
> *At the going down of the sun, and in the*
> *morning*
> *We will remember them.*
>
> *Laurence Binyon*

1914–1918

Arthur John Bennet; was born at Morestead, the grandson of William and Sarah Betteridge. He enlisted in 15th Service Battalion, Hampshire Regiment and was killed in action in Flanders, 22nd October, 1918, aged 19. He lived at *Old Wells Cottage*.

Edwin Fletcher; was born at *Rose Cottage*, Owslebury. He became a carpenter and married Lucy Harfield. He enlisted in the Hampshire Regiment and was killed in Mesopotamia, 20th September, 1916.

William Gale; was born in Winchester. He enlisted in the Hampshire Regiment and was killed in action in Flanders at the Battle of the Somme, 1st July, 1916. He lived at Owslebury Bottom.

Basil Plowman; was born and lived at *Baybridge Farm*. He was a Lance Corporal when killed in action in Flanders at the Battle of the Somme.

J Dorling; lived at Longwood and worked as a gamekeeper there. He enlisted in the Royal Fusiliers.

Arthur H. Emmet; served in the Gloucestershire Regiment.

William Tuffs; enlisted in the Hampshire Regiment. He died of heat stroke in Mesopotamia, 22nd July, 1915, aged 42. He lived at Owslebury Bottom, then *Yew Tree Cottages*, where he left a wife, Clara, and twelve young children.

E A Chandler; served in the Australian Imperial Force.

W P Le Mercier; enlisted in the Royal Engineers.

Frederick W Read; served in the Royal Navy. He lived at *Lower Farm Cottages*, the son of Elizabeth and Henry Read.

A R Welsh; enlisted in the Yorkshire Regiment. He lived at *Owslebury Farm*.

There are two more Owslebury men who gave their lives during the First World War but who, for some strange unknown reason, are not recorded on the memorial plaque. Their names and details **are** recorded in a list of monumental inscriptions from the churchyard and are as follows:

C.S.M. George Taylor R.G.A.; served in the Heavy Artillery, Signalling Depot and died 14th April, 1918, aged 40.

Hugh Prior; was the son of Henry and Mary Prior, who fell in action, September, 1916

1939 –1945

George Leslie Guy; served in the 1st Wiltshire Regiment, 4th battalion. He was killed in France, 5th August, 1944, aged 40, and is buried at Calvados. He was born in Hensting, the son of Philip and Jane Guy. He lived in Owslebury at *Yew Tree Cottages* with his wife, Emily, and daughter, Vera. Vera was three years old when her father died.

Edmond Jack Macdonald Lucas; served in the Royal Navy, and was the eldest son of Edward Macdonald Lucas from Baybridge.

Arthur Sylwood Lush; served in the RAF. He lived at Number 1 *Bankside Cottages*, the only son of Albert and Florence Lush and brother to Thora. He was shot down over Germany in 1942, aged 22 years.

Memorials in the Churchyard and Around the Village

Cliff Bradshaw; Cliff Bradshaw lived in the village for some considerable time with his wife, Gladys. For many of those years he served as a verger in the church. After his death Gladys planted a maple tree just inside the church gates in his memory but sadly this did not survive.

Louisa Leeks; Just by the little iron gate linking the churchyard with the Glebe Field, stands a flowering cherry tree which is a picture each springtime. This tree was planted in 1988 in loving memory of Louisa Leeks (née Read). The Reads were a village family in days gone by. Louisa's parents were Elizabeth and Henry Read and she had five brothers, Tom, Arthur, Ted, Fred and Will as well as several sisters. Henry Read was a foreman for Charles Anstey at *Lower Farm* and the family lived in a cottage there. When Louisa married she moved away from Owslebury. Her last years were spent in Cambridgeshire where she died, aged 92. The tree has been planted by her children as a memorial not only to Louisa but to all the family.

Mary Shaw; The gates leading to the Glebe Field have a small brass plaque fixed to them to inform villagers that they were placed in loving memory of Mary Shaw who was a District and City Councillor from 1972 until 1983. She lived in the village for many years at *The Cricketers* with her husband, Jack, and son, John. Mary and Jack were both well-known village folk. Mary died in 1983, aged 71.

Walter and Daisy Trott; The church notice board was erected in loving memory of Walter and Daisy Trott.

 Walter was a London boy who joined the navy when aged 16 and so came to Portsmouth. He was of an age that he would fight for his country in **two** World Wars. He became friends with Alfred Glasspool who invited him to come home with him one day to Owslebury. Walter thus met Alfred's sister, Daisy, and was straight away smitten. Daisy had been born in 1900 and belonged to a family who had lived in Owslebury for over 300 years. At the time of their marriage, Daisy was in service with the family of the Mayor of Winchester. They insisted that she was married in the city and then had the reception at their house in St Cross.

Walter and Daisy began their married life in Portsmouth but came back to Owslebury in 1941 after their house was bombed. They had four children, Vera, Walter, Joyce and Roger. The two sons live in the village today and it was they who organised the making of the board for the church in memory of Walter and Daisy. Walter died in 1962 and Daisy in 1986. They are buried in the churchyard.

In this millennium year, Roger Trott is making a new board for the church.

Fred Merritt; On the Cricket Down are two seats, placed there by the village in loving memory of Fred Merritt.

Fred was born at *Little Lodge*, Belmore Lane and thus grew up as a local lad. Fred's father, William, at one time owned *Holly Hatch* on the corner of Crabbes Hill. After Fred was married to Phyllis they lived for six months in a little wooden bungalow down Pitcot Lane where *Pitcot House* is now located. They then moved to Mr Sawyer's Shop, now *Bressay*, before finally making a home in Beech Grove.

As a boy Fred was a scout in Twyford and thus began his life-long involvement with the scout movement. He became a scout leader and it was Fred who was responsible for gaining the Jubilee Hut on the Cricket Down for cubs and scouts in the village. Much of his spare time was dedicated to scout work and his wife, Phyllis, remembers *'many a Sunday dinner spoilt because he **had** to finish something!'* He was always anxious to help others and even after his leg was amputated he would chop bags of kindling wood and take it to elderly folk. After his death in 1981, a moving tribute was written by Paul White in the Newsletter, when he described him as a much loved, tireless worker who had given so much of his time to village boys.

The seats on the Cricket Down are worthy reminders of this kind and hard working man. Revd Geoffrey Holland and John Richman, who was chairman of the Scout Committee at the time, presided at the dedication ceremony.

Iris and Lawrence Edwards; A seat on the Glebe was placed there in loving memory of Iris and Lawrence Edwards.

Iris Edwards came to live in Hilly Close shortly after the death of her husband, Lawrence, in 1969. She came to Owslebury from not very far away, for Iris and Lawrence had lived first in *South Lodge,* Hurst Lane, when Lawrence was head gardener for Colonel Harrison at *Marwell Hall*, and then at *Marwell Farm Cottages* when he later worked for Lady Kelburn. They came to the village regularly, particularly to go to church. Iris had a niece, Sheila Norgate, who was already living in the village. Lawrence was a member of the Horticultural Committee and entered vegetables and flowers in the shows for both Colonel Harrison and Lady Kelburn, winning many First Prizes with them. It was after Iris' death in 1983 that her daughter, Rosemary, now living at Colden Common, had the seat placed on the Glebe in memory of her parents. It has given her much pleasure to see the seat well used. Both Iris and Lawrence are buried in the churchyard.

June Rhyder; When entering the school drive one passes on the left-hand side a small ornamental pond. It is known as the June Rhyder Pond. June was a village 'mum' with two young sons, Colin and Robert, still at primary school, when she suddenly collapsed and died. Her premature death shocked and saddened village folk and the school knew they had lost a real friend. Not only was June always on hand to help out with various school activities, but she was also a parent representative for the school governing body.

The pond was dug out by villager Dave Edwards, and the planting organised by Jill Hancock who was a teacher at the school at the time. It was officially 'opened' in the summer of 1986 and a seat was placed alongside. They remain today as a permanent memorial to June.

Jack Shaw; Tucked away in a small corner behind Hilly Close is a children's playground. As well as play equipment for the children, a seat may be found there as a welcome resting place for parents and grandparents. The wood is engraved with Jack Shaw's name, and the seat was placed here in loving memory of this villager. Jack lived in Owslebury for many years with his wife, Mary, and son, John. The family lived at the *Cricketers* on Crabbes Hill. Jack died in 1984, aged 71 years.

Ian Robinson; In the far corner of the Cricket Down, furthest away from the road under the shade of the trees there, is a seat which is in constant use by cricket spectators during summer months. This was placed here in loving memory of Ian Robinson. Ian was not actually a native of Owslebury but came from nearby Fair Oak regularly for many years to score for the village team. It is inscribed *'In loving memory of Ian Robinson, 1935 – 1991'.*

12: BEGINNINGS AND ENDINGS

"There is a season for everything, a time for every occupation under heaven:
A time for giving birth, a time for dying, a time for planting, a time for uprooting what has been
planted . . . a time for tears, a time for laughter, a time for mourning, a time for dancing".
From the Book of Ecclesiastes, chapter 3

As the second millennium drew to its close and the third millennium began we had to say goodbye to many of our oldest village residents. However, we have also celebrated the births of many new babies who are just starting out on their life's journey. Several couples have made a commitment to marriage during these two years also. All three major happenings of life remind us of the continuity of life, of what one generation leaves as a heritage for the next.

The following names have been recorded from church registers and village Newsletters. There may be some happenings that have not been recorded publicly in these documents, and so are not recorded here.

1999

Deaths

January	Elizabeth Hannah 88 years
February	Jack Churchill 82 years
April	Allan Peachey 83 years
May	Leslie Arthur Thatcher 70 years
December	James Pritchard 71 years

Weddings

March	Peter Taylor and Catherine Clayton
May	Adam Richards and Tina Lloyd
June	Becky Hamilton and Matthew Webb
December	Anne De Salis and Iain Wright

Births

June	James Tickle
July	Charles Oliver Gwynn

2000

Deaths

January	Joyce Wayment 90 years
February	Harry Willis 70 years
March	Nessie Brinton 85 years
April	Alan Harfield 70 years
June	Ann Lightfoot 66 years
July	Sydney Street 88 years
	Frederick Gray 74 years
	Edith Briercliffe 87 years
September	George (Nobby) Clark 92 years
December	William Gough 75 years

Weddings

June	Sean Taylor and Georgina Hopkins
August	Jolene Conway Miller and Steven Gibbs
September	Emma Hall and Steven Large

Zoe Mansell-Carter, born January, 2000 –
Owslebury's first millennium baby, aged 10 months (EH)

Births

January	Zoe Rebecca Mansell-Carter
February	Maria Elise Green
June	Mason Ken Tyler Smith
	Toby Rivett
July	Theo Mitchell
	Todd Kennedy
September	Angus Joseph Baker

'Pop' Britton – born in 1903
and Owslebury's oldest resident in 2000 (EH)

A Time Line

Contributed by Nick Perry

The Time Line below includes a miscellany of milestones and memories on the way to the third millennium, to which families of Owslebury might relate in the past or in the present, might have been affected by in some way or which might just be markers in their minds.

1901   Death of Queen Victoria; Edward VII accedes to the throne on same day, 22nd January.
Statue of King Alfred erected in Winchester.

1902   Coronation festivities; lunch and tea for Owslebury, Morestead and Lane End residents on Owslebury Down.
Coronation of King Edward VII and Queen Alexandra on 9th August.
Beatrix Potter publishes *The Tale of Peter Rabbit*.

1903   Suffragette Movement founded.
Rolls Royce cars launched.

1904   **New Mail Collection Service between Winchester and Owslebury on weekdays.**
J M Barrie's *Peter Pan* first performed in London.

1905   **Mr G W Pierce appointed Headmaster of Owslebury School. Three new bells added to St Andrew's Church - now a peal of six.**

1907   New Parish Hall opened by Captain Faber, MP.
Song *The Teddy Bears' Picnic* written.

1908   **Whooping cough epidemic closes Owslebury School for two weeks.**

1909   **Owslebury Cricket Club's first season on the Cricket Down instead of Longwood**
Bleriot flies across the English Channel.

1910   Edward VII dies and is succeeded by George V, 6th May.

1911   **Village Coronation Festivities on 11th August.**
Coronation of King George V. 22nd June.

1912   **Vestry added to St Andrew's Church.**
Loss of RMS *Titanic*.
Scott's ill-fated expedition reaches South Pole.

1914   **New playing field for Owslebury School established.**
First World War begins on 3rd August.

1915   *Owslebury School Headmaster, Mr Pierce, enlists for war service*.
New Zealand-born British surgeon, Harold Delf Gillies, pioneers plastic surgery for war casualties.

1918   Armistice between Allies and Germany comes into force at 11am on 11th November.
World pandemic of Spanish 'Flu.
Married Love published by Dr Marie Stopes in Britain.

1919   **Mr Pierce returns from the war to resume duties as Headmaster of Owslebury School.**

Englishman Francis Aston splits the atom.

1920 **Revd. Edward Flower – last rector of Morestead as a single parish retired.**

Morestead Stables built.

1921 **Owslebury and Morestead Women's Institute formed.**

Dutch Elm Disease first described in the Netherlands.

Chanel No 5 perfume launched.

1922 BBC founded.

British horologist John Harwood invents the self-winding wristwatch.

Production of first British massed produced car the Austin Seven begins at Cowley, Oxfordshire.

1923 **Owslebury and Morestead become one benefice under the Vicar, Revd Albert Briggs.**

English FA Cup final held at Wembley for first time; Bolton Wanderers beat West Ham United 2-0.

1925/6 Baird demonstrates television.

1926 General Strike.

1928 **First six council houses built in Hilly Close**

Alexander Fleming discovers penicillin.

Whittle develops the jet engine.

Women's voting rights in UK equal with those of men (21yrs)

1930 **New weather vane pole erected on the church tower.**

1931 **Mr James Matthews appointed headteacher.**

School dinners begin to be served

in the Parish Hall.

1932 King George V makes first Christmas broadcast by a British head of state.

1933 *The Cricketers* **ceases to be a Public House; Mr Wort being the last landlord**

Grantley Dick-Read's book '*Natural Childbirth*' published.

1936 Mars of Slough introduces Maltesers.

1938 Nestle produces the first instant coffee.

1939 Second World War begins on 3rd September.

1940 Population (in millions) of England 39.2, Wales 2.5, Scotland 4.9, Northern Ireland 1.4.

Songs *We'll meet Again* and *White Cliffs of Dover* popularised by Vera Lynn.

Rationing of basic food in UK begins with bacon, butter and sugar.

1941 Age of call-up lowered to 18½ and of single women (aged 20-30) liable for military service.

1943 *Bevin Boys* system of National Service introduced to provide extra manpower for coal mines.

1944 **Drama Club formed; first performance, a one act play 'The Colonel's Consent'**

First of 1,115 V2 rockets fired against London.

D-Day 6th June.

1945 **5 Tilley lamps purchased for the Church; 'lighting much improved'**

Atomic Bomb used at Hiroshima

End of Second World War VE Day, 8th May

VJ Day, 2nd September

Clement Attlee formed Labour Government.

BBC *Radio Home Service and Light Programme* introduced

1946 **Mothers' Union banner dedicated on 6th November.**

Doctor Benjamin Spock publishes *The Common Sense Book of Baby and Child Care.*

1947 **Parish Hall registered as a charity with a new constitution.**

1948 **Mains Water Supply laid to Owslebury village.**

Gorse Down houses built; the first with modern plumbing and flush toilets installed.

National Health Service came into being on 5th July.

Olympic Games, Wembley.

1949 **Mains water turned on at Owslebury School, 14th September.**

Mains electricity switched on in main village, 29th October.

1950 **Electricity switched on in the church.**

Populations in millions; England 41.1, Wales 2.5, Scotland 5.2, Ireland/ Northern Ireland 1.4.

1951 Festival of Britain.

1952 **Beech Grove Council Estate built**

4,000 people died as a direct result of the London smog.

King George VI died, 6th February.

1953 **Commemorative Iron Gates to St Andrew's Church erected.**

Mount Everest climbed, 29th May.

Coronation of Queen Elizabeth II, 2nd June.

Structure of DNA discovered.

1954 Roger Bannister breaks 4 minute mile barrier (3 mins 59.4 sec).

1956 **Electricity supplied to Owslebury Bottom and Baybridge.**

St Andrew's Church nave roof restored and iron columns encased in wood.

1957 **Electricity supplied to Hensting Lane.**

1959 **Owslebury Youth Club formed.**

First publication of the Newsletter.

Beryl Roff appointed Headmistress of Owslebury School.

1960 **Bridle's Mill, the wind pumping mill behind the Parish Hall, demolished.**

1961 **Archaeological excavations at *Bottom Pond Farm* reveal Iron Age/ Romano British farming settlement.**

1963 **Old people's bungalows built in Beech Grove.**

President John F Kennedy assassinated 22nd November.

1965 Film '*Sound of Music*' released.

1966 England won the World Cup.

1968 **Opening of Jubilee Hut for Owslebury Scouts and Cubs.**

1969 **Public meeting to discuss proposed wild-life park at Marwell.**

First landing on the moon, 20th July.

US Department of Defence establishes

a computer network which is the basis of the *Internet*.

1970 **Mr P J Langler appointed Owslebury School Headteacher and work started on temporary classroom in Glebe Field.**
Longwood House demolished early in the decade.

1971 Decimalisation of British currency effective 15th February.
Population of Great Britain and Northern Ireland 55.5 million.

1972 **Marwell Zoological Park opened 22nd May; admission 30 pence.**

1973 **Old Vicarage sold.**
New Owslebury vicarage (Glebe House) built

1974 British Airways formed from BOAC (British Overseas Airways Corporation) and BEA (British European Airways).

1975 **Plans for new school confirmed.**
Owslebury and Morestead join Twyford in sharing the same vicar.
House of Commons confirm UK partnership of the European Economic Community by 396 votes to 170, 9th April.

1976 **Use of new school begins 22nd October.**

1977 **New Owslebury School officially opened on 27th January, by Mr R Dulson, Area Education Officer, and dedicated by the Right Reverend C A Cavell, Bishop of Southampton.**
Silver Jubilee carnival, June.

1978 **Mrs Adrienne Caplin appointed Owslebury School Head Teacher.**

1979 Margaret Thatcher elected first woman Prime Minister, 4th May.

1980 **New Vicarage sold in June.**
Church kneelers and new Brownie flag dedicated, 1st June.

1982 Falkland's War.

1984 **Last big Owslebury and Morestead Horticultural Show held.**
IRA bombing of Grand Hotel, Brighton, killed five people during Conservative Party Conference, 12th October.

1987 **New church organ dedicated in memory of Dick Boston.**
Hurricane hits Britain 16th October.

1988 **Parish Appraisal survey.**
Terrorist bomb killed all 259 passengers of Pan Am 747 and 11 people on the ground at Lockerbie, 21st December.

1989 **David White appointed Owslebury School Head Teacher**
Last remaining village shop closed 31st October.

1990 East and West Germany formally reunited 2nd October.

1991 The Gulf War.

1992 Separations of Prince and Princess of Wales and of the Duke and Duchess of York. Divorce of Princess Royal and Captain Mark Phillips.

1994 **Floodlighting installed outside the church.**
Final (Winchester) section of M3 opened.

1995 **Owslebury Cubs disestablished.**

1996 **Old Parish Hall demolished. New Parish Hall opened on 9th November.**

Cloning of Dolly the sheep.

1997 **Jubilee Hut demolished.**

Princess of Wales killed in car crash, 31st August.

1998 **Owslebury and Morestead Women's Institute disestablished.**

Refurbishment of mains water system.

Newbury (A34) bypass opened.

1999 **New and strengthened electricity cables installed in Owslebury.**

Christmas illuminations switched on, 13th December.

Total eclipse of the sun 11th August.

2000 **Service for the new millennium in St. Andrew's Church January 2nd.**

Presentation of old Owslebury map to the village in the Parish Hall, January 2nd.

St Andrew's Church Millennium Wallhanging dedicated 26th November.

Millennium Dome opened at Greenwich.

Queen Elizabeth the Queen Mother 100 years old, 4th August.

Olympic Games, Sydney, Australia.

BIBLIOGRAPHY

Many stories included in this book were gleaned from past village Newsletters and correspondence from previous residents. Many other stories have been passed by word of mouth to be retold here.

Various books and articles have also been used and have proved an invaluable source of information. Such writings are as follows:

'Owslebury Bottom', by Peter Hewett 1991

'Owslebury Remembers' by Betty Harfield 1994

'Owslebury School' by Betty Harfield 1990

Owslebury and Morestead WI scrapbook

Parish Notes compiled between 1884 and 1961 by various vicars of Owslebury

Victoria County History of Hampshire 1908

Notes by Michael Houghton, compiled for a Duke of Edinburgh Gold Award 1987

A thesis on Marwell Woodlock, by Stan Waight 1997, which included details concerning *The Farm House* and *Chestnut House*

Twyford, Owslebury and Morestead Parish Magazines

Notes compiled by Frank Williams after interviewing various villagers in the 1960s

The Marwell Hall Estate Sale Schedule 1934 – kindly lent by Dick Lush

The Longwood Estate Sale Schedule 1972 – kindly lent by Walter Trott

Back numbers of The Hampshire Chronicle

Monumental Inscriptions of St Andrew's Church, Owslebury, recorded by Clive Colpus and Joy Hobbs 1981, for the Hampshire Genealogical Society

'Twyford, 20th Century Chronicles', ed. by Stanley Crooks 2000

'Twyford, Ringing the Changes', by Doreen Pierce and Stanley Crooks, 1999

Notes on the Parish of Morestead begun in 1920 by Revd F G L Lucas of Morestead Grange

'The Story So Far' by John Adams, published by Marwell Zoo

ILLUSTRATIONS

Cover illustrations:

front top, The Ship Inn, c1902 (BN)

front bottom, The Ship Inn, 2000, with the landlord and his family – Clive and Ali Mansell with

Katy and Zoe (EH)

back, Owslebury Millennium Tapestry (EH)

Text illustrations *(page / description)*:

Index

Note: maiden names are indexed under née

Y